Building Websites with PHP-Nuke

Douglas Paterson

PUBLISHING

BIRMINGHAM - MUMBAI

Building Websites with PHP-Nuke

First published: November 2005

Published by Packt Publishing Ltd.
32 Lincoln Road
Olton
Birmingham, B27 6PA, UK.

ISBN 1-904811-05-1

www.packtpub.com

Cover Design by www.visionwt.com

Dinosaur Portal topic images created by James Turner, of www.beaverandsteve.com

Credits

Author
Douglas Paterson

Reviewers
Stoyan Stefanov
Bill Wong

Technical Editor
Nikhil Bangera

Editorial Manager
Dipali Chittar

Indexer
Ashutosh Pande

Proofreader
Chris Smith

Production Coordinator
Manjiri Nadkarni

Cover Designer
Helen Wood

About the Author

Douglas Paterson is a full time development editor and part-time author for Packt Publishing. He is a doctor of Mathematics and has over five years experience working on programming books across a range of subjects.

He lives in Birmingham, England with his girlfriend, and his unusually hairy dog Zak. He can be reached at doug@packtpub.com.

Table of Contents

Preface

PHP-Nuke is a free tool to manage the content of dynamic websites, and allows you to create a dynamic, interactive website with minimum effort and programming knowledge.

As one of the most popular applications on the Internet, PHP-Nuke has grown into a complex, powerful tool with an extraordinary range of features, and a loyal community of supporters. Users can edit and manage their site through a web-based interface, without the need for any knowledge of web programming. PHP-Nuke is ideal for running a community-driven website, where visitors create accounts, contribute material, and interact with the site.

This book is packed with practical steps for you to learn how to build your own website with PHP-Nuke. From the basics of installing and configuring PHP-Nuke, you will learn how to manage your site, add content to it, and then customize its look.

What This Book Covers

The book begins with an overview of PHP-Nuke; what it is, and what it can do to help you build your own community-driven website. We shall learn all the features and functionality provided by PHP-Nuke by developing an example site, the Dinosaur Portal, as we progress through this book.

In *Chapter 2*, you will learn how to install and configure PHP-Nuke, apply patches, and also create the database. At the end of this chapter you will have a fully operational PHP-Nuke site, ready to go!

In *Chapter 3* you will begin to explore the many features of PHP-Nuke, create the super user (an all-powerful administrator of the site), and make your first modifications to the site. You will also learn about the ways in which PHP-Nuke restricts access to the site.

Chapter 4 introduces you to the administration area of PHP-Nuke, which allows you to manage your site from the comfort of your web browser. You'll see how to configure your site, back up the database, and manage blocks and modules.

Your site is created for visitors and *Chapter 5* shows you how to manage them. You will learn how to create users, explore the Your Account module, which is the user's private 'space', and set up other administrators to perform limited administrative tasks on the site.

Chapter 6 is where we really start adding content to the site. In this chapter, we have a thorough walkthrough of story management, from both the visitor and administrator viewpoint. A story is PHP-Nuke's most versatile type of content, and we explore how to add, edit, and manage stories, and the features that allow visitors to interact with the stories.

Chapter 7 covers some of the other standard modules for adding content in PHP-Nuke. The Content, FAQ, Encyclopedia, Web Links, Downloads, and Reviews modules are all covered in this chapter, from both the visitor and administrator viewpoint. Each of these modules handles a different type of content, and you will see the functionality they offer for visitors to interact with the content, and also how each module organizes its content.

PHP-Nuke has a fully featured discussion board module, the Forums module. In *Chapter 8*, you will take a tour of setting up a new forum, assigning moderators, and setting permissions to these forums.

Before *Chapter 9*, you've been working with the standard-looking PHP-Nuke site. In *Chapter 9*, it's time to unleash your creativity and create a new look for the site. This is done through customizing a PHP-Nuke theme. In this chapter, we race through a range of customizations, from changing the site logo, to adding and styling a navigation bar, creating new blocks, and changing the format of stories on the homepage, among others. This chapter features a lot of coding in HTML and CSS, in addition to some changes to PHP files, and there are clear instructions to help you through.

Chapter 10 shows you how to program PHP-Nuke to create new blocks and modules. You will see how PHP-Nuke handles page requests, data access, and language files. You will also see how code is organized in a module for both the visitor end and the administrator end.

Appendix A has a walkthrough of installing the XAMPP package, which provides a working installation of PHP, MySQL, and Apache, ready configured for you to test your PHP-Nuke site on.

What You Need To Use This Book

You will need access to an installation of PHP-Nuke. PHP-Nuke can be freely downloaded from www.php-nuke.org, and there are more details of how to do this in *Chapter 2*. PHP-Nuke requires a working installation of PHP, MySQL, and the Apache web server to run. In *Appendix A*, you will find instructions on how to download the XAMPP package, which has all of these ready configured.

Basic knowledge of HTML will help if you intend to explore customizing your own theme, and a basic knowledge of PHP will help if you want to get the most from *Chapter 10*.

Conventions

In this book, you will find a number of styles of text that distinguish between different kinds of information. Here are some examples of these styles, and an explanation of their meaning.

There are three styles for code. Code words in text are shown as follows: "… the database access variables, $prefix and $db, and it needs the module name, $module_name."

A block of code will be set as follows:

```
if ($numrows)
{
    $row = $db->sql_fetchrow($result);
    $dino_title = $row['title'];
    $image = $row['image'];
}
```

When we wish to draw your attention to a particular part of a code block, the relevant lines or items will be made bold:

```
if ($numrows)
{
    $row = $db->sql_fetchrow($result);
    $dino_title = $row['title'];
    $image = $row['image'];
}
```

New terms and **important words** are introduced in a bold-type font. Words that you see on the screen, in menus or dialog boxes for example, appear in our text like this: "clicking the Next button moves you to the next screen".

Tips, suggestions, or important notes appear in a box like this.

Reader Feedback

Feedback from our readers is always welcome. Let us know what you think about this book, what you liked or may have disliked. Reader feedback is important for us to develop titles that you really get the most out of.

To send us general feedback, simply drop an email to feedback@packtpub.com, making sure to mention the book title in the subject of your message.

If there is a book that you need and would like to see us publish, please send us a note in the SUGGEST A TITLE form on www.packtpub.com or e-mail suggest@packtpub.com. If there is a topic that you have expertise in and you are interested in either writing or contributing to a book, see our author guide on www.packtpub.com/authors.

Customer Support

Now that you are the proud owner of a Packt book, we have a number of things to help you to get the most from your purchase.

Errata

Although we have taken every care to ensure the accuracy of our contents, mistakes do happen. If you find a mistake in one of our books—maybe a mistake in text or code—we would be grateful if you would report this to us. By doing this you can save other readers from frustration, and help to improve subsequent versions of this book. If you find any errata, report them by visiting http://www.packtpub.com/support, selecting your book, clicking on the Submit Errata link, and entering the details of your errata. Once your errata have been verified, your submission will be accepted and the errata added to the list of existing errata. The existing errata can be viewed by selecting your title from http://www.packtpub.com/support.

Questions

You can contact us at questions@packtpub.com if you are having a problem with some aspect of the book, and we will do our best to address it.

1
An Introduction to PHP-Nuke

PHP-Nuke is a free tool to manage the content of dynamic websites. To be more specific, PHP-Nuke is an open-source content management system. In fact, you could say it is 'the' open-source content management system. Since it is vastly popular, a number of other similar systems have sprung from it, and even similar systems based around very different technologies that owe nothing to it in terms of code have added 'Nuke' to their name as homage.

Although the first paragraph conveys something of the history and grandeur of PHP-Nuke, it doesn't answer the basic question of what it can actually do for you.

PHP-Nuke allows you to create a dynamic, community-driven website with minimum effort and programming knowledge. To get the most out of PHP-Nuke, a knowledge of web development will prove to be useful, but even then, PHP-Nuke is written in the PHP scripting language (as can be deduced from the name), which is probably the most popular and straightforward language for creating websites and web applications.

The first PHP-Nuke release in June 2000 was created by a developer named Francisco Burzi to power his site, Linux Preview. Since then, PHP-Nuke has evolved under his guidance to the system it is today.

PHP-Nuke is truly one of the Internet's legendary applications. In this chapter, we will take our first look at PHP-Nuke, understand what it can do, find out where to go for further resources, and briefly discuss the site we will create in this book.

What PHP-Nuke Can Do for You

PHP-Nuke is ideal for creating community-driven websites.

The 'community' part of 'community-driven' means that the site is geared towards a particular group of people with similar interests. Maybe this community is concerned with wine making, flowers, programming, zombie films, or even dinosaurs. Maybe the community is actually a group of customers of a particular product. Of course, we are talking about an online community here.

Whatever the community is into, the site can be structured to hold information relevant to the members; maybe it will be news stories about a forthcoming zombie film, links to other zombie sites, reviews, or synopses of other zombie films.

The 'driven' part of 'community-driven' suggests that the information available on this site can be extended or enhanced by the members of the community. Members of the community may be able to shape what is on the site by posting comments, contributing or rating stories, and participating in discussions. After all, communities are made up of people, and people have views and opinions, and often like to express them!

This is exactly what PHP-Nuke enables. More than being just a website, a PHP-Nuke site provides a rich and interactive environment for its visitors.

The best bit is, you don't have to be an expert programmer to achieve all this. With only rudimentary knowledge of HTML, you can engineer a unique-looking PHP-Nuke website.

The Visitor Experience

The standard installation of PHP-Nuke provides many features for its visitors. Some of them are:

- Searchable news articles, organized into topics
- Ability of visitors to create an account on the site, and log in to their own personal area
- Ability of visitors to rate articles, and create discussions about them
- Straw polls and surveys
- Ability of visitors to submit their own stories to be published on the site
- An encyclopedia, in other words, a collection of entries organized alphabetically
- A catalog of web links or downloadable files
- Discussion forums
- Ability of visitors to select their own look for the site from a list of different 'themes'
- RSS syndication of your articles to share your content with other sites

This is not a complete list either. And these are only some of the features that come with the standard installation. PHP-Nuke is a **modular** system; it can be customized and extended, and there is a huge range of third-party customizations and extensions to be found on the Internet. Any of these can add to the range of features your site provides.

The Management Experience

As a potential 'manager' of a PHP-Nuke site, as you read through the list of features above you may think they sound rather attractive, but you might also wonder how you will handle all of that.

PHP-Nuke provides a web-based management interface. You, as the manager of the site, visit the site and log in with a special super user, or site administrator, account. After this, from the comfort of your web browser, you run the show:

- You can add new information, and edit, delete, or move existing pieces of information.
- You can approve articles submitted by the user to be shown on the site.
- You can decide the features of the site.
- You can control what is displayed on the pages.
- You can control who is able to see what.

With the possibility of adding so much to the site, you might think it will be difficult to keep track of everything, and make sure that everything is linked. This is also done for you by PHP-Nuke, and it creates navigation menus for the visitor, and displays lists of articles and other information, automatically setting up the links for visitors to move from one place to another.

Of course, PHP-Nuke cannot do everything you imagine, and it has its limitations. For example, PHP-Nuke is very good for adding text content to the site. However, it is not so good (in the default setup) for adding images and other resources to the site; it supports them once they are available, but the management interface does not really help with adding them. To add images and other resources such as Flash movies or banners, you will need to access the web server directly using an FTP client.

However, the power and flexibility PHP-Nuke offers you to manage a complex website would be difficult to achieve without many, many hours of careful programming.

What Exactly is PHP-Nuke?

PHP-Nuke is a collection of PHP scripts that run on a web server, connect to a database, and display the retrieved data in a systematic way. In other words, PHP-Nuke is a data-driven PHP web application.

PHP-Nuke can be downloaded for free, and then installed to your local machine for testing and development. The files and the database can be uploaded to a web hosting service, so that your site will be available to anyone on the Internet. There are even web hosting services that offer PHP-Nuke installation at the click of a button.

Modular Structure

PHP-Nuke is built around a 'core' set of functions, which perform mundane tasks such as selecting what part of the application the user should be shown, checking who the user is, and what they can do on the site. The thing that makes PHP-Nuke exciting to the world is the set of modules that comes with it. These modules provide the real functionality of the site, and include ones for news and article management, downloads, and forums, among others. The modules can be switched on and off with ease, and other modules can be added to the system.

There is no shortage of third-party modules on the Internet, and you can find a PHP-Nuke module for almost any imaginable purpose.

Themed Interface

The look of a PHP-Nuke site is controlled by a theme. This is a collection of images, colors, and other resources, and instructions that determine the layout of the page. A new theme can be selected, and your site will be transformed immediately. Visitors with a user account on the site are able to select their own personal theme.

Multi-Lingual Interface

PHP-Nuke comes with many language files. These contain translations of standard elements on the site interface. The availability of these translations reflects the international nature of the PHP-Nuke community.

PHP-Nuke as an Open-Source Content Management System

We used the expression 'open-source content management system' earlier in the chapter to describe PHP-Nuke. Let's take a closer a look at this term.

Open Source

PHP-Nuke is free, and it is also open source. After downloading PHP-Nuke, all the source code of the application is there in front of you. This means, if you are so inclined, you can dig around to see how it works, or check why something is not working as it should. PHP-Nuke is not a perfect application (what is?), and there will always be parts that do not work as they should. Since there are many people using PHP-Nuke on the Internet, the problem is usually spotted and the solution is posted on one of the PHP-Nuke forums.

Another advantage of having the source of the application (the code) available to you is that you can modify (hack!) it, or extend it in whichever way you choose.

PHP-Nuke is released under a license, the **GNU General Public License (GPL)**. The GPL bestows much freedom in the way that you can work with PHP-Nuke, and it also brings along some restrictions. The ins and outs of the GPL are pretty complex, and we aren't even going to attempt an in-depth discussion of the consequences of this. For more information about the GPL visit http://en.wikipedia.org/wiki/GPL.

The GPL should always be respected. The GPL is one of the cornerstones of the Free Software movement, which was set up to promote rights to use, modify, and redistribute computer programs. The GPL offers you almost complete freedom in your use of the software, and means, basically, that PHP-Nuke will not be going away. Even if some future version of it were to become completely commercial, the existing code could be taken and modified to create a new version, also released with a GPL license. This process, known as forking, accounts for a number of the PHP-based content management systems that can be found on the Web today. A number of other established systems, such as XOOPS and PostNuke, began life as 'forks' of PHP-Nuke, and have evolved in their own particular direction.

There are a couple of restrictions with PHP-Nuke, involving copyright messages. For example, the copyright message displayed at the foot of each page should not be removed from your page:

> PHP-Nuke Copyright © 2004 by Francisco Burzi. This is free software, and you may redistribute it under the GPL. PHP-Nuke comes with absolutely no warranty, for details, see the license.

If you wish to remove this message (and others like it), you should visit http://php-nuke.org to find out about the commercial license. You should not find these requirements restricting your use of PHP-Nuke.

Content Management System

We have spoken a lot about adding and editing 'information' on a website. A broader term for information here would be 'content'. To summarize our earlier discussions of PHP-Nuke, it allows you to manage the content of your site. In other words, it's a content management system.

According to Wikipedia, a **Content Management System (CMS)** is a 'system used to organize and facilitate collaborative creation of documents and other content' (http://en.wikipedia.org/wiki/Content_management_system).

Well, it is difficult to define content management system and avoid the words 'a system for managing content'!

You can think of a content management system as playing three roles:

- **Capturing** content
- **Maintaining and Organizing** content
- **Serving** content

Capturing the content is usually done by users entering data in forms in a web browser. This content is then stored in a database for later retrieval. Serving the content allows the right data to be selected, sorted, and ordered, and then displayed to the visitor in a coherent and consistent way.

PHP-Nuke achieves all of these. Visitors or the site administrator can input content from a range of places on the site. This content can be maintained and organized from the web-based administration interface by the site administrator. When a visitor requests a page from the site, PHP-Nuke will determine which content should be displayed and how it should be ordered. It then handles the output of the content, along with the rest of the page.

Getting Help in the PHP-Nuke Community

PHP-Nuke has a substantial user base. There is a large group of people who run PHP-Nuke sites, develop extensions to PHP-Nuke, and create visual customizations, among other activities. All this leads to a vibrant community that pushes the product forward, helps to address the problems faced by people working with PHP-Nuke, and offers support and encouragement to users.

There are a number of sites dedicated to PHP-Nuke that contain a range of PHP-Nuke resources, such as add-ons, bug fixes and patches, tutorials, and so on. You will also find the option of paid support for PHP-Nuke, and since PHP-Nuke is such a popular and widespread application, it will not be difficult to find a PHP developer who has experience of working with PHP-Nuke.

Each of these sites is well worth a visit to see what they offer:

- `http://phpnuke.org`: This is the home of PHP-Nuke, run by Francisco Burzi, the creator and maintainer of PHP-Nuke. From here, you can download the latest version of PHP-Nuke. This is also a good place to find news of the latest offerings from the PHP-Nuke community, including new sites running on PHP-Nuke.

- `http://www.nukecops.com`: There is a particularly large forum here, with many posts on problems encountered by PHP-Nuke users. If you find yourself with a problem, then the `Nukecops.com` forums are a good bet to find a solution.

- `http://www.nukeresources.com`: This is the home of the PHP-Nuke patches that we will use when installing PHP-Nuke. There is also an extensive list of downloads here, as well as a number of tutorials.

- `http://www.karakas-online.de/EN-Book/`: This is the PHP-Nuke HOWTO. This is a massive collection of tips and tricks for working with PHP-Nuke, solving common problems, and useful hacks. This document is also found on a number of other PHP-Nuke websites as the PHP-Nuke HOWTO.

- `http://thethemes.cc/`: This is a site with dozens of PHP-Nuke themes aimed at gaming sites.

- `http://ravenphpscripts.com/`: NukeSentinel, a security add-on for PHP-Nuke, can be found here.

Many of the PHP-Nuke sites will have links to other recommended PHP-Nuke sites. In addition to providing valuable resources and information, all these sites will give you a good idea of what it is possible to accomplish on a PHP-Nuke site.

The Dinosaur Portal

We're going to create an example site, the Dinosaur Portal, as we move through the book. The Dinosaur Portal does not have an extensive list of requirements; we simply want to create a site with features such as a structure for adding dinosaur-related stories and a place for entering information about various dinosaurs. We also want to make sure that the site looks very distinctive, and is fun.

The Dinosaur Portal is based around the premise that 'just because you haven't seen a dinosaur, it doesn't mean they've all died out'. It will be a place where people can explore a range of rather fantastical theories about dinosaurs and their interactions with other life forms.

A web portal is a site that is a gateway to other resources on the Internet (or possibly an intranet). The features of PHP-Nuke are ideal for creating web portals, and the Dinosaur Portal will be a gateway to a whole host of eclectic, dinosaur-based resources.

Summary

This first chapter has introduced PHP-Nuke. PHP-Nuke is an open-source content management system; you can also think of it as a free tool for managing the content of websites.

We looked at what PHP-Nuke offers in terms of a visitor experience, and also what this will mean for the person who is in charge of maintaining the site. PHP-Nuke has functionality to make site maintenance easy, and the site can be run from a web-based interface. We found out about the PHP-Nuke community, and where to go for help or further PHP-Nuke resources.

The chapter concluded with a quick description of the Dinosaur Portal—the site we are going to create in this book. We are ready to begin on this journey, so the next step is to actually get PHP-Nuke up and running.

2
Installing PHP-Nuke

In this chapter we will cover how to install PHP-Nuke on a local machine running an Apache/MySQL/PHP (AMP) environment. We will not cover the installation of AMP here; you can find a walkthrough of installing the XAMPP package in Appendix A. This package includes PHP, MySQL, Apache, and much more, and is a quick way to get yourself a working AMP development environment.

The steps to install and configure PHP-Nuke are simple:

1. Download and extract the PHP-Nuke files.
2. Download and apply ChatServ's patches.
3. Create the database for PHP-Nuke.
4. Create a database user, and fill the database with data.
5. Make some simple changes to the PHP-Nuke configuration file.
6. Copy the PHP-Nuke files to the document root of the web server.
7. Test it out!

Let's get started.

Downloading PHP-Nuke

The latest version of PHP-Nuke can be downloaded at phpnuke.org downloads page:

    http://www.phpnuke.org/modules.php?name=Downloads&d_op=viewdownload&cid=1

You can also obtain older versions of PHP-Nuke, including version 1.0, from SourceForge:

    http://sourceforge.net/project/showfiles.php?group_id=7511&package_id=7622

SourceForge is the world's largest home of open-source projects. Many projects use SourceForge's facilities to host and maintain their projects. You can find almost anything you want on SourceForge—whether it is in a usable state or has been updated recently is another matter.

Extracting PHP-Nuke

Once you have downloaded PHP-Nuke, you should extract the contents of the PHP-Nuke ZIP archive to the root of your c:\ drive. You will have to create a folder called PHP-Nuke-7.8 in the root of your c:\ drive. (If you extract the files elsewhere, create the folder PHP-Nuke-7.8 and copy the contents of the main unzipped folder to this new folder).

> If you don't have a tool for extracting the files, you can download an evaluation edition (or buy a full edition) of WinZip from www.winzip.com.
>
> There are also free, powerful, extracting tools such as ZipGenius (http://www.zipgenius.it/index_eng.htm) and 7-Zip (http://sourceforge.net/projects/sevenzip/) among others.

In the PHP-Nuke-7.8 folder, you will find three subfolders called html, sql, and upgrades. The upgrades folder contains scripts that handle upgrading the database between different versions, the sql folder contains the definition of the PHP-Nuke database that we will be working with, and the html folder contains the guts of your PHP-Nuke installation.

The html folder contains all the PHP scripts, HTML files, images, CSS stylesheets, and so on that drive PHP-Nuke. Within the html folder are further subfolders; some of these include:

- modules: Contains the modules that make up your PHP-Nuke site. Modules are the essence of PHP-Nuke's operation; we look at them from Chapter 3 onwards.
- blocks: Contains PHP-Nuke's blocks. Blocks are 'mini-functionality' units and usually provide snippet views of modules. We will look at blocks in Chapter 4.
- language: Contains PHP-Nuke language files. These allow the language of PHP-Nuke's interface to be changed.
- images: Contains images used in the display of the PHP-Nuke site.
- themes: Contains the themes for PHP-Nuke. The use of themes allows you to completely change the look of a PHP-Nuke site with a click of a button.
- includes, db: Contain code to support the running of PHP-Nuke. The db folder, for example, contains database access code.
- admin: Contains code to power the administration area of your site.

Downloading the Patches

No software is without its flaws, and PHP-Nuke is no exception. After a release, the large user community invariably finds problems and potential security holes. Furthermore, PHP-Nuke also contains features such as its forum, which is in fact the phpBB application specially modified to work with PHP-Nuke. phpBB itself is updated on a regular basis to correct critical security vulnerabilities or to fix other problems, and consequently the corresponding part of PHP-Nuke also needs to be updated. Rather than releasing a new version of PHP-Nuke for these situations, patches for its various parts are released.

ChatServ's patches from www.nukeresources.com are mostly concerned with variable validation, in other words, making sure that the variables used in the application are of the right type for storing in the database. This has been an area of weakness with many earlier versions of PHP-Nuke. The patches are often incorporated into subsequent versions of PHP-Nuke so that each new version becomes more robust.

Note that you don't have to apply the patches, and PHP-Nuke will still work without them. However, by applying them you will have taken a good step towards improving the security of your site.

If you navigate to http://www.nukeresources.com, there is a handy menu on the front page to access the patches:

To obtain the patch corresponding to your version, click the link and you will be taken to the relevant file (of course, www.nukeresources is a PHP-Nuke powered site!). Click on the Nuke 7.8 link to go to the Downloads page of www.nukeresources.com. On this page, clicking the Download this file Now! link will download the patches for PHP-Nuke 7.8. The name of this file will be of the form 78patched.tar.gz. This is a GZIP compressed file that contains all the patches that we are about to apply. The GZIP file can be extracted with WinZip, or any of the other utilities we discussed earlier.

The patches are simply modified versions of the original PHP-Nuke files. The original files have been modified to address various security issues that may have been identified since the initial release, or maybe since the last version of the patch.

Applying the Patches

To apply the patches, first we need to extract the 78patched.tar.gz file. We will extract the files into a folder called patches that we will create in the PHP-Nuke-7.8 folder.

After extracting the files, copy the contents of the patches folder to your html folder. Do not copy the patches folder, copy its *contents*. The patches folder contains files that replace the files in the default installation, and you get a Confirm File Replace window. Select Yes for all the files, and when the copying is complete, your installation is ready to go.

We have performed this patching immediately after installing PHP-Nuke, but we could have done this at any time. Doing it at this point is more sensible as it means that we are working on the most secure version of PHP-Nuke. Also, the patch process we have described here overwrites existing

PHP-Nuke installation files. If you have modified these files, then the changes will be lost on applying the patch. Thus applying the patches later without disturbing any of your changes becomes more demanding.

There is one further thing to watch for after applying the patches. You may find that the patched files have had their permissions set to read-only, and that you are unable to modify the files. To modify the files (and we do have to modify at least the config.php file in this chapter) you will need to remove this setting. You can do this on Windows by right-clicking on the file, selecting Properties from the menu, unchecking the Read-only setting, and clicking the OK button:

We've done almost all the work with the files that we need to; now we turn our attention to creating and populating PHP-Nuke's database.

Preparing the PHP-Nuke Database

We'll be using the phpMyAdmin tool to do our database work. phpMyAdmin is part of the XAMPP installation (detailed in Appendix A), or can be downloaded from www.phpmyadmin.net, if you don't already have it. phpMyAdmin provides a powerful web interface for working with your MySQL databases.

First of all, open your browser and navigate to http://localhost/phpmyadmin/, or whatever the location of your phpMyAdmin installation is:

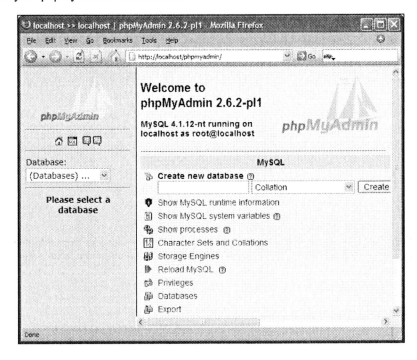

Creating the Database

We need to create an empty database for PHP-Nuke to hold all the data about our site. To do this, we simply enter a name for our database into the Create new database textbox:

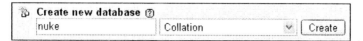

We will call our database nuke. Enter this, and click the Create button. The name you give doesn't particularly matter, as long as it is not the name of some already existing database. If you try to use the same name as an already existing database, phpMyAdmin will inform you of this, and no action will be taken. The exact name isn't particularly important at this point because there is another configuration step coming up, which requires us to tell PHP-Nuke the name of the database we've created for it.

After clicking Create, the screen will reload and you will be notified of the successful creation of your database:

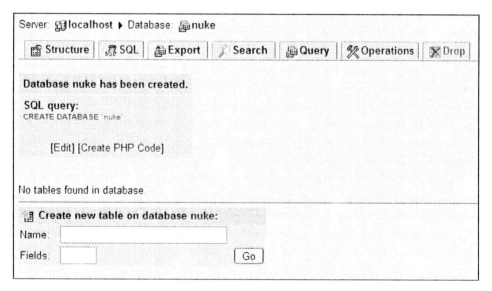

Creating a Database User

Before we start populating the database, we will create a database user that can access *only* the PHP-Nuke database. This user is not a human, but will be used by PHP-Nuke to connect to the database while it performs its data-handling activities. The advantage of creating a database user is that it adds an extra level of security to our installation. PHP-Nuke will be able to work with data *only* in this database of the MySQL server, and no other. Also, PHP-Nuke will be restricted in the operations it can perform on the tables in the database.

We will need to create a username for this boxed-in user to access the nuke database. Let's call our user nuker and go with the password nukepassword. However, in order to add an extra level of security we will introduce some digits into nukepassword, and some other slight twists, to strengthen it, and so use the word No0kPassv0rd as our database user password.

To create the database user, click the SQL tab, and enter the following into the Run SQL query/queries on database textbox:

```
GRANT ALL PRIVILEGES ON nuke.* TO nuker@localhost
                IDENTIFIED BY 'No0kPassv0rd'
                WITH GRANT OPTION
```

Your screen should look like this:

Click the Go button, and the database user will be created:

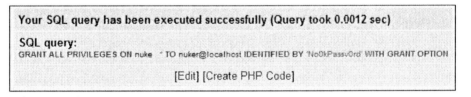

Populating the Database

Now we are ready to fill our database with data for PHP-Nuke. This doesn't mean we start typing the data in ourselves; the data comes with the PHP-Nuke installation. This data is found in a file called nuke.sql in the sql folder of the PHP-Nuke installation. This file contains a number of SQL statements that define the tables within the database and also fill them with 'raw' data for the site.

However, before we fill the database with the tables from this file, we need to make a modification to this file.

By default, the name of each database table in PHP-Nuke begins with nuke_. For example, there is a table with the name nuke_stories that holds information about stories, and a table called nuke_topics that holds information about story topics. These are just two of the tables; there are more than 90 in the standard installation. The word nuke_ is a 'table prefix', and is used to ensure that there are no clashes between the names of PHP-Nuke's tables and tables from another application in the same database, since the rest of the table name is descriptive of the data stored in the table, and other applications may have similarly named tables.

What this does mean is that unless this table prefix is changed, the table names in your PHP-Nuke database will be known to anyone attempting to hack your site. Many of the typical attacks used to damage PHP-Nuke are based around the fact that the names of the tables in the database powering a PHP-Nuke site are known. By changing the table prefix to something less obvious, you have taken another step to making your site more secure.

Before we fill our PHP-Nuke database, we will change the table prefix from nuke_ to dinop_ (for the Dinosaur Portal). This requires us to make a change to the nuke.sql file first, and then a configuration change later.

Open the nuke.sql file in a text editor (such as Wordpad), and use the find and replace feature (Edit | Replace in Wordpad) to replace all occurrences of nuke_ with our chosen prefix dinop_. Make sure that you include a space before nuke_, and for the replacement prefix, include a space before its name. The image below shows the Replace dialog in Wordpad for changing the prefix to dinop_:

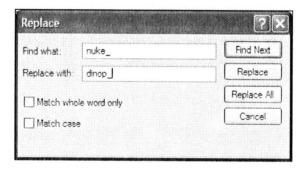

Clicking the Replace All button will make all the changes within the file, and then we can save this new file as dinop.sql in the sql folder, and we will have a new set of tables with a different prefix.

Now the prefix has been changed, we can return to phpMyAdmin and continue with populating the database. To get the data into the database, click the SQL tab, as shown in the figure overleaf:

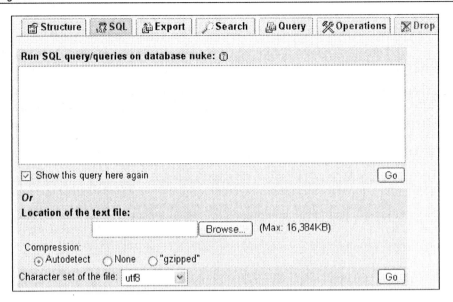

Click the Browse button, navigate to the sql subfolder in the PHP-Nuke-7.8 folder, and double-click on the dinop.sql file. Click the Go button, the screen will reload, and in the left-hand panel of the browser you will see the tables in your fully populated database:

Our database is now ready. There are still two more steps before we are ready to run PHP-Nuke.

Configuring PHP-Nuke

We need to tell PHP-Nuke where to get its data from, and how to get that data. This requires us to provide the name of the database and the database user we just created. We add this information into the config.php file located in the html folder of your PHP-Nuke installation.

To do this, open the config.php file in your favorite text editor (Notepad or Wordpad will do fine).

Scroll down to find these five consecutive lines:

```
$dbuname = "root ";
$dbpass = "";
$dbname = "nuke";
$prefix = "nuke";
$user_prefix = "nuke";
```

These five lines are PHP variable definitions that determine the username and password of the database user account that will access the database, and the name of the database that we will be accessing, and the table name prefix. PHP-Nuke uses these to connect to its database, so they had better be correct.

The first thing we will do is change the database username and database password to those of the database user we created earlier. Edit the lines as follows:

```
$dbuname = "nuker";
$dbpass = "NoOkPassvOrd";
```

Next, we should set the database name by changing the variable assigned to $dbname to the name of the database we just created. We have named our database the same as the one specified here, nuke. If we had chosen a different name for the database, we would have had to set the value of the $dbname variable to that name.

The $prefix variable holds the value of the table name prefix, which by default, is set to nuke. We discussed the table name prefix earlier, and how all the table names in the standard setup are prefixed with nuke_. (The _ character does not need to be included in the $prefix variable). Whenever there is any attempt to access a table from within the PHP-Nuke code, the $prefix variable is used. We set the value of the $prefix variable to our changed prefix, dinop:

```
$prefix = "dinop";
```

The fifth variable, $user_prefix, is also a table prefix. There is a pair of tables in the PHP-Nuke database, nuke_users and nuke_users_temp (with the default prefix) that hold information about each user and users waiting to be registered on the site respectively. Whenever these tables are queried in the code of PHP-Nuke, the $user_prefix variable is used to get their table prefix rather than the $prefix variable. This means that these tables could have a different table prefix from the rest of the tables in the PHP-Nuke database. A consequence of this is that you could have several PHP-Nuke sites stored in the same database, each with different table prefixes, but the user prefix could be the same. This would mean that a user could have a single user account valid across all these sites. This is a more advanced use of PHP-Nuke that we won't have the space to go into any greater detail.

For now, we set the $user_prefix variable to be the same as the $prefix variable:

```
$user_prefix = "dinop";
```

For completeness, we will make a change to another configuration variable, the site key. This is a long string used in the random generation of the graphical security code that prevents automated registration or login attempts to your site. The site key can just be a random string of text, provided you don't add any quotes. The default value is this:

```
$sitekey = "S·kQSd5%W@Y62-dm29-.-39.3a8sUf+W9";
```

Let's change its value with some random pressing of the keyboard to:

```
$sitekey = "78W f7sys f89s fsd sj hjsg sdfw3p;";
```

We've told PHP-Nuke the name of the database to use, the prefix of the name of the tables, and also the name and credentials of the database user to access the database with. Our configuration is done, so let's save the file config.php and we are ready to move on.

Putting PHP-Nuke Files into the Web Server Root

In this book, we are going to access the homepage of our local PHP-Nuke site with this URL:

```
http://localhost/nuke/
```

In order to do this, we will create a folder called nuke in our web server root (\xampp\htdocs\ if you are using XAMPP), and copy the contents of the \PHP-Nuke-7.8\html\ folder into this folder. Do not copy the html folder itself, but the *contents* of the folder.

We will refer to the nuke folder in the web server root as the 'root of our PHP-Nuke installation'.

Testing the Installation

Finally, we are ready to go.

Open up your web browser and navigate to http://localhost/nuke/. You should see the following screen:

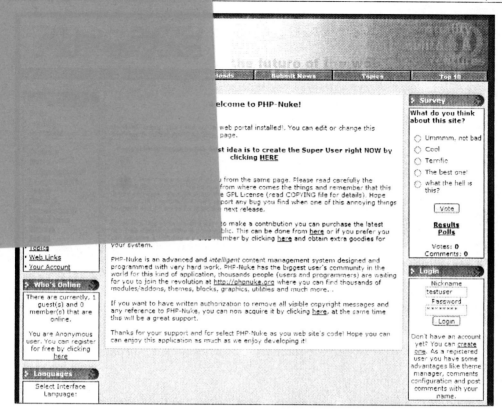

If this is what you see in your browser, then you are ready to go, and you can move on to the next chapter. If you see something different from this image in your browser, we may have to perform some troubleshooting. Here we'll look at some of the more common problems that users encounter with their PHP-Nuke installations.

Database Connection Problem

If you see this in your browser:

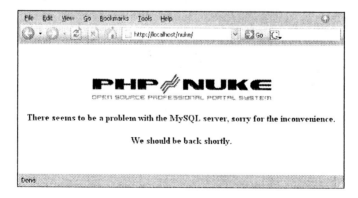

then there might be a problem with your database server or, more likely, your connection information. If the MySQL server is running (navigate to `http://localhost/phpMyAdmin/` to see if phpMyAdmin is working), then it's likely that you specified the wrong database name, wrong username, or possibly the wrong password in the `config.php` file, so go back and check them.

No Data in the Database

You might get a blank screen or receive error messages like these in the browser window:

```
Warning: main(language/lang-.php): failed to open stream: No such
file or directory in \xampp\htdocs\nuke\mainfile.php on
line 183
...

Fatal error: Call to undefined function: themeheader() in
\xampp\htdocs\nuke\header.php on line 47
```

This probably means that your database is actually empty. Ensure you have added the data as we did earlier. Another possibility is that you have incorrectly specified the table prefix in the file `config.php` file. That line should look like this:

```
$prefix = "nuke";
```

Still Having Problems?

If PHP-Nuke is still not working, and you have followed the steps in this chapter, then there is something wrong elsewhere, but it is likely that you will find the answer by scouring the forums at `http://www.nukecops.com/forum2.html`. This is the Installation for Newbies forum on nukecops. This contains many questions (and solutions) from new users attempting to get their site running.

Summary

In this chapter, we have walked through the typical steps to install PHP-Nuke on a local machine running an AMP environment.

After obtaining and installing the PHP-Nuke application from the PHP-Nuke main site, `phpnuke.org`, we also installed ChatServ's patches so as to minimize possible security issues.

The next thing we did was to create the database for PHP-Nuke and populate it using phpMyAdmin—a web-based tool for working with MySQL databases. As you will see in later chapters, almost everything about your site is stored in this database.

Finally, we moved the folder containing PHP-Nuke's code into the document root of our web server. We also looked at some troubleshooting issues to check that everything is working OK. With everything working fine, we can start exploring PHP-Nuke!

3
Your First Page

In the previous chapter you learned how to install PHP-Nuke. In this chapter you'll familiarize yourself with a visitor's-eye view of the PHP-Nuke world and make your first modifications to the site.

We're going to look at our new homepage and from there move on to look at some of the main concepts of PHP-Nuke: blocks, modules, themes, and site security. Along the way, we're going to create the **super user**, a user with absolute power over our site; we will edit our first piece of content in PHP-Nuke, and begin the construction of the Dinosaur Portal.

Your New Homepage

Navigate to your site's homepage in your browser. For our newly installed PHP-Nuke site, this will be http://localhost/nuke/. You should be presented with the following screen, which we saw at the end of the last chapter:

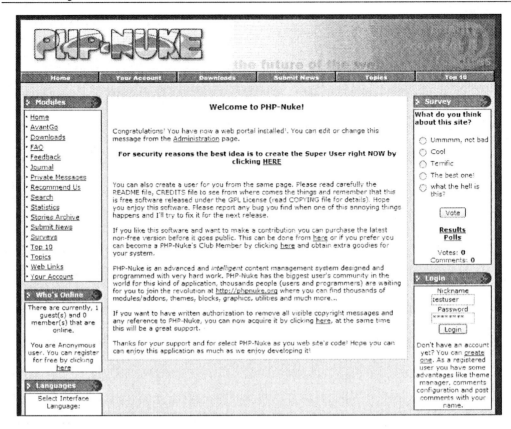

Considering that we've not really done anything, this is impressive. I'm sure you won't be able to resist clicking on some of these links and seeing what PHP-Nuke has in store for us. Currently, the system is 'empty', so it has a rather cold and eerie feeling about it. Rest assured that it will start to warm up over the next few chapters as we add content to the site.

> By the way, if you are impressed with the features you're seeing right now, let me tell you that there are others that haven't yet been activated. Also, there are many other add-ons that we can find from various PHP-Nuke resource sites across the Internet.

Let's now talk about some of the PHP-Nuke bits that we see on the front page.

First of all, there's the look of the page. There is the banner at the top, a site logo, and a horizontal navigation bar:

The page 'body' begins below the navigation bar. You can see a three-column layout with a big chunk of information in the middle column. The page layout of a PHP-Nuke site need not always look this; the arrangement of the elements, the choice of color, text styles, and images is controlled by the **theme**. A different theme can be selected for the site, and immediately, the look and feel of your site is changed.

Blocks

The elements that you see in the left- and right-hand columns are known as **blocks**:

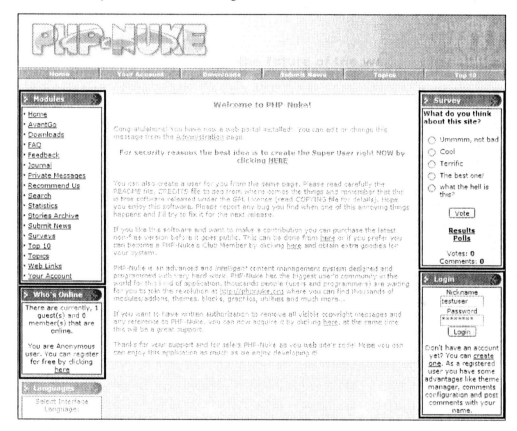

Blocks in PHP-Nuke are little nuggets of information positioned at the sides or sometimes at the bottom of a page. They often provide 'navigation', linking to other parts of the site, and provide a report or summary of the content that is available either on your site or, possibly, on another site. Typically, many blocks are displayed on a single page.

An important block is the **Modules** block in the left-hand column:

This block shows a list of the active modules on your site, and is the standard navigational element of a typical PHP-Nuke site. Each entry in the above list is a link to a module on your site, and by clicking on the links the visitor is able to move between the modules.

Modules

PHP-Nuke is a modular system. Each module is like a mini website in itself, performing different tasks and working with different types of content. The PHP-Nuke 'core' provides a central mechanism for handling these modules, so that they work together sharing data and user information, and ensuring a consistent look and operation throughout your site.

> In short, the modules define your site.

The good thing with PHP-Nuke is that you can add and remove modules as needed, selecting the best range of features to suit your site and its visitors. We will discuss the standard PHP-Nuke modules over the next few chapters.

When viewing a page on a PHP-Nuke site, the module currently in play can be known by looking at the URL of that page. For example, if you are looking at the Downloads module, the URL will be something like this:

```
http://localhost/nuke/modules.php?name=Downloads
```

The part of the URL after the ? character is the query string. The query string contains variables that are separated by the & character. In the above URL, the query string contains a single variable, name, which has the value Downloads. PHP-Nuke switches between modules according to the value specified in the name variable. The other query string variables determine what else is to be displayed on that page, such as the required news story for example. (Handling these query string variables appropriately has traditionally been a security weakness in PHP-Nuke, but that is true for many other web applications).

The output of the module being currently viewed is displayed in the middle column of the web page.

A Fistful of Default Modules

Let's have a quick overview of what some of the standard modules offer:

- **Home**: Shows the homepage of the site. There isn't actually a Home module but some particular module is associated with the homepage. The homepage actually has the URL index.php, rather than modules.php?name=xxxx.

- **Downloads and Web Links**: Allow you to create and maintain categorized lists of downloadable resources or links to other sites. Possibly you have already seen the Downloads module in action when you downloaded PHP-Nuke itself from a PHP-Nuke powered site. This is another 'interactive' module—visitors can submit their own downloadable resources or links here.

- **Recommend Us**: Allows the visitor on your site to send a message to their friends suggesting that they come and visit your site.

- **Search**: Allows the visitor to search the contents of your site.

- **Statistics**: Provides site statistics like the number of visits to your site, the different browsers used by visitors, and the most-viewed stories on your site.

- **Stories Archive**: Contains an archive of past stories that have appeared on the site, arranged by month of publication.

- **Submit News**: Allows visitors to submit a news story to the site through a form, after which the story goes straight onto the site provided it is acceptable. The story is then said to be **published**.

- **Surveys**: Displays the results of polls that have appeared on the site. Polls can be attached to stories and other pieces of content.

- **Topics**: Provides a different view of the stories, this time arranged by their topic.

- **Your Account**: Allows visitors to your site to register and create their own accounts. All visitors that register at your site can have their own area, which is accessed through this module. They can customize their own area, including their own Journal.

That's not even all of the modules, but it's enough to give you an idea of the breadth of the functionality that PHP-Nuke offers and the kind of experience that your visitors can look forward to.

Coming back to the homepage, have a look at the message in the middle that says:

> For security reasons the best idea is to create the Super User right NOW by
> clicking HERE

It's not everyday that we're invited to create a super user, so I think we should get on with that, especially as the word NOW is in upper case; that always suggests a sense of urgency.

Clicking on the word HERE in that message will take you to the page `http://localhost/nuke/ admin.php`; and we can begin creating our super user.

Creating the Super User

PHP-Nuke enables visitors to your site to create their own user account, and add and maintain their own personal details. The user account is required to identify them for posting news stories, making comments, or contributing to discussions in the forums, among other activities. By registering on the site and creating a user account, the visitors are given greater freedom on the site. However, their freedom has limits.

We are about to create a special type of user, the super user. This is a registered user of the site who has almost total freedom on the site and absolute power over it. The super user can access, add, remove, and modify any part of the site, and can configure and control anything on the site. Given the nature of this power, there comes the obvious responsibility of ensuring that the identity of this user is kept a secret.

Anyone obtaining these account details will be able to do almost anything to your site, and that could be *worse* than it sounds, so you must ensure that these details do not fall into the wrong hands.

The super user is a site administrator, in fact, *the* site administrator. We will use the term administrator and super user interchangeably. It is also possible to create other, less powerful, site administrators who can manage various parts of the site, such as approving bits of content submitted by visitors.

We shall now create the super user account. As with any user account on PHP-Nuke, it will consist of a username ('nickname', as it is also known in PHP-Nuke) and a password.

On the page `http://localhost/nuke/admin.php`, you will be presented with a form asking you to choose a super user Nickname, the HomePage of that user, a contact Email address and a Password. The password should only contain alphanumeric characters (letters and numbers). This is how the form looks:

There are no Administrators Accounts yet, proceeed to create the Super User:

Nickname: [   ]
HomePage: [http://   ]
Email: [   ]
Password: [   ]
Do you want to create a normal user with the same data? ⊙Yes ○No
[Submit]

The super user account is not the only type of user account that can be created with PHP-Nuke. Visitors to your site can register and create their own user accounts, which make them **Registered Users** of your site. When creating the super user there is an option to create a registered user with the same details, although obviously that user doesn't have the extended power of the super user. This does mean that when you log in with this administrator account, you will enjoy all the personalization benefits of the standard user account.

We will create the nickname and password for the super user account now.

> Do not use nicknames like admin, super user, or root for the super user; these would be the first guess of any miscreant attempting to break into your system. Also, make your password difficult to guess; make it long with a mixture of digits and letters, both upper and lowercase (definitely do not use the word password as your password!). Making the password secure is another vital step toward the overall security of your site.

In the page, we will enter dinoportmeister for the nickname, and use the password Pa2112cktXog. You can enter your own nickname and password here if you like, but make sure you remember them!

Your email address needs to go into the Email field, this is another required field. The HomePage field does not have to correspond to the address of this site; this is for informational purposes only.

The option to create a normal user with the same data will do just that, it will create a user with the same username and password as the administrator account. However, the two accounts are distinct, and changing the password for either account will not affect the other.

Click Submit and the super user is created.

Becoming the Administrator

After you have created the details for the super user, you still have to log yourself in with these details. On the admin.php page, you will find a form for entering the administrator username and password. Hopefully you haven't forgotten them already!

After entering the details here, click the Login button and you will pass over to the other side: the administration area of the site.

The admin.php page is where you need to log in to access the administration area. Whenever you want to log in as an administrator to perform some site maintenance, you do so from this page. Logging in from any other place on the site will log you 'normally' into the site, as if you were a standard visitor to the site, even if the administrator username and password is accepted.

If you think about it, this suggests that unless it has been specially customized, any PHP-Nuke site has an administrator login page at admin.php. This means that anyone intent on accessing the administrator area of that site does not have to look far to find the administrator login (of course, getting the right username and password combination is another matter). To counter this, from PHP-Nuke 7.6 onwards, if you want to rename the admin.php file, you can do so by storing the new name of the file in the $admin_file variable in the config.php file. This relocates your administrator login page.

Once you have entered the administration username and password, you will get your first taste of the administration area:

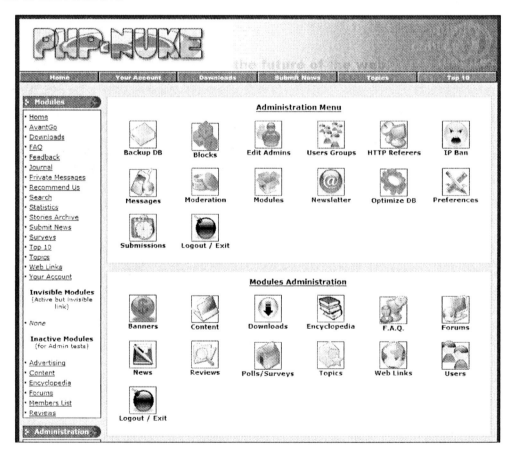

That might be more than you were expecting. We are presented with two towering graphical menus; the Administration Menu and the Modules Administration menu, the main navigation tools for the site administrator. (In versions of PHP-Nuke earlier than 7.5, these menus were one—the Administration Menu).

We'll dig into more detail about these menus in the next few chapters. This is the place where you will spend most of your PHP-Nuke life, so you will need to get comfortable with it.

Before we go any further, click the Home link in the Modules block to return to the homepage of your site.

A New Welcome

When you return to the homepage, you will notice that some extra text has appeared at the bottom of the welcome message:

[View: All Visitors - Unlimited - Edit]

This text is evidence of the super user's extra powers. If you click on the Edit link, you can begin changing the site. The presence of the Edit link is an example of 'in-position' editing, whereby as you browse the site you can quickly edit or delete the content you see. This link is not available to normal users of the site and is a pretty neat feature of PHP-Nuke.

When you click the Edit link, you will be taken back to the administration area.

The place we're after, the Edit Message box, is actually tucked away underneath the Modules Administration menu, so you'll need to scroll down in your browser to find the Messages Administration panel.

```
┌─────────────────────────────────────────────────────────┐
│                 Messages Administration                  │
├─────────────────────────────────────────────────────────┤
│                                                           │
│                      Edit message                         │
│  Title:                                                   │
│  ┌─────────────────────────────────────────────────────┐ │
│  │Welcome to PHP-Nuke!                                 │ │
│  └─────────────────────────────────────────────────────┘ │
│  Content:                                                 │
│  ┌─────────────────────────────────────────────────────┐ │
│  │Congratulations! You have now a web portal installed!.│ │
│  │You can edit or change this message from the          │ │
│  │Administration page.                                  │ │
│  │                                                      │ │
│  │  For security reasons the best idea is to create the │ │
│  │       Super User right NOW by clicking HERE          │ │
│  │                                                      │ │
│  │You can also create a user for you from the same page.│ │
│  │Please read carefully the README file, CREDITS file to│ │
│  │see from where comes the things and remember that this│ │
│  │is free software released under the GPL License (read │ │
│  │COPYING file for details). Hope you enjoy this        │ │
│  │software. Please report any bug you find when one of  │ │
│  │this annoying things happens and I'll try to fix it   │ │
│  │for the next release.                                 │ │
│  └─────────────────────────────────────────────────────┘ │
│   B  I  U  ABC  ≡ ≡ ≡ ≡  ⋮≡ ⋮≡  ↶ ↷  ∞ ⊗  ✎ HTML         │
│                                                           │
│  Expiration: Unlimited ▼                                  │
│                                                           │
│  Active? ◉ Yes ○ No                                       │
│                                                           │
│  Change start date to today? ○ Yes ◉ No                   │
│                                                           │
│  Who can View This? All Visitors            ▼             │
│  [ Save Changes ]                                         │
└─────────────────────────────────────────────────────────┘
```

This is the 'raw data' that made up the welcome message we saw on the homepage. This piece of content is an example of a PHP-Nuke **message**. This is just one of the many types of content that PHP-Nuke handles, and we'll see more over the next few chapters.

Editing Text in PHP-Nuke

The large textbox containing the Content text is our first experience of editing content in PHP-Nuke. Before we go any further, it's worth taking a moment to understand what you can and cannot do when editing textbox content in PHP-Nuke.

HTML Rules

Firstly, all the text you enter will be displayed as HTML on the site, so multiple spaces will be displayed as a single space, and breaking lines by simply pressing *Enter*, as if you were using a word processor, won't work. (The text will be stored in the format you enter it in but isn't displayed as you intend it to be.)

To introduce line breaks, use the
 HTML tag. More elegant is to enclose paragraphs in <p> and </p> tags, which inserts line breaks between paragraphs. You can enclose text with <b> and </b> tags to produce bold text, <i> and </i> tags to produce italics, and <u> and </u> to underline text.

Forbidden Tags

For anyone other than an administrator of the site, there are some HTML tags that cannot be used when submitting content to PHP-Nuke through a form. For example, you cannot use the `<script>` tag to include any JavaScript in your text; PHP-Nuke will reject this. Also, you can't define the style of any elements with the `style` attribute, thus something like:

```
<p style="font-size:1000px">Big Text</p>
```

will be rejected. Using any of the forbidden tags will produce the following error message:

PHP-Nuke rejects these kinds of tags to avoid cross-site scripting (intriguingly acronymed XSS to avoid clashing with the CSS of Cascading Style Sheets) attacks, a traditional security vulnerability of many web applications. These restrictions are intended not only for security reasons but also to prevent people from creating disturbing-looking content through creative use of the `style` attribute.

These constraints aren't specific to the editing we're doing now—these rules apply wherever content is entered by a user and posted back to PHP-Nuke. Since these restrictions prevent people going overboard with the use of excessive styles, we get consistent looking pages.

The ability for administrators to use these otherwise-forbidden tags is new to PHP-Nuke 7.8.

Adding Links

You can add links to textbox content just as you would with HTML, through the `<a>` tag. You do not need to prefix links to pages on your own site with your site's domain name. In other words, if your site is at www.thedinosaurportal.com, you do not need to use a link like this to link to another page on your site:

```
<a href="http://www.thedinosaurportal.com/modules.php?name=Content">
```

You can simply use relative links:

```
<a href="modules.php?name=Content">
```

There is a good reason to not hardcode your domain name into such links. If you move your site to a different domain name, such as when moving from a local version of the site to a web hosting environment, your links will still work.

Note that PHP-Nuke doesn't check any links that you add to textbox content—if the link is broken (that is, there is no longer a page at that URL), PHP-Nuke will not alert you about it.

Don't forget the closing `</a>` tag for links!

Adding Images

You can add images through the `<img>` tag as you normally would in HTML. However, PHP-Nuke does not usually offer you the facility to upload any accompanying images. If you want to display an image on your site in some piece of content, you must upload it yourself at some other time.

HTML Editor in PHP-Nuke 7.7

From PHP-Nuke 7.7, a **WYSIWYG (What You See Is What You Get)** HTML editor has been introduced, which replaces the large multi-line textboxes everywhere:

This allows the users to see their text as HTML as they type it, and provides a more familiar editing environment to work in, with buttons for adding bold, italics, and so on. The HTML editor is quite restrictive of the types of HTML that can be used in entries, and does not allow editing of the source HTML.

In PHP-Nuke 7.8, you can turn off this HTML editor by adding the highlighted line in the `config.php` file located in the root of our PHP-Nuke installation (we've added it underneath the definition of the site key we created in the last chapter):

```
$sitekey = "78w f7sys f89s fsd sj hjsg sdfw3p;";
define('NO_EDITOR', 1);
```

The highlighted line defines a PHP constant called NO_EDITOR, and gives it the value 1. This indicates to PHP-Nuke that the HTML editor should not be used. If you change the value 1 to 0, then you will restore the HTML editor.

Throughout this book, we have used this line to turn off the HTML editor, and our screenshots will show the standard textboxes, as found in all the PHP-Nuke versions before 7.7.

Time For Action—Changing the Welcome Message

1. Change the Title field of the message from Welcome to PHP-Nuke! to Welcome to the Dinosaur Portal.

2. Click in the Content field, press *Ctrl+A* to select all the text in that box and then press *Delete*. Now, in the empty box, enter the following:

```
The Dinosaur Portal is a site dedicated to dinosaur-related information.
Its founding principle is that...<br><br>
<i>Just because you haven't seen a dinosaur, it doesn't mean they've all
died out....</i>
```

Edit message

Title:

Welcome to the Dinosaur Portal

Content:

The Dinosaur Portal is a site dedicated to dinosaur-related
information. Its founding principle is that...

Just because you haven't seen a dinosaur, it doesn't mean
they've all died out....

---

3. Click the Save Changes button.

4. When the page reloads, scroll down the screen to see your message listed:

Overview messages

ID	Title	Language	Visible to	Active	Functions
1	Welcome to the Dinosaur Portal	All	All Visitors	Yes	(Edit-Delete)

5. Now click on the Home link at the top of the Modules block to go back to our homepage. The new welcome message is displayed in the middle of the page:

Welcome to the Dinosaur Portal

The Dinosaur Portal is a site dedicated to dinosaur-related information. Its founding principle is that...

Just because you haven't seen a dinosaur, it doesn't mean they've all died out....

[View: All Visitors - Unlimited - Edit]

We have edited our first piece of PHP-Nuke content: an existing **message**. A message is a simple type of PHP-Nuke content that is displayed (usually) at the top of the homepage, under the site banner. In this case we were editing the first message, which has special importance.

The first steps were simply entering some text into the Title and Content fields, thus populating the message with some content and replacing the existing content.

After that, we clicked the Save Changes button to persist our new content to PHP-Nuke's database. We also saw the list of current messages stored in PHP-Nuke. After entering a piece of content to be stored, PHP-Nuke will usually present you with a list of the stored content, often with links or buttons to operate on that content. For example, in the list of messages shown in the screenshot before last, you can see Edit and Delete links in the Functions column. There were a number of other options at the bottom of the Edit Message panel that we did not touch. Let's discuss them now.

Messages can be set to expire after a certain length of time, and the Expiration field can be used to set this time period. If we want our message to remain present indefinitely, we can set this value to Unlimited. (You may think Unlimited is a confusing value for the expiry date and that a value like Never is more suitable, as it is in keeping with the other values that you find in the dropdown. If so, you've had a PHP-Nuke moment).

We left the Active option set to Yes so that our message is available. Selecting No would make it disappear from the homepage, but the message itself wouldn't be deleted.

The Change start date to today? field resets the expiration 'counter'. This means that if the message is to expire, the expiry period will be calculated from the moment you save this changed version of the message, rather than being calculated from the moment the message was originally created. If a message had been previously deactivated, and you were reactivating it, the start date would automatically be set to 'today'.

The final option, Who can View This? brings us to another very important concept of PHP-Nuke sites.

Restricting User Access

Security in your PHP-Nuke site controls 'who can do what' in a particular place. There are two fundamental problems of security here:

- **Authentication**: The problem of deciding if the user is who they claim to be
- **Authorization**: The problem of what that user is able to do when browsing the website

PHP-Nuke solves the authentication problem with **user accounts.** It authenticate users (when necessary) by asking for a username and password combination.

PHP-Nuke solves the authorization problem by classifying the status of the visitor into one of the following:

- **Registered Users:** Visitors with a user account who have logged in with a valid username and password.

- **Administrators:** Users who are logged in with an administrator account (in other words a username and password that are valid on the admin.php page).

- **Anonymous Users:** People who have not logged into the site. Until a visitor registers and logs in, he or she has no identity and is hence anonymous.

- **Subscribed Users:** This is a special type of Registered User who has been given a special type of access, a *subscription*, which is valid for a certain period of time. Subscriptions are usually offered to fee-paying customers, and these users can benefit not only from exclusive access to certain parts of the site, but are also not shown adverts.

Anybody browsing the site falls into one of these categories. There is another category, which covers anybody visiting the site at all: All Visitors. Any visitor having either a user account or an administrator account, who might or might not be logged in, falls into the All Visitors category.

There are many opportunities within PHP-Nuke to restrict access or contributions. These restrictions or 'permissions', if you like, rather than being assigned on an individual user basis are assigned to one of the above categories of users. In this way, access to parts of your site can be restricted and these restrictions can be easily managed.

Restricting access so that only visitors from a particular category can view certain content is commonplace in PHP-Nuke.

Returning to our welcome message, we were presented with these options:

- All Visitors
- Anonymous Users Only
- Registered Users Only
- Administrators Only
- Subscribed Users

We wanted everyone to see our message, regardless of who they were, so we left All Visitors selected. We will see these options again in other areas of the site when we need to restrict access to some operation of the site.

Summary

This has been a short chapter, since we had only one task to accomplish—changing the welcome message on the homepage. This was our first attempt at modifying the content of the PHP-Nuke site, but in doing so we were introduced to many things that we will see again in the next few chapters, and which you will be using frequently as you work on your own PHP-Nuke sites.

Before we began editing the message, we created the super user account. The super user account has ultimate control over a PHP-Nuke site, and it is particularly important that this account information is kept secure.

In the role of the super user, we edited the welcome message from the homepage through a link that had appeared exclusively for that user. We had our first look at the administration area, and entered content into PHP-Nuke.

Finally, we discussed how PHP-Nuke classifies visitors to the site, and how permissions to parts of the site or pieces of content can be managed through this classification.

4
Managing the Site

In this chapter, we will begin to acquaint ourselves with PHP-Nuke's administration area, which allows you to manage your site from the comfort of your web browser. We'll look first at the website configuration settings. These options control many global properties of the site.

Then we will look at block and module administration. The tools available here let you change the functionality of your site with ease, and customize the site's features to your liking.

Your Site, Your Database

The database that we created when we installed PHP-Nuke in Chapter 2 is PHP-Nuke's storage repository.

That may sound like a rather trivial remark; we know PHP-Nuke is a database-driven web content management system. However, it is worth understanding the nature of what PHP-Nuke stores. PHP-Nuke stores not only information about registered users of the site, and such things as your news stories, features about you, your company, or your club, your photos and other images, but also stores *all* the information about your site and the content it holds.

In its database, PHP-Nuke stores such things as the name of your site, the site URL, the site logo, how many stories are displayed on the front page, whether users can comment anonymously on stories, the footer text displayed at the bottom of the page, how many people have read the stories, the voting information about stories, and also what layout and choice of colors are used to display the site. There are many, many more things PHP-Nuke squirrels away into its database, but the point in general is that your site is determined by the contents of its database.

This may sound rather overwhelming, particularly if you are new to databases—but this is precisely where the real power of PHP-Nuke lies. You don't have to be a MySQL master or know anything about the finer points of database theory; in fact, you generally won't be touching the database yourself. PHP-Nuke has a powerful web-based administration tool that lets you control and maintain your site. Through it you are effectively managing the database but this is happening behind the scenes and it is not something that you need to overly concern yourself with.

Visiting the Administration Area

With PHP-Nuke's awesome administration tool, you manage your site through your browser, controlling almost every aspect of its behavior, as well as adding and maintaining the content that is displayed. This doesn't mean that anyone can mess with your site; access to the administration area is restricted. You, the super user, as head of administrators have supreme power and can even appoint other people to act as limited administrators, with specific abilities to moderate and approve content for certain parts of the site.

PHP-Nuke's administration area can sometimes feel too comprehensive and often be overwhelming, occasionally counterintuitive in its behavior. This is the jungle we will beat our way through in the next few chapters, and in fact, it's where you will spend most of your PHP-Nuke life (the administration area, not these chapters!).

The first thing to do is to log in to the administrator account. Enter the following URL into your browser:

```
http://localhost/nuke/admin.php
```

If you are not already logged in, you will be prompted for the administrator username and password created in the previous chapter. Enter these and click the Login button to proceed.

Once you log in, you will be in the administration area and are confronted with two monstrous administration menus in the center of the screen:

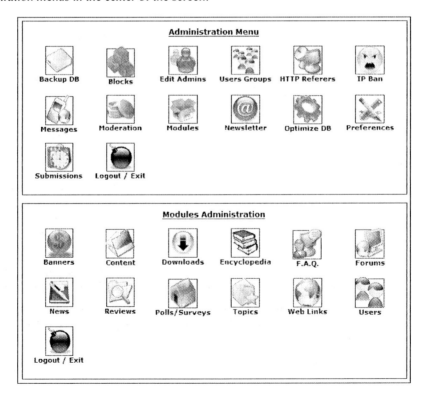

This is the central hub of the administration interface. Each of the icons you see on screen is a link to specific parts of the administration area, responsible for the control and management of particular features. If you scroll down the page, you will find some panels with information about the current home module, how many users are online, and some details of recently published stories, although at the moment, there is not much to see in any of these displays since we have no content or users!

The top menu of the administration interface, the Administration Menu, has icons for general 'system' management functions. These control the 'core' operations of PHP-Nuke, such as:

- Block and module management
- Database backup and optimization
- Banner management, users and user groups, and newsletters
- Site configuration
- Logging out of the administrator account

The lower menu, Modules Administration, has icons that take you through to the administration areas of individual modules. There is also another logout link.

> Note that if you are using a version of PHP-Nuke earlier than 7.5, there is only one large menu, the Administration Menu, and this contains all the above icons mixed in together.

The two-menu split emphasizes the division of labor for managing a PHP-Nuke.

- The top menu has tasks for maintaining and configuring the site.
- The bottom menu has tasks for maintaining and configuring individual modules.

First experiences of the administration menu are often perplexing—you click on one of the images and the page reloads, but nothing seems to have happened. The menus are still there in the middle of your page, grinning at you. (Particularly the rather gruesome looking IP Ban icon; you may begin to believe its eyes follow you around the room.)

What you're actually after is displayed below the menus. By default, the administration menus are always displayed at the top of the page in the administration area; the action you're trying to do is contained in the panels underneath, and you will generally have to scroll down to get at what you want. Possibly, if your screen resolution is sufficiently high and your browser window sufficiently sized, then you won't get this problem, but for most of us, we will find ourselves wondering if anything has happened.

The advantage of these ever-present menus is that if you suddenly find yourself needing to switch to another task, you simply scroll back up to the top of the page and click on the desired icon.

If you want to return to the administration homepage at any point, you can either enter the URL of the administration homepage (http://localhost/nuke/admin.php) or if you glance to the left-hand side of your page, you will see the Administration block.

The top link in this block, Administration, returns you to the administration homepage. This block is ever present if you are logged in as the administrator. Administrator movements are not necessarily restricted to the 'back end' (the administration interface) of the site. You can also visit the 'front end' of the site and view the site as your visitors see it. However, for the administrator, extra, context-sensitive links appear on various items that provide you with a fast track to the administration area, and let you control that item. We'll see more of these links as we look in detail at the default modules over the next few chapters.

Also, there are special blocks that are only visible to the administrator, the Administration block being one of them.

You can replace the graphical administration menus by a more manageable text menu, but for now we will be working in the more familiar graphical environment, at least until we know our way round.

Site Preferences

Our first job will be to change some global settings of our site; we do so by clicking on the Preferences option:

When you do this, the page will reload and the Administration Menu will reappear, and then you should scroll down to the Web Site Configuration menu. This is a long list of options; the top part is shown in the following figure:

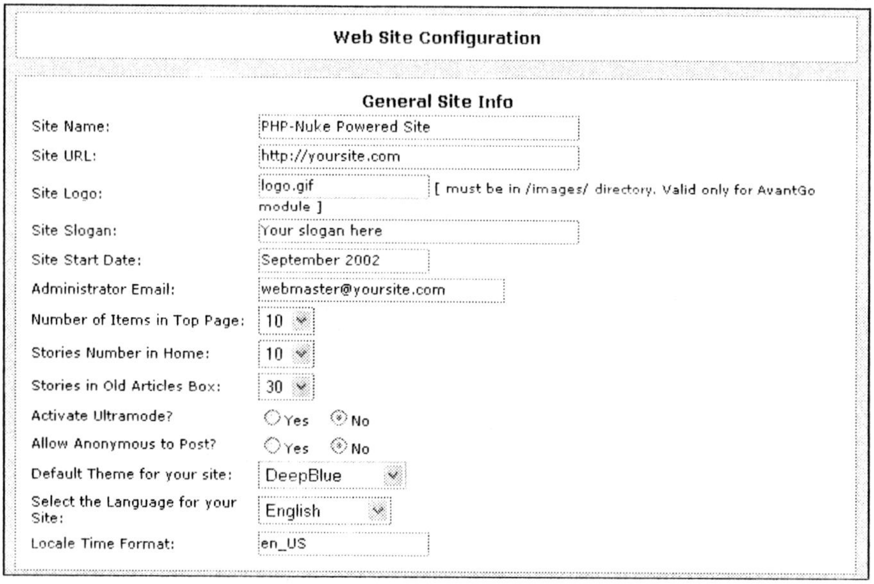

```
                          Web Site Configuration

                            General Site Info
   Site Name:          PHP-Nuke Powered Site
   Site URL:           http://yoursite.com
   Site Logo:          logo.gif                  [ must be in /images/ directory. Valid only for AvantGo
                       module ]
   Site Slogan:        Your slogan here
   Site Start Date:    September 2002
   Administrator Email: webmaster@yoursite.com
   Number of Items in Top Page:  10 ▾
   Stories Number in Home:       10 ▾
   Stories in Old Articles Box:  30 ▾
   Activate Ultramode?           ○ Yes  ⊙ No
   Allow Anonymous to Post?      ○ Yes  ⊙ No
   Default Theme for your site:  DeepBlue    ▾
   Select the Language for your  English     ▾
   Site:
   Locale Time Format:           en_US
```

At the foot of the list is a **Save Changes** button (not seen in the screenshot as it is too far below). This button has to be clicked for any changes to persist.

The list of Web Site Configuration options is divided into a number of panels, grouping together options for particular tasks:

- General Site Info
- Multilingual Options
- Banners Options
- Footer Messages
- Backend Configuration
- Mail New Stories to Admin
- Comments Moderation
- Comments Option
- Graphics Options
- Miscellaneous Options
- Users Options
- Censure Options

We won't look at all of these panels now; instead we will look at them as we need them. For example, when covering story management in Chapter 6, we'll explore the Comments Moderation, Comments Option, Censure Options, Backend Configuration, and the Mail New Stories to Admin panels.

We shall now look at some of the options in General Site Info; these control some basic options for our site.

First up is the Site Name option. This is the name of your site, and is usually displayed in the title-bar at the top of the browser. It also used in any text referring to your site, such as email messages automatically sent out by the site (for example, the confirmation message sent to a user who has created an account on your site).

Let's stamp the identity of this site, by changing the Site Name value to the Dinosaur Portal:

General Site Info	
Site Name:	the Dinosaur Portal

Now scroll to the bottom of the list of preferences where you see the Save Changes button. Click this to update your site. After the page reloads, you should see that the title bar in your browser has changed from PHP-Nuke Powered Site to our new site name—the Dinosaur Portal.

When the page reloads, you are still on the Web Site Configuration menu page. This is good in case you need to make any further changes, or if you got something wrong with the last change you made. There are some parts of the PHP-Nuke administration interface where clicking a Save or Ok button does not keep you in the same part of the administration interface but returns you to the administration homepage. This kind of thing can make you lose your bearings early on.

> Although we only made one change before clicking the Save Changes button, you can, of course, make as many changes to the preferences as you like before clicking the button.

The Site URL is important too. This field holds the URL of your site homepage (without the index.php bit). If you specify the wrong Site URL or, more likely, forget to change it from http://phpnuke.org, then the consequences are not drastic; visitors will not suddenly find themselves transported to another site when they click a link on your site. However, the Site URL is used in emails sent to newly registered users with a link to confirm their registration. With the wrong Site URL here, people will go to the wrong site to register (and fail!). We will remind you of this when we discuss emails sent out by the system.

Let's change the Site URL before we forget. Since our site is at http://localhost/nuke, enter that into the Site URL field, and then scroll down and click the Save Changes button.

The Site Slogan, Site Start Date, and Administrator Email are straightforward to change. The Administrator Email account is the email account that will be used to send out user registration confirmations. The Site Slogan value is used in the META DESCRIPTION tag in the page header of your page:

```
<META NAME="DESCRIPTION" CONTENT="Your slogan here">
```

This tag is used by some search engines to create the description of your page in its listing. (That is *when* you are visited by search engines, which is still a long way off!)

By default, the value of the META DESCRIPTION tag is fixed for all pages in PHP-Nuke, and takes the value of your Site Slogan field.

The Site Logo specifies an image used by some modules to 'stamp' their pages. This value does not control any site logo image that may appear in the site banner at the top of your page.

Another interesting option is the Default Theme for your site. This gives you a drop-down box with a list of the currently installed themes. Select NukeNews from the list, scroll down, and click Save Changes. When the page reloads, it looks rather different:

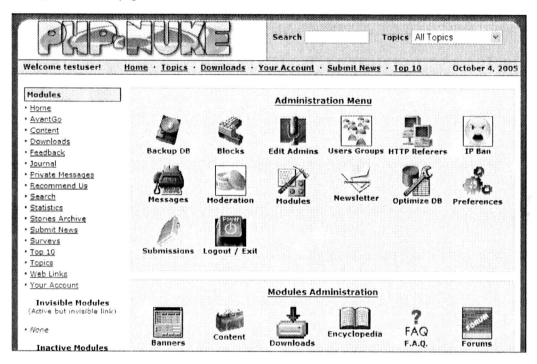

Not bad for two clicks of a mouse. We just changed the site's default theme and immediately the new theme has been applied, and we now have a very different looking site. It still 'works' the same, but it looks very different. One of the most obvious changes is the icons in the Administration Menu. There are some standard images in PHP-Nuke that can be overridden by images from the theme. The icons in the Administration Menu are one set of images that can be overridden like this.

Every visitor sees the theme that is specified as the default theme. Registered users have the option to choose their own theme, to personalize the site to their liking.

Now let's select the DeepBlue theme from the list of themes and click the Save Changes button. In the next few chapters we're going to see a lot of screenshots from the PHP-Nuke administration interface and the front end, and they're all going to be taken with the DeepBlue theme. If you're not using this theme as you follow along, things could look different. The DeepBlue theme is the default theme.

Turning off the Graphical Icons

For future reference, if you get sick of the Administration Menu icons (perhaps the terrifying IP Ban icon is finally getting to you), the Graphics Options panel is where you can turn off the graphical administration menu:

Graphics Options

Graphics in Administration Menu? ⦿ Yes   ○ No

We will leave it set to Yes for now as we explore the administration interface. When you feel more confident, you can return here and set it to No to replace the graphical menu by a text menu.

The Cookie Crumbles

That's enough of the Web Site Configuration menu for now. Don't worry; we will come back to it over the next few chapters. Your next task is to close your browser.

Now open a new browser window, and navigate to your site's homepage (http://localhost/nuke/). You will notice that you are still logged in as the administrator—you can see the Administration block in the left-hand side column.

You may find this rather strange—you didn't enter a username or a password or go through the admin.php page, so how did it know? The answer is a cookie. PHP-Nuke issues cookies to visitors, which contain a number of user preferences, including their login details. This means that when the visitor returns to the site they are identified, and dealt with accordingly. This explains why you are logged back in as an administrator without having taken any action.

An annoying side-effect is that if you wanted to view the site as a visitor and administrator at the same time, you would have to log out and log in again before viewing. Should you find yourself doing this often, an obvious solution is to use two different types of browsers—say Mozilla Firefox and Internet Explorer (cookies are distinct on the two applications)—so one can be your administration browser and the other can be your visitor browser.

Backing Up the Site Database

It's not an exciting activity, but backing up your database is essential for the continuous running of your site. Almost everything about your PHP-Nuke site is stored in the database, and if there's some problem with the database, it will surely translate into a big problem on your site. Also, creating a backup of the database is not only to prevent a catastrophe; if you plan to develop your site locally (as we are doing) before uploading to your web host, then you will want a backup of the local database with you. This copy can be directly uploaded to the web host database server so that your site is ready to go without having to go through the entire configuration setup again.

You can create a backup of the database from within PHP-Nuke's administration area. Doing this creates a copy of the database in the same format as the nuke.sql file that you used to construct the original PHP-Nuke database. This file should then be stored safely, ready to be used in case of a database emergency.

Creating a database backup is a one-click process. You simply click the Backup DB icon in the Administration Menu:

After a moment, a Save dialog box will open in your browser. The database backup is a text file having the default filename of Save.

You can give the file a name in the format <databasename>_backup_<date>.sql, and then open it in a text editor to check what it contains.

Once you have the backup of the database, restoring the database is similar to the process of creating the original PHP-Nuke database that we saw in Chapter 2. The only difference is the choice of file to upload, and the fact that you will have to remove the existing data in the database before 'applying' the backup.

You can easily remove all the data, in fact the entire database, from phpMyAdmin. Simply open it up in your browser, and select your PHP-Nuke database from the drop-down list on the left-hand side of databases. Once it is selected, and all the tables are displayed, click the Drop tab on the right-hand side:

An alert message will appear:

The use of uppercase for DESTROY signals that you are about to perform a drastic operation. Clicking OK will remove the database from your database server, but this is not a problem since you did make a backup copy of it.

To recreate the database, simply retrace the steps outlined in Chapter 2 to create the database (you will have to define the database user and role again), and then to create the tables and fill them with the data from the backup, click the SQL tab, click the Browse button, and navigate to your database backup file. Selecting this and clicking Go will restore your database. Removing the database will, of course, mean your PHP-Nuke site is temporarily broken, and any visitors will see one of the data access error screens that we saw in Chapter 2.

Note that you can zip up the database backup and upload the ZIP file to phpMyAdmin rather than the plain text file. phpMyAdmin will automatically extract the text file and process it. However, it is possible that when you are attempting this on a web hosting provider, the server may not be able to work with the ZIP file in this way; it should become obvious that this is a problem, since you will get a page full of error messages, and you will have to upload the file in the standard text format.

Be careful about the size of the file you upload when working with a hosting provider; it is also likely that there will be some restriction on the size of file that you can upload to the server—typically 2MB.

You should get in the habit of backing up the database once your site is up and running. How often you back up will depend on how busy your site is, and how often new content is added or changes are made, but a daily backup is wise for any active site.

There is also an Optimize DB (Database) option in the PHP-Nuke Administration Menu:

As the name suggests, clicking this icon will have PHP-Nuke go through all the tables in the database in an attempt to 'optimize' them. In fact, PHP-Nuke issues a MySQL OPTIMIZE TABLE statement against every table in the database, and reports any space saved in the database by doing this. You can read more about exactly what the OPTIMIZE TABLE statement does, and when you may want to use it, in the MySQL manual at:

```
http://dev.mysql.com/doc/mysql/en/optimize-table.html
```

Managing Blocks

Blocks are a key part of the layout of a PHP-Nuke website, and you have a great deal of ability to customize the way in which they are displayed. We've already seen the Modules block; this is the main navigational control in PHP-Nuke. Here are some of the other blocks shown on the default homepage to a visitor:

Languages: This block is placed on the left of the page. This block allows you to choose the PHP-Nuke interface language.

Survey: This block is placed on the right-hand side of the page. This allows visitors to take part in straw polls on some pressing matter of the day. The default poll is the question we're all asking at this point in the book.

If you are logged in as an administrator, you will also see blocks such as the Administration block that we saw earlier, and the Waiting Content block in the left-hand column.

This block shows a summary of any pending user-submitted content that needs to be moderated and approved before publishing. We'll find out more about this 'workflow' in the next few chapters.

You will notice that all the blocks on the page look the same as this, and the overall columnar layout is a hallmark of most PHP-Nuke sites.

You will also notice that each block consists of two parts—one part is the **title** (Languages or Survey for example), and the other part, the body of the block, is the **content**. A block does not concern itself with how it is displayed; this is taken care of by the PHP-Nuke theme. The pictures below show the Languages block when it is rendered in two different themes; 3D-Fantasy and Karate in these cases:

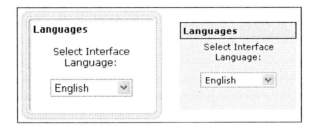

Although the blocks look different, you can see that the title-content split persists.

Types of Blocks

A block's job is to produce its content. This content may come from one of three places, and the origin of the content determines the type of block:

- HTML stored in the database
- Dynamic content created by PHP files
- RSS feeds from other sites

Let's talk about the third option for a moment. RSS is a standard format for sharing web content or summaries of web content, together with data about the content such as a link to the full version of the content. Typically, the content changes often, such as news stories, latest postings to a personal weblog, or assorted new additions to a site. RSS stands for Really Simple Syndication; you can read more about its definitions (the specification) and its history at http://blogs.law.harvard.edu/ tech/rss. The site http://www.whatisrss.com/ has more information about RSS. You can also refer to *RSS and Atom* by Heinz Wittenbrink from Packt Publishing (ISBN 1-904811-57-4).

The information is delivered via an RSS feed, and using such a mechanism allows a site to make its content available to others without having to notify them when new material is published. In other words, the receiver of the feed can have up-to-date information about the content available on the feeding site.

The process of making these headlines available is known as 'syndicating content', and is becoming an ever more popular way of distributing information without actually doing anything; anyone interested will consume the news feed.

PHP-Nuke's RSS blocks allow you to include RSS feeds on your site, so that you can suck up the headlines of stories from relevant sites and display them on your own site, creating a network of content for visitors to your site.

PHP-Nuke also provides facilities for syndicating news stories on your PHP-Nuke site via RSS; we'll look at that in Chapter 6.

Block Positioning

To determine where a block is displayed on the page, the block is given a position (left, right, or center), and a number called its weight. Blocks with a lower weight are displayed first; we'll see that changing the weight of a block moves it up and down the page.

Block Visibility

Blocks have a property that determines who is able to see the block. The administration blocks, for example, are only visible to the administrator and not to any other user. A block that contains the details of a logged-in visitor should only be displayed to that visitor—for an unregistered visitor this block would be meaningless. Also, it is often wise to not show advertising blocks to paying subscribers of your site.

The Blocks Administration Area

To set about our work with blocks, click on the Blocks icon in the Administration Menu:

Blocks

This brings up the Blocks Administration area. From here you can control all the blocks on your site. You can change the position of a block, the order in which it appears, its visibility to users, or even activate or deactivate the block.

The top part of the Blocks menu is show here:

Title	Position	Weight		Type	Status	Visible to	Functions
Modules	◁ Left	1	⬇	FILE		All Visitors	
Administration	◁ Left	2	⬆ ⬇	SYSTEM		Administrators Only	
Who's Online	◁ Left	3	⬆ ⬇	FILE		All Visitors	
Search	◁ Left	4	⬆ ⬇	FILE		All Visitors	
Languages	◁ Left	5	⬆ ⬇	FILE		All Visitors	
Random Headlines	◁ Left	6	⬆	FILE		All Visitors	

If the icons themselves aren't clear enough, hovering your mouse cursor over the graphic will display a tooltip explaining the function of that graphic.

Let's have a run-through of the columns in the table of blocks.

We have already seen the Title and the Position attributes of the block; the Weight column determines a logical ordering of the blocks within their 'column'. The order in which the blocks appear can be adjusted with the up and down arrows in the Weight column. In this way, you can reorder the blocks as you please, moving them up and down your page.

The Type column specifies the type of block: FILE, HTML, RSS/RDF, or SYSTEM. We discussed the first three types of block earlier; SYSTEM blocks are added by PHP-Nuke itself.

If the block Status is shown as ⚙, then the block is active and is displayed on the site. If this icon ⚙ is shown in the Status column, then the block is inactive. If the block is inactive, the next block (namely the block with the next lowest weight) will be displayed in its place—there is no gap left where an inactive block should be. Thus blocks can be removed from the page without leaving unsightly holes in the layout.

The Visible to column determines which group of visitors can see the block; the groups are, as we know, All Visitors, Registered Users Only, Administrators Only, or Anonymous Users Only.

The last column, Functions, is where the fun starts. Each block has four icons in the Functions column:

From left to right these icons allow you to:

- Edit the details of the block
- Activate or deactivate the block (depending on whether it is currently active)
- Delete the block
- Preview or 'show' the block

The preview icon is only enabled when the block is currently deactivated; clicking this icon gives you a view of what the block will look like when activated on your site. When the icon is not enabled, it will be grayed out.

If you forget which icon is which, then hover your mouse cursor over it, and the action of the icon will be displayed—Edit, Activate (or Deactivate), Delete, or Show.

We've talked about how we can reorder and reorganize the blocks, so let's actually have a go at it. Our first task will be to swap the order in which the Who's Online and Languages blocks appear on the page. The inactive Search module in sandwiched between them, but that isn't going to concern us at the moment.

Let's see how we can change the position of the Languages block:

1. Click on the up arrow in the Weight column of the Languages block in the block table. As your mouse cursor hovers over the arrow, you should see the helpful Block UP text popup, to let you know what clicking that image will do:

Who's Online	◁ Left	3	⇧ ⇩	FILE	⚙	All Visitors	📝 ⚙ 🗑 🔍
Search	◁ Left	4	⇧ ⇩	FILE	⚙	All Visitors	📝 ⚙ 🗑 🔍
Languages	◁ Left	5	⇧ ⇩	FILE	⚙	All Visitors	📝 ⚙ 🗑 🔍
Random Headlines	◁ Left	6	Block UP FILE		⚙	All Visitors	📝 ⚙ 🗑 🔍

2. When the page reloads, the Languages and Search block have swapped weights in the blocks table, as seen in the picture below. Since the Search block is inactive, it is not displayed, so at this point you cannot see any change to the look of your page.

Who's Online	◁ Left	3	⇧ ⇩	FILE	🗑	All Visitors	📝 🗑 📑 🔍
Languages	◁ Left	4	⇧ ⇩	FILE	🗑	All Visitors	📝 🗑 📑 🔍
Search	◁ Left	5	⇧ ⇩	FILE	🗑	All Visitors	📝 🗑 📑 🔍

3. Click on the up arrow for Languages, and when the page reloads, our work is done.

Languages	◁ Left	3	⇧ ⇩	FILE	🗑	All Visitors	📝 🗑 📑 🔍
Who's Online	◁ Left	4	⇧ ⇩	FILE	🗑	All Visitors	📝 🗑 📑 🔍
Search	◁ Left	5	⇧ ⇩	FILE	🗑	All Visitors	📝 🗑 📑 🔍

If you glance to the left-hand side of your page, you will see that the Languages and Who's Online blocks have switched positions. The picture below shows a 'before and after' shot of these two blocks on the page (the before shot is on the left):

That's moving blocks up. You go through a similar process for moving blocks down.

Occasionally, things don't quite go to plan when moving blocks down, and you may find that you have two blocks with the same weight. To resolve this problem, there is a way to 'rebalance' the weights. At the bottom of the blocks table you will find a Fix Block's Weight Conflicts link. Clicking this link, as the name suggests, corrects the list of block weights, ensuring that each block has a distinct weight.

Time For Action—Changing Block Position

Now we've made the Languages block move up the page, let's move it to the other side of the page.

1. To see the properties of a block, we click its Edit icon in the Functions column. Click the Edit icon of the Languages block now. You should see the Edit Block panel appear:

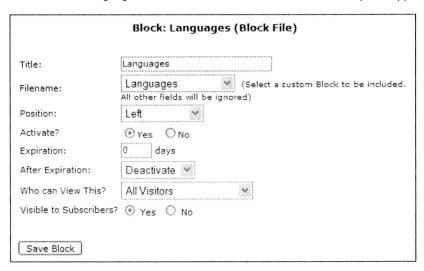

2. Select Right from the Position drop-down box:

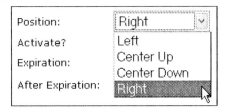

3. Click the Save Block button at the bottom of the panel.

4. When the page reloads, the Languages block has moved way down the list of blocks in the table, and also it has vanished from the left-hand column of the page. You will now find the Languages block along with other blocks whose Position is Right:

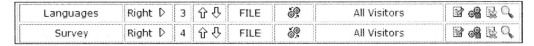

5. Now open a new browser window and go to your site's homepage. The Languages block is now on the right-hand side column, at the top of that column at the moment in fact. (The blocks above it in the list are either inactive or are displayed to registered visitors only.)

Welcome to theDinosaurPortal	Languages
Welcome to **theDinosaurPortal**. This site is founded on the premise that...	Select Interface Language:
Just because you haven't seen a dinosaur, doesn't mean they've all died out....	English
[View: All Visitors - Unlimited - Edit]	
	Survey
	What do you think about this site?

The process to change the block position was straightforward. This combined with the ability to reorder the blocks on the page means that you have great control over where blocks go on your page. In addition to Left and Right, there are two other positions for blocks:

- Center Up: In this position the block appears *before* the main module output.
- Center Down: In this position the block appears *after* the main module output.

Blocks in these last two positions are only shown on the site homepage. On the homepage of your site, blocks will be displayed in any of the four positions. In general, when you are looking at any of the modules, only the left-hand block column is displayed (Downloads, Feedback, and Web Links are exceptions to this).

An interesting thing to note about the repositioning of a block is the new weight it is given.

- When you change the position of a block, its weight *remains the same*.
- Any blocks of your target position whose weight is equal to or more than your block's weight will have their weight increased by one; they will all shuffle down to make room for your block.
- Any block in the same position as your block's original position whose weight is more than your block's weight will have their weight's decreased by one; they will all shuffle upwards to fill in the gap left by the moving block.
- If the weight of your block is higher than the maximum weight of any block in the target position, then your block will be given a new weight that is one more than that highest weight, so that again there is a nice sequence of consecutive weight values.

In short, when you change the position of blocks, PHP-Nuke will make some adjustments to all the other weights to retain sequences of consecutive weight values, which keeps things tidy.

Adding Blocks

The interface for adding new blocks to PHP-Nuke is the Add a New Block panel, found underneath the list of blocks in the Blocks Administration area.

Add a New Block

Title:	[ ]
RSS/RDF file URL:	[ ] Custom ▼ [Setup] (Select Custom and write the URL or just select a Site from the list to grab news headlines)
Filename:	None ▼ (Select a custom Block to be included. All other fields will be ignored)
Content:	[text area] If you fill the URL the content you write will not be displayed!
Position:	Left ▼
Activate?	⦿ Yes ○ No
Expiration:	0 days
After Expiration:	Deactivate ▼
Refresh Time:	1 Hour ▼ (Only for Headlines)
Who can View This?	All Visitors ▼
Visible to Subscribers?	⦿ Yes ○ No

[Create Block]

There are lots of options on this panel; some of the options apply to all types of block, and some only to certain types of block. This can be rather confusing to start with and is something that can make block management tricky for the beginner.

> There is also no option to specify what kind of block you are creating (HTML, RSS/RDF, FILE); this is because the type of block you create is determined for you by PHP-Nuke based on what you put into the fields of the Add a New Block panel.

Options for All Blocks

Here are the options that apply to all blocks, followed by a description of their purpose:

Option	Description
Title	This is the title of the block; this appears in the list of blocks in the Blocks Administration menu, and usually identifies the block on the page when it is displayed. You have to choose the value for Title. A block cannot be created without a title. It is possible to create two different blocks with the same title.

Option	Description
Position	Here you select from Left, Right, Center Up, or Center Down. This determines where the block appears on the page when displayed.
Activate?	Determines whether the block should be activated now. Once activated, a block can be deactivated from its Functions column. The default setting for this option is Yes—the block will be activated once it is created.
Expiration	Allows a time period—specified as a number of days—after which the block will be deactivated. The default value is 0, and this means the block will remain indefinitely. Note that if you set an expiration date, you cannot modify this value by editing the block properties.
After Expiration	Determines what action should be taken after the block expires, if an expiration time period has been set. This can be one of two values; Deactivate or Delete. Deactivate means the block will be deactivated and no longer visible once it expires; this option can be set on any type of a block. The Delete value is only applicable to HTML or RSS/RDF blocks, and will actually remove their details from the database.
Who can View This?	Determines the type of visitor that can view this block. The value is chosen from the categories we saw at the end of the previous chapter; Anonymous Users Only, Registered Users Only, Administrators Only, or All Visitors. The default value is All Visitors. Thus any freshly created block is visible to any visitor to the site.
Visible to Subscribers?	Determines if the block can be seen by subscribers. If it is set to No, then subscribers will not be able to see the block, regardless of the Who can View This? setting. This is commonly used to hide advertisement blocks from subscribers who will have already paid a fee for their subscription. The default value is Yes.

We will cover the options that apply to specific types of blocks as we come across them.

Time For Action—Adding a Static Block

Our first attempt at creating a block will be a simple HTML block; for this we simply use a lump of HTML. This will be stored in PHP-Nuke's database, and then retrieved and displayed when this block is output on the page. The HTML block cannot take advantage of any 'server-side' PHP processing, so the output is always fixed. The block will always look the same, whenever you look at it, whoever you are. The block is truly 'static'.

First of all, let's make sure we're in the Blocks Administration area; click on the Blocks icon in the Administration Menu just to make sure, and scroll down to the Add a New Block panel.

Our block will be a 'Dinosaur of the Day' block, displaying an image of today's dinosaur, and its name. We're going to position the block on the left-hand side of the page, and make it available to every visitor, and it shall remain on the site indefinitely.

1. Enter Dinosaur of the Day into the Title field.

2. Ignore the next two fields (RSS/RDF file URL and Filename); these have nothing to do with our HTML block.

3. Enter the following text into the Content field:

```
Today's dinosaur is
<br><center><b>Tyrannosaurus Rex</b></center><br>
<center><img src="images/dinosaurs/dotd.gif"
                alt="Tyrannosaurus Rex"></center><br>
```

4. Leave the Position field set to Left, and leave Activate? set to Yes.

5. Leave all the other fields as they are—the block is to remain indefinitely so we leave Expiration set to 0. Hence the After Expiration field is redundant and Refresh Time does not apply to this type of block. The block is to be visible to everyone, so leave All Visitors selected in Who can View This?

6. Click the Create Block button.

When the page reloads, you will see your new block added to the list of blocks:

And if you glance over the left of your page, you will see the block displayed:

Immediately, you can see the kind of limitations static HTML blocks have—if we want a different dinosaur displayed on a different day, we would have to edit the block text itself. We could change the image, but still the name of the dinosaur remains.

> Be careful when creating HTML blocks—if you enter anything into the RSS/RDF file URL field, whatever you type into the Content field will be ignored, and you will not create an HTML block but an RSS/RDF block. There is a warning about this at the foot of the Content field, so pay attention!

Adding Other People's News with RSS/RDF Blocks

OK, we've added our static HTML to the site. The next thing we'll do is genuinely impressive—we will add a news feed from an external site to our page. This is accomplished with the RSS/RDF block.

As we mentioned earlier, RSS feeds are a method for syndicating content. (Note that RDF is essentially a variation of RSS.) The data from an RSS feed is just a text file, in XML format, although that is something that doesn't concern us for now.

XML stands for Extensible Markup Language, a general-purpose markup language for carrying data between different sources and platforms. You can read more about XML at http://www.w3schools.com/xml/default.asp.

The first thing we'll need is a good news source. We'll grab the information about the latest adventures of the cartoon pair, Beaver and his dinosaur pal Steve from www.beaverandsteve.com. This news feed is found at:

http://www.beaverandsteve.com/rss.xml

Let's get back to the Blocks Administration area by clicking on the Blocks icon in the Administration Menu, and scroll down to the Add a New Block panel.

There are two ways we can store the URL of a target news feed in PHP-Nuke; we can either enter the URL directly into the RSS/RDF file URL field in this panel, or else we can create a new **headline** site. A headline site is just a named site with a URL for its news feed.

The advantage of creating a new headline site is that the URL is stored independent of the block; if you delete the block, then you can easily create a new block with the same news feed, without having to type (or maybe find!) the URL of the news feed again. Using a headline site also gives you the block title for free, as we will see now.

Time For Action—Creating a New Headline Site

1. From the Add a New Block panel, click on the Setup link on the right-hand side of the panel:

Add a New Block

Title:

RSS/RDF file URL: [   ] [Custom ▾] [Setup]
(Select Custom and write the URL or just select a Site from the list to grab news headlines)

2. The Headlines Administration panel is displayed. This is a list of the currently defined headline sites; there are some twenty or so sites already defined, some of which are related to PHP-Nuke (PHP-Nuke, NukeCops, and NukeResources for example) while others are about general open-source news or just general news. The top of this list is shown here:

Headlines Administration

Site Name	URL	Functions
AbsoluteGames	http://files.gameaholic.com/agfa.rdf	[Edit	Delete]
BSDToday	http://www.bsdtoday.com/backend/bt.rdf	[Edit	Delete]
BrunchingShuttlecocks	http://www.brunching.com/brunching.rdf	[Edit	Delete]
DailyDaemonNews	http://daily.daemonnews.org/ddn.rdf.php3	[Edit	Delete]
DigitalTheatre	http://www.dtheatre.com/backend.php3?xml=yes	[Edit	Delete]
DotKDE	http://dot.kde.org/rdf	[Edit	Delete]

3. If you scroll to the bottom of this list, you will see the Add Headline panel. This is where we define our headline site. Enter BeaverAndSteve into the Site Name, and into the RSS/RDF file URL field enter our news feed URL:

Add Headline

Site Name: | BeaverAndSteve.com |

RSS/RDF file URL: | http://www.beaverandsteve.com/rss.xml |

[Add]

4. Click the Add button, and when the page reloads, you will see our new news feed added to the bottom of the list of headlines:

| BeaverAndSteve.com | http://www.beaverandsteve.com/rss.xml | [Edit | Delete] |

You can use the Edit or Delete links to amend the details of the news feed link. Clicking on the link itself will open the news feed in a new browser window. This is useful for checking if you've actually got the URL correct—if you specify an incorrect URL for an RSS/RDF block, then your page output can be severely disrupted, so it's wise to check that you're actually pointing at the news feed.

Curiously, there is no link to the Headlines Administration panel in the Administration Menu by default. You will have to come through the Blocks Administration area by clicking the Setup link, or bookmark the Headlines Administration page in your browser.

Time For Action—Adding the RSS/RDF Block

Now our headline site has been defined, let's get back to creating the RSS/RDF block. Since we are currently in the Headlines Administration area you will have to click on the Blocks icon in the Administration Menu to get back to the Blocks menu, and then scroll down to our Add a New Block panel and follow these steps:

1. There is a drop-down box to the right of the RSS/RDF file URL field currently holding the value Custom. This contains a list of all our defined headlines. From this box, select BeaverAndSteve.com (it's right at the bottom!):

2. Let's leave the block on the Left, and set Activate? to Yes, and leave Refresh Time set to 1 Hour. We will also set this block to be viewable by All Visitors.

3. Click the Create Block button.

4. When the page reloads, you will see your newly created block in the list of blocks. Note that the block is of type RSS/RDF, and the Title has automatically been assigned from the name that we gave to the headline site:

| BeaverAndSteve.com | ◁ Left | 7 | ⇧ | RSS/RDF | 🙊 | All Visitors | 📝 🐾 🔖 🔍 |

Glance to the left of your page, and you will see the block in action. This is what the block displayed at the time of writing—when you see the block's output, the news will be different:

If you hover the mouse cursor over any of these links, you will see that these are links to the actual news stories on www.beaverandsteve.com, and clicking one will open that story in a new window. There is a read more... link at the foot of an RSS/RDF block that takes you to the homepage of the source site. We did not add any information about the URL for this homepage ourselves—this information is contained within the news feed itself, and was read and processed by PHP-Nuke for us.

Note that PHP-Nuke does not suck in the news feed from the source site every time the block is displayed. The operations of acquiring and processing the RSS feed every time the block was displayed would adversely affect the performance of the web server running PHP-Nuke, and so PHP-Nuke caches the feed in its database to use subsequently.

However, the Refresh Time setting of the block determines when PHP-Nuke should obtain a new version of the feed to keep it 'fresh'. When PHP-Nuke needs to display the RSS feed in the block, it will check the time it last stored the feed. If the time elapsed exceeds the Refresh Time value, PHP-Nuke will get a new version of the feed, and cache that. The Refresh Time setting doesn't have any effect on the other types of blocks.

Adding a File Block

A file block is a PHP script that is stored in the blocks folder of the PHP-Nuke installation. At this point, we're not going to create a new block of this type; we'll see that in Chapter 10. There are a number of file blocks already in the blocks folder, provided by PHP-Nuke. We will choose one of those.

Time For Action—Adding the Total Hits Block

The Total Hits block simply displays the number of times the site has been accessed. PHP-Nuke maintains a counter that is updated whenever any page is requested from the site. This is the number that is displayed by the Total Hits block.

From the Administration Menu, click on the Blocks icon to get back to the blocks menu, and then scroll down to our Add a New Block panel.

1. Select Total Hits from the Filename drop-down list:

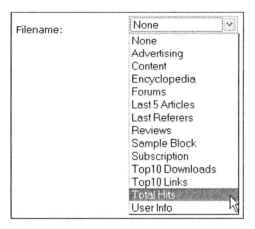

2. Let's leave the block on the Left, and set Activate? to Yes. We will also set this block to be viewable by All Visitors.

3. Click the Create Block button.

4. When the page reloads, you will see your newly created block in the list of blocks. Note it is of type FILE, and the Title has been provided from the filename:

5. A glance over to the left of your page, and you will see the Total Hits block is in place:

What Just Happened?

We just added a file block, and it was very simple. PHP-Nuke helps by providing a list of the available file blocks in the Filename drop-down list, and all you have to do is to select the filename from the list.

The names in the list correspond to PHP files in the blocks folder, and PHP-Nuke checks this list of files every time you come to the Blocks Administration area, and the drop-down list is populated. To show up in this list, the name of the file in the blocks folder must be of the form block-NAME.php, where NAME is the name of the block that shows up in the drop-down list. The block does not take its title from this part of the filename, you still have to add that yourself in the panel. If you have a quick look in the blocks folder in your PHP-Nuke installation, you will see that all the files are named like this.

Installing a new file block is simply a case of copying the required PHP file into the blocks folder. There are some example blocks in the code download for this book, and you can experiment with them. If you have placed a file into the blocks folder but it is not showing in the Filename drop-down list, then the file is likely to have its name in the wrong format for PHP-Nuke to pick up.

Managing Modules

Modules are like limbs to the body of your PHP-Nuke site; they kind of stick out and do stuff for you. However, PHP-Nuke allows your system to have an almost indefinite number of limbs, er, modules, and also allows you to add or remove them with ease. In this section, that's exactly what we're going to look at.

First of all, return to the Administration Menu and click on the Modules icon:

This brings you to the Modules Administration area. This area is for administration of all modules, not the properties of individual modules. Individual modules such as Downloads, FAQ, and so on have their own sections in the administration area.

Visiting the Module Administration area like this also 'refreshes' PHP-Nuke's module list. If you have installed any new modules, then PHP-Nuke will detect them and add them to its list.

In the Module Administration area you will see some helpful text, describing some general instructions for module administration, and below that is a table from which you can actually control your modules:

Title	Custom Title	Status	Visible to	Group	Functions
Advertising	Advertising		All Visitors	None	
AvantGo	AvantGo		All Visitors	None	
Content	Content		All Visitors	None	
Downloads	Downloads		All Visitors	None	
Encyclopedia	Encyclopedia		All Visitors	None	
FAQ	FAQ		All Visitors	None	
Feedback	Feedback		All Visitors	None	
Forums	Forums		All Visitors	None	
Journal	Journal		All Visitors	None	
Members_List	Members List		Registered Users Only	None	
News	**News**		**All Visitors**	None	
Private_Messages	Private Messages		All Visitors	None	
Recommend_Us	Recommend Us		All Visitors	None	

This table is similar to the one we saw for managing blocks in the Blocks Administration area. Each module has a Title and Custom Title; the Title actually refers to a folder in your PHP-Nuke installation, and to avoid spaces in the filenames, underscores are used, and the Custom Title provides a friendlier name for the module with the use of spaces instead of underscores.

The Status column has an icon, similar to the blocks table, indicating whether the module is Active or Inactive. Active modules are visible on the site, and can be accessed by visitors. Inactive modules are generally not visible to the visitor, but can be accessed by the administrator. If you glance to the left-hand column of your page, at the bottom of the Modules block you will see a list of the inactive modules:

```
Inactive Modules
   (for Admin tests)

• Advertising
• Content
• Encyclopedia
• FAQ
• Forums
• Members List
• Reviews
```

As an administrator, you can still visit and test these modules, either by clicking on these links or directly entering a URL. This list of inactive modules is only visible to the administrator, and should a sneaky visitor manage to find their way to an inactive module, they will be confronted with the following statement, and they are unable to use the module any further:

```
Sorry, this Module isn't active!

         [ Go Back ]
```

Making a module inactive does not 'remove' it from the site as you can see—it's still there, just sleeping. You can remove modules completely from the site, but this requires you to physically delete some files from your PHP-Nuke installation.

As with blocks, access to modules can be restricted to groups of users, as shown in the Visible to column. The group can be chosen from All Visitors, Registered Users Only, Administrators Only, and Subscribed Users.

Unlike the access restriction for blocks, whereby if a visitor is not permitted to see the block, the block itself will not be displayed, attempts to access a restricted module will display a message like this:

```
┌─────────────────────────────────────────────────────────────────┐
│                                                                   │
│  ┌─────────────────────────────────────────────────────────────┐ │
│  │             the Dinosaur Portal: Access Denied                │ │
│  └─────────────────────────────────────────────────────────────┘ │
│                                                                   │
│  ┌─────────────────────────────────────────────────────────────┐ │
│  │           You are trying to access a restricted area.          │ │
│  │                                                                │ │
│  │   We are Sorry, but this section of our site is for Registered Users Only.  │ │
│  │                                                                │ │
│  │       You can register for free by clicking here, then you can │ │
│  │           access this section without restrictions. Thanks.    │ │
│  │                                                                │ │
│  │                        [ Go Back ]                             │ │
│  └─────────────────────────────────────────────────────────────┘ │
│                                                                   │
└─────────────────────────────────────────────────────────────────┘
```

Module access can be restricted to registered users of your site, but you can also restrict access even further through the use of **user groups**. When users contribute to your site by posting a news story, commenting on a story, or recommending the site to a friend, they can earn points for themselves, as reward. When they have collected enough points, they become members of a particular user group.

Being a member of this group may be prestigious enough for some people, but it also means that you can allow these 'worthy' people access to parts of your site that are forbidden to those who haven't yet earned the privilege. The user group (and it can be only one group) that has exclusive access to a module is indicated by its Group column in the modules table. By default, this is set to None, meaning that no group has exclusive access. We'll look at creating user groups in the next chapter.

The Functions column has icons similar to the blocks table, and plays the same role as the Functions column in the blocks table. From here we can manage the properties of an individual module, in the same way that we edited the properties of blocks. Modules can be activated or deactivated, edited, or set as the default module—the 'home' module. You will notice that one of the modules (currently News) is highlighted in the table, and its Status has an Active (In Home) icon. This is the current default module, and is the module displayed when a visitor comes to the home page index.php. Thus this module will be the first thing that a new visitor sees. Clicking the Put in Home icon ▤ from the Functions column of a module will allow you to set that module as the default module.

> If you attempt to set an inactive module as the home module, PHP-Nuke will kindly activate it for you. Note that the module will remain active should you then choose another module as your home module.

Time For Action—Activating Modules

Before we go any further, let's take a moment to activate some modules. We'll want to look at some of these modules in the next few chapters, the Content, Encyclopedia, FAQ, Forums, Members_List, and Reviews modules, so we may as well activate them now. We'll only go through activating the Content module; the other modules can be similarly activated.

1. Ensure that you are in the Module Administration area, by clicking the Modules icon in the Administration Menu.

2. Scroll down the list of modules to find the Content module. It is currently marked as inactive in the list:

Content	Content		All Visitors	None	
Downloads	Downloads		All Visitors	None	

3. Click the Activate icon in the Functions column of the Content module. When the page reloads, you will see that the Content module is now marked as Active in the list:

Content	Content		All Visitors	None	
Downloads	Downloads		All Visitors	None	

4. The Content module is now showing in the Modules block:

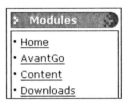

That's all there is to activating an already installed module. Deactivating is similar; you simply click the deactivate icon in the Functions column. This icon is only shown when the module is active.

Editing Module Properties

The Top 10 module has a potentially confusing name. It isn't the list of top 10 singles or DVDs; it shows lists of the top 10 pieces of content on the site. Once you know what it shows, the title makes sense, but until then, it doesn't really. This kind of title won't help new visitors feel particularly comfortable navigating around your site. Let's start by getting that name changed to something that is more descriptive of its function.

In the Modules Administration table, find the module with the Title of Top, and click on the Edit icon in its Function column. You'll be presented with a list of options like this (remember to scroll down from the admin menu!):

Modules Edit

Change Module Name
(Top)

Custom Module Name: Top 10

Who can View This?   All Visitors

Visible in Modules Block?   ⦿ Yes   ○ No

[Save Changes]

[Go Back]

Here we can see that we can edit the Custom Module Name (its Custom Title in the modules table), which category of visitors is able to see the module, and also, if the module is to be Visible in the Modules block?.

Invisible Modules

If you were to set a module to be not visible in the Modules block, then it still remains active and usable. However, there is no link to the module in your main navigational device, the Modules block. You will have to direct visitors to the module by some other means. Modules like this are listed in the administrator's version of the Modules block, just above the list of inactive modules:

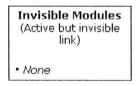

Invisible Modules
(Active but invisible link)

• *None*

These modules are called Invisible Modules. A rather colorful title, but it simply means that there is no explicit link to them in the list of active modules in the Modules block. Remember that an invisible module may still be accessible, and no extra security is placed upon the module. You might want to use this if you wanted a select group of people to preview a module before you unleashed it on the world, for example, and send them the URL to visit it directly. However, the 'no one will ever guess the name of that page' school of security is not a particularly advisable way of thinking.

Time For Action—Editing the Top 10

Now let's edit the properties of the Top 10 module. At the moment, you should still be on the Modules Edit page. If you're not, make your way there by clicking on the Modules icon in the Administration Menu, and in the table of modules, click the Edit icon in the Functions column of the module with the Title of Top 10.

1. Change the Custom Module Name to Top 10 Bits of Content

2. Select All Visitors for Who Can View this?.

3. Leave Visible in Modules Block? set to Yes.

4. Click the Save Changes button.

After you click the button, the page will reload, and you will be back at the Modules Administration page. You will see the properties of the former Top 10 module have now changed in the modules table:

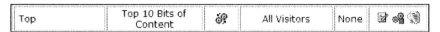

And if you glance to the left of your screen to the Modules block, you will see the Top 10 entry has been replaced by our new title:

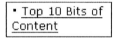

That makes it so much clearer. Now everyone should understand exactly what that link is pointing to.

Adding New Modules

The standard installation of PHP-Nuke probably isn't going to do everything you want. Although that isn't part of its appeal, the fact that you can write your own modules and add them to your system is. That doesn't just mean you, but anybody with some PHP know-how. Besides, there is a vast library of PHP-Nuke modules available on the Internet.

> Take due caution when downloading third-party modules, especially executable files, as they might not be thoroughly tested and it is possible that they contain spyware or viruses.

Generally, adding and installing third-party modules involves more work than we will do here, because there will often be database tables to be created, and files to be copied into different folders.

Time For Action—Installing a Simple Module

1. From the code download for this book, find the folder called MyModule in the ch04 folder.

2. Copy the MyModule folder into the modules folder of your PHP-Nuke installation.

3. Open your browser (make sure you are logged in as the super user) and click the Modules link in the Administration Menu.

4. Scroll down the list of modules to find the MyModule entry:

5. Click the Activate icon in the Functions column.

6. When the page reloads, MyModule will have appeared in the Modules block, and clicking its link will take you to the MyModule front page.

What Just Happened?

We just added a new module. The first stage was simple, copying the module files into the modules folder. A module is a set of files contained in a folder that goes in the modules folder, with PHP-Nuke picking up the name of the module from the name of the folder. For our module, it picks up the name MyModule.

Once the folder has been placed in the modules folder, the list of modules is refreshed by visiting the Modules Administration area. The list of modules is refreshed by PHP-Nuke going through all the folders in the Modules folder to see if there are new folders added, and if so, adds them to the list of installed modules. By default, these newly found modules are not activated. After we clicked the Activate icon and the page reloaded, a glance over to the Modules block showed that the MyModule module has been registered as an inactive module:

```
Inactive Modules
(for Admin tests)

· MyModule
```

This module now also appears in the list of modules in the Module Administration table, and from here, you can activate it or edit its properties like any other module.

Note that removing a module also works in the same way. To remove a module, simply remove its folder from the modules folder. When PHP-Nuke refreshes its list of modules, that module will removed from the database.

In general, installing third-party modules involves more steps than we have seen here, particularly depending on the version of PHP-Nuke the module was originally written for. Usually, you will have to create some database tables for the module, since a module of any complexity will involve storing and retrieving data. (Our module has very little complexity!)

With third-party modules, there will often be instructions along with the module in the form of a README file or INSTALL.txt that provide specific guidelines on where to put various files, and the steps you must take to get the module up and running.

Summary

In this chapter we have had a lengthy tour of the PHP-Nuke administration interface, and accomplished some of the basic tasks of site management.

We looked first at the Web Site Configuration menu in the site Preferences. From here we set a number of global properties of the site, such as its name, its URL, and its description. It is important to set these early on when creating a new site, particularly since the URL of the site appears in emails generated by the system. There were a number of panels in the Web Site Configuration menu; we will encounter more of them as we move through the book.

Next we looked at creating a backup of the database. This is a very important task and should be performed regularly, since the PHP-Nuke database *is* your site. If something were to happen to it, you would lose all your site content, users, configuration settings, and so on, so taking regular backups will be important as soon as your site has any amount of traffic.

Block and module management were the next stops. We saw how to position and order blocks on the page, and how to set up the different types of blocks: static blocks of HTML stored in the database, RSS feeds from other sites, and PHP script blocks. The RSS block is particularly interesting, because it allows us to display details of content on other sites from the pages of our site.

Modules perform the main functionality of our site. We saw the Modules Administration area, from where we are able to activate or deactivate modules, or change some of their properties, such as which groups of users are able to access them.

Now it's time to move on to those whom your site is really for—the visitors.

5
Managing Users

So far your site feels rather lonely. Sure we've added some new blocks, and moved some around, activated and deactivated modules until we are blue in the face, but there is something missing (apart from content, I know—that comes in the next chapter!). What's missing is your site's users.

PHP-Nuke is about web communities, and communities need members. PHP-Nuke enables visitors to your site to create and maintain their own user account, and add their personal details. This is usually required for them to post their own new stories, make comments, or contribute to discussions in the forums. Those annoying little tasks like managing lost passwords are also taken care of for you by PHP-Nuke.

User accounts can be created in two ways:

- By the super user (that's you)
- By the user registering on your site

The second method involves a confirmation email sent to the user's email account. This email contains a link for them to click and confirm their registration to activate their account (this needs to be done within 24 hours or the registration expires).

Once a visitor is registered on your site, the gates to enjoy the full glory of your site will be thrown wide open. Visitors, or users as you could now call them, will be able to contribute to discussions on forums, add comment on posted stories, even add their own new stories, as well as access parts of the site that are off-limits to the 'riff-raff' unregistered visitor.

In this chapter, we will walk through the creation of new users, both by the super user and also by registering as a new user from the standard visitor interface on the site. We will also look at the basics of subscribing users to the site.

Once we have some users in place, we will look through the Your Account module, which provides a personal area for each user within the site, and allows them to personalize the site.

We will also look at the system of points awarded to users for interacting with the site, and the benefits this brings them through user groups.

The final part of the chapter covers setting up other administrator accounts for managing individual modules rather than the entire site.

Ingredients of a User

Every user requires a certain amount of information to uniquely identify them in PHP-Nuke. There are the usual three things required of every user in PHP-Nuke:

- A nickname: This is an alias or username if you like. This identifies who the user is, and is their online identity in PHP-Nuke.
- A password: This is required to verify that the user is who they claim to be.
- A valid email address: This is where the confirmation email is to be sent.

Once the user account is created for a user, the user is of course able to modify their details, and also view the details of other users.

Information such as the URL of the user's own website, messenger ID (MSN, AIM, and others), their location, and interests are also part of the user 'profile', but are not compulsory.

By default, the real email address of any user is never made public, for both security and to prevent harvesting by spammers. Users can specify a 'fake email' address, possibly in spam-obfuscated form (for example, address_at_mydomain.com) which will be displayed to other users, although this is not required. A user's privacy is always protected.

Setting Up a New User

User management starts by clicking the Users icon in the Modules Administration menu:

Users

Clicking this icon brings you to the User's Administration panel. This panel consists of two mini-panels, Edit User and Add a New User, whose use is given away by their titles.

We'll start by setting up a new user. Our user will imaginatively be called testuser.

Time For Action—Setting Up a New User Manually

1. If you're not at the User's Administration panel, click the Users icon in the Modules Administration menu.
2. In the Add a New User panel, enter testuser into the Nickname field.
3. Enter Test User into the Name field.
4. Enter your own email address into the Email field.

Edit User

Nickname: [   ]   Modify ▼   [Ok!]

Add a New User

Nickname	[ ]	(required)
Name	[ ]	
Email	[ ]	(required)
Fake Email	[ ]	
URL	[ ]	

5. Scroll down to the Password field. Enter testuser as the password.

6. Click the Add User button. When the page reloads, you will be taken straight back to the administration homepage.

What Just Happened?

We created a new user. For this simple user, we only specified the required fields Nickname, Email, and Password, and provided a single piece of personal information, Name. Failing to specify the required fields will mean that the user is not set up, and you will be prompted to go back and add the missing fields.

No email notification is sent to the user when the user is set up in this way, and no confirmation of the registration is required. As soon as you click Add User, provided all the required fields have been entered, the user is ready to go.

Editing the details of a user is equally easy, but you do have to know their nickname to edit the details. Simply enter this into the Nickname field of the Edit User panel, select Modify from the drop-down box and click Ok! If you have taken a sudden dislike to a particular user, enter their nickname into the Nickname field and select Delete from the drop-down box, click Ok! and they are gone forever (the account, not the person).

Subscribing a User

Once a user has been created, you have the option to subscribe this user. We mentioned the idea of Subscribed Users in earlier chapters; it's a mechanism for restricting module access to specific groups of people, such as fee-paying customers. There is only one group of Subscribed Users in PHP-Nuke at present, so once a user has a subscription, they are able to access any module restricted to Subscribed Users only.

The option to subscribe a user is not available when you create the user manually, as we did above. To find the option, you have to edit the user's details. This is done by entering their username into the Edit User panel, selecting Modify from the drop-down box, and clicking the Ok! button.

The subscription options are near the bottom of the user details, underneath the newsletter option. The Subscribe User option does not refer to 'subscribing to' the newsletter; you sign up the user or remove them from your newsletter mailing list with the Newsletter option. The Subscribe User option makes the user into one of the site's elite, a Subscribed User.

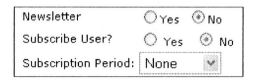

If you subscribe the user, then you must specify the Subscription Period. This is the length of time that the user remains subscribed, and ranges from 1 year to 10 years, in yearly increments. If you leave the Subscription Period at None then the user will not be subscribed.

Once a user has been subscribed, you can change their subscription details from the same panel:

You can unsubscribe the user, or extend their subscription period. To shorten the subscription period, you would have to unsubscribe the user, subscribe them again, and then set the new period.

Subscribed users are reminded of the passing of time and the impending expiry of their subscriptions when they visit the Your Account module—we'll further explore this module later in the chapter:

> **Your subscription will expire in:**
> 364 days, 23 hours, 51 minutes, 34 seconds
>
> **Subscribed User!**
>
> **Subscription Expire in:**
> 364 days, 23 hours, 51 minutes, 34 seconds

Time For Action—Registering as a User

This time we'll register to create a user account as a normal visitor would. We'll call the user account userdude. If you do not have your mail server set up, then you will just have to follow the text and screenshots for now. The confirmation email sent by PHP-Nuke is a key part of the registration process, and includes a special link for the visitor to click to activate their account. Don't worry though, when your site is live on your web hosting account, you will undoubtedly be able to access a mail server.

1. If you are still logged in as the super user, logout by clicking the Logout icon in either of the administration menus, or click the Logout link in the Administration block.

2. If you are still logged in as testuser, logout by clicking on the Your Account link in the modules block, then click the Logout/Exit link in the navigation bar that appears:

Alternatively, you can enter the logout URL directly:

`http://localhost/nuke/modules.php?name=Your_Account&op=logout`

3. You will be redirected to the site homepage. Now click the Your Account link in the Modules block:

User Registration/Login
User Login
Nickname:
Password:
Login
[Lost your Password? | New User Registration]

4. Click the New User Registration link. This brings you to the New User Registration panel. The top part of that panel is shown here:

User Registration/Login
New User Registration (All fields are required)
Nickname:
Email:
Password:
Re-type Password: (Leave blank for auto-generate your password)
New User

5. Enter the Nickname of userdude.

6. Enter your own email address into the Email field.

7. We are going to use userdude for the password as well as the nickname. If you think of another password at this point, enter it instead. Then put the password into the Re-type password field as well.

8. Click the New User button. You will come to the final step of the registration process:

New User Registration: Final Step

userdude, please check the following information. If all is correct you can proceed with the registration by clicking on "Finish" button, otherwise "Go Back" and change whatever information is needed.

User Name: userdude
Email: myaddress@packtpub.com

Note: You will receive a confirmation email with a link to a page you should visit to activate your account in the next 24 hours.

Finish   [Go Back]

---

9. Click the Finish button.

10. Open up your email client, and log in to check your mail. You should find a mail with the subject New User Account Activation waiting for you. It will be from the email address you specified in the Administrator Email field in the Site Configuration Menu. The body of that email will look something like this:

```
Welcome to the Dinosaur Portal

You or someone else has used your email account
(myaddress@packtpub.com) to register an account at the Dinosaur
Portal

To finish the registration process you should visit the following
link in the next 24 hours to activate your user account,
otherwise the information will be automatically deleted by the
system and you should apply again:
http://thedinosaurportal.com/modules.php?name=Your_Account&op=activate&use
rname=userdude&check_num=64ad845758d7f8f572b12800f60842ba

Following is the member information:

-Nickname: userdude
-Password: userdude
```

11. Click the link in the email, or copy the link and paste it into your browser, and you will be taken to the New User Activation page where you will see a message of the form:

userdude: Your account has been activated. Please login from <u>this link</u> using your assigned Nickname and Password.

12. Clicking this link takes you back to the User Registration/Login page of the Your Account module, and you can use your nickname and password to login.

What Just Happened?

You just created a new user account. The page for logging in is the homepage of the Your Account module. We'll talk more about this module in a minute; as you could guess, it handles everything to do with 'your' user account.

If the visitor is not logged in, they are presented with the login panel when they visit the Your Account module page. From here they can enter their nickname and password to log in, or click the New User Registration link to register a new user account, as we did.

For visitors that have forgotten their password, clicking the Lost your Password? link will take them to a screen where they can enter their nickname, and an email will be sent to their registered email address containing a confirmation code, a random-looking 10 digit string; with this code they can have their password changed. A new, random password is generated and emailed to them. PHP-Nuke never stores raw passwords in its database, so it can never reveal any password. With the new password, the user can log in and change their password to something easier to remember.

The registration process for the user is straightforward; they only require a nickname, a valid email address, and a password. There are certain rules, however, that are followed by PHP-Nuke:

- Only one occurrence of an email address is allowed on the system; if someone uses an email address that belongs to another user account that address will be rejected, and the user will have to choose another.

- Only one occurrence of a particular nickname is allowed as well; the system will check the uniqueness of the nickname before creating the account.

After the visitor clicks Finish on the final step, the user account is created. Following that, the confirmation email is sent to the email address. If the email address specified is invalid, or not the visitor's email address, then that visitor will have to create their account with a new email address. If the user doesn't mind being embarrassed, they can contact the site administrator, or wait 24 hours for the account to be deleted from the list of 'waiting to be activated' accounts, and then try again.

You will notice that the link to activate the account contains the URL of your PHP-Nuke site:

```
http://thedinosaurportal.com/modules.php?name=Your_Account&op=activate&usernam
e=userdude&check_num=64ad845758d7f8f572b12800f60842ba
```

It is very important that you have configured your Site URL option correctly in the Web Site Configuration menu (we saw this in Chapter 4). If you haven't done that, then the activation link will point to the wrong site!

The check_num part of the URL is what identifies the unregistered visitor to the system. When the visitor registers their details, PHP-Nuke stores them in the database along with the check_num value. When the visitor visits the above link, PHP-Nuke will check the value of check_num against the values stored in the database, and if it finds a match, it will move that visitor's details to the proper users table in the database, and remove them from the table of visitors waiting to confirm their registration.

That's all there is to creating user accounts. It is possible to turn off the registration, so that only the administrator can create accounts. If you feel the need for this, you can read more about it in the PHP-Nuke HOWTO:

http://www.karakas-online.de/EN-Book/disable-registration.html

That section of the PHP-Nuke HOWTO also has a number of other user account hacks that you can make use of.

Graphical Code for User Registration

PHP-Nuke enables you to add a security code to the login or registration pages on the site. The security code is a small graphic with some digits, and is shown under the password fields, along with a textbox for the visitor to type in the digits from the graphic.

The point of this device is to prevent automated registrations; without typing the correct digits into the Type Security Code field, the submission will not be accepted. The digits displayed in the image are not part of the page HTML, and the only way for the digits to be read is to actually see them when they are displayed on a monitor.

Use of the security code is controlled by a setting in the file config.php in the root of your PHP-Nuke installation. (This was the file in which we made some database settings in Chapter 2.) The setting to change is the value of the $gfx_chk variable. By default, it looks like this in the file, which means that the security code is not used:

```
$gfx_chk = 0;
```

The config.php file itself has a description of the values for this variable as seen in the table:

Value	Effect on the Security Code
0	Security code is never used.
1	Security code only appears on the administrators login page (admin.php).
2	Security code only appears on the normal user login page.
3	Security code only appears for new user registrations.
4	Security code appears for user login and new user registrations.

Value	Effect on the Security Code
5	Security code appears for administrator and user logins.
6	Security code appears for administrator and new user registrations.
7	Security code appears at every login opportunity, and also on new user registration page.

Thus to have the security code appear only at the administrator login, you would set $gfx_chk to 1 and then save the config.php file:

```
$gfx_chk = 1;
```

For the graphical code to function properly, the GD extension will need to work properly with PHP on the web server. The GD extension takes care of drawing the graphics, and if this isn't functioning for whatever reason (possibly it's not installed), then the graphic will not be displayed properly, and it will be impossible to determine the security code. In that case, you will have to change the setting in config.php to remove the graphical code.

If you are running your site on a web hosting account and the graphical security code is not being displayed when it should, then you should contact your host's technical support to find out if there is a problem with the GD extension. You can tell if the GD extension is installed by using the phpinfo() PHP function. Open a text editor and enter the following code:

```
<?php
phpinfo();
?>
```

Save this file as phpinfo.php in the web server root (\xampp\htdocs\). When you navigate to that page in your browser, a number of PHP settings are displayed, including the status of the GD extension:

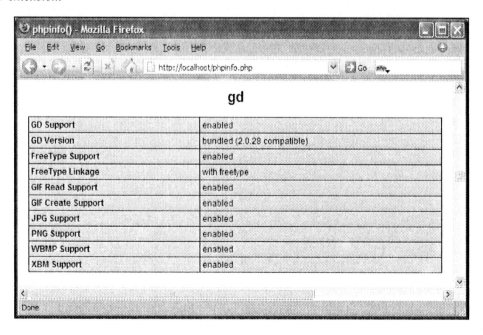

If you do not see a table like the one above on the page, or if it does not say enabled next to GD Support, then contact your host's technical support. The XAMPP package we install in Appendix A has GD installed and working.

Seeing Who's Who

Log in to your site as the super user and activate the Members List module (deactivated by default). After activation there will be an additional option available in the Modules block called the Members List module, which provides anyone able to view this module with a list of the registered users:

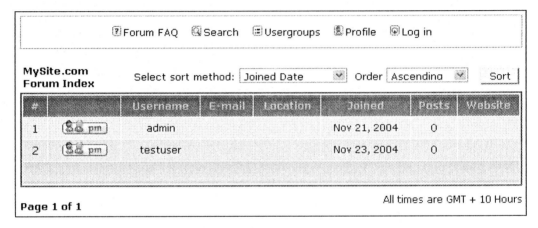

Clicking on the username will bring up a view of that user's profile:

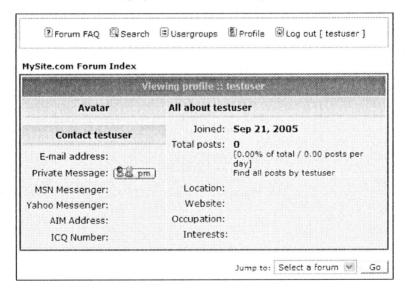

This is only a *view* of the user profile, and it is not an editable form. You will notice the word Forum in the above screenshot. The user profile displayed here is actually the user profile from the Forums module (and note also that the Forums module needs to be activated for this screen to be seen). You will also notice that the name of the site is wrong—it says MySite.com, which is not the value we set for our site name. This is because the Forums module has its own set of configuration settings. We will see how to set these in Chapter 8. Also note that the Members List module takes information from the Forums module configuration settings.

The Forums module is a complete application—phpBB, one of the best pieces of free, open-source forum software around—integrated into PHP-Nuke. One aspect of the integration is the shared user account—the user account you create for the PHP-Nuke site also functions as a user account on the forums. As a user, it is possible to work with your details in two places in PHP-Nuke— from the Your Account module and also from within the Forums module.

Although there are two views of information, and two places to edit your details, there is still only one user account. At the moment, the Your Account module offers more user details than are found in the Forums module, such as newsletter subscription information.

The integration between the PHP-Nuke user account and the user account for the Forums module has gradually become tighter over the versions of PHP-Nuke, and they are likely to 'converge' further in future versions of PHP-Nuke.

Once a user account is created, and the user has logged in, a whole new world opens up to them.

The Your Account Module

The Your Account module is a visitor's space. The visitor is guided round their space by a graphical navigation bar as seen below:

Before we look at each of these links, let's mention what else is on the front page of the Your Account module:

My Headlines

Select the site from which you want to read the headlines:

[Select a Web Site ▾]

Or type the headlines RSS/XML url of your prefered site:

[http://] [Go]

Broadcast Public Message

You can send a *Public Message* from here (255 characters max). This message will be displayed to all online users in the next 10 minutes. Any user online will see you message just once in a red bar under the site's logo. Any user can deactivate this feature from <u>here</u>. Please don't abuse. HTML code isn't allowed here.

[   ] [Send]

- My Headlines: The user can view a list of headlines from an RSS news feed of another site. The user can select from one of the headline sites that we saw in the previous chapter, or enter the URL of the site directly.

- Broadcast Public Message: The user can enter the text of a public message to be shown to all current visitors of the site. We'll look at this in a moment.

These two features are not always displayed; their display is controlled by options in the Web Site Configuration menu that we'll see in a moment. However, the user is always able to see their Last 10 Comments posted and their Last 10 News Submissions on this page.

Returning to our discussion of the links in the navigation bar of the Your Account module, we've already seen what the Logout/Exit link does; it logs the visitor out.

The Themes link takes the visitor to a page from where they can choose one from the list of themes installed on the site.

We'll look at the Comments link in detail in the next chapter; it leads to options for viewing and posting comments on stories.

Note that when you are logged in as the super user, the Your Account module displays another panel called Administration Functions. This panel allows you to modify certain details of that user. We will talk about these in the next chapter and meet them in their natural context.

Editing the User Profile

The Your Info link takes the user to their user profile. We saw some of the options here when we looked at creating the user manually. These options are generally for personal details (name, email, and so on), newsletter subscription, private message options, and forum configuration, among others. The options themselves are straightforward. A number of options in the user profile correspond to forum profile options, and don't particularly affect the user outside of the Forums module.

After making any changes to a user profile, the Save Changes button needs to be clicked to save these changes. Note that the Save Changes button is not the button at the very bottom of the user details page—the Save Changes button is above the Avatar Control Panel:

Password: (type a new password twice to change it)

Save Changes

Avatar control panel

The button at the bottom of the form is marked Submit, and is only active when the options in the Avatar Control Panel are enabled.

The Avatar Control Panel seen at the bottom of the user profile contains an interesting option. An avatar is a small graphic, representing you as an online character. You can choose a graphic from the already existing library by clicking on the Show Gallery button next to the Select Avatar from gallery option:

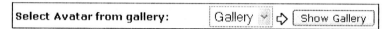

Select Avatar from gallery: Gallery ⌄ ⇨ Show Gallery

Clicking this button brings up a selection of little images for the user to choose from. Simply click on the required image and this will be assigned to the user profile:

Avatar for testuser Saved!

Your New Avatar:

[Back to Profile | Done]

Clicking the Back to Profile link will return you to the Your Info page.

The library of images you just saw can be found in the `modules\Forums\images\avatars\gallery\` folder of your PHP-Nuke installation. If you want you can add in more images here, but make sure your image is a GIF file, and that it isn't more than 80 pixels wide or 80 pixels high.

Your Account Configuration

The Your Home link provides some options for configuring Your Account further:

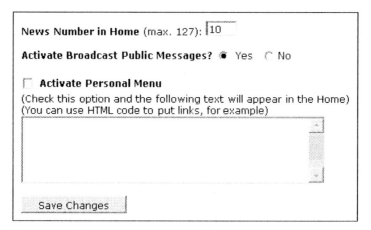

From this panel, the number of news stories displayed on the homepage of the site can be controlled. Remember, this setting only applies to you—and only when you are logged in.

Talking to the World with Public Messages

You can activate or deactivate public messages from Your Home too. Public messages are displayed to every visitor to the site They appear near the top of the page on the homepage of the site and remain there for 10 minutes, or until another public message appears:

> **Public Message from testuser: "There's a monster loose on the site!!!!!"**
>
> [Turn Off Public Messages]

Public messages can be entered from the front page of the Your Account module page:

Broadcast Public Message

You can send a *Public Message* from here (255 characters max). This message will be displayed to all online users in the next 10 minutes. Any user online will see you message just once in a red bar under the site's logo. Any user can deactivate this feature from <u>here</u>. Please don't abuse. HTML code isn't allowed here.

| There's a monster loose on the site!!!!! | Send |

Simply type in the text of your message and click the Send button, and your public message is broadcast to all and sundry.

You can imagine having a message that is displayed to every single user on the front page of your site may be a bit too much. Fortunately, users cannot 'spam' the public message feature by constantly submitting public messages—once they have submitted a message they must wait for that message to expire before another is accepted from them.

Also, any user can turn off the public messages by setting to No the Activate Broadcast Public Messages? option in the Your Account module. This turns off the display of public messages to everyone. However, any user can turn them back on again by setting this option back to Yes!

The administrator can override all of this from the Web Site Configuration menu. The Activate Broadcast Messages option in the Users Options panel allows public messages to be turned off for everyone, with nobody other than the administrator able to turn them back on. The image below shows this panel in the Web Site Configuration menu:

This setting, unlike the one in Your Home above, will prevent public messages from being entered and not just from being broadcasted. The Activate Broadcast Public Messages? option in Your Home is also not made available to users, since public messages have been banned anyway.

In the Users Options panel of the Web Site Configuration menu, the Activate Headlines Reader? option controls the display of the My Headlines panel on the front page of the Your Account module. Setting this to No means that no user can see or select other site headlines to be displayed in the Your Account module. The Let users change News number in Home option is simple; if set to No a fixed number of stories will be displayed to all users.

It's My Block and I'll Cry if I Want to...

The final option in the Your Home area, Activate Personal Menu, allows the user to enter some HTML that will be displayed as a block on the homepage of the site. This block can be used for easy access to handy links. By checking the box and entering some text your block will be created. We have inserted links to two articles here:

When Save Changes is clicked, and you return to the homepage of your site, your block can be seen (by default it is on the right-hand side of the page):

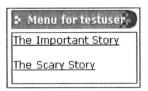

Remember that this block is seen only by you, the current user. In this way, every user can have a personal block.

Private Messages

Visitors can send messages to each other through the Private Messages conduit. It's a kind of site-specific email system, except that you can only send a message to one recipient at a time, and you can't send attachments.

While going through the Your Info module, you would have seen some options for visitors to be notified of any private messages sent to them; Notify on new Private Message by Email and Pop up window on new Private Message. If the administrator has activated the Private_Messages module, then the homepage of a user's Your Account displays a count of the private messages sent to them, and allows them to send a new message:

Your Private Messages
You have **1** private message(s).
Send a Private Message to: [   ]   [Search Users]

Sending a private message from here can be confusing—there is no Submit or Send Message button. To send a private message, you simply enter the nickname of the intended visitor into the Send a Private Message to box and press the *Enter* key to submit the page. Provided there is some text in that box, PHP-Nuke will interpret that as a user nickname and move you to a screen for entering your message.

If you have any private messages, the number of messages is displayed as a link in the You have ... private messages(s) text. Clicking this link takes you to your private messages inbox:

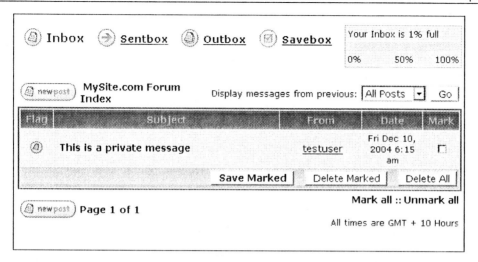

From here you can manipulate private messages in much the same way as you work with emails in any email client, although the Outbox and Sentbox deserve mention. Messages you have sent will first appear in the Outbox. However, once the recipient reads the message, that message moves into your Sentbox and you immediately know that your message has been read.

If the idea of private messages disturbs you as an administrator—after all, there is no option for a user to not receive private messages—then your only option is to turn them off for everyone by deactivating the Private_Messages module from the Module Administration area.

Note that the Private_Messages module is very different from the Messages functionality that we saw at the end of Chapter 3, do not get them confused. The Private_Messages functionality is also tied to the Forums module; that's why the screenshot above shows the wrong site name, as we explained earlier for the Members Lists module.

User Journal

In PHP-Nuke, every registered user is able to keep a **journal**. This is supplied by the Journal module and can also be accessed from within the Your Account module, which is why we are discussing it here. Rather confusingly, clicking on the Journal link in the Modules menu brings you to the Journal page, but with the same navigation bar of the Your Account module, so you feel like you are in the Your Account module. Note that if the Journal is deactivated, it will not be displayed in the navigation bar of the Your Account module.

In their journal a user can enter their thoughts and opinions, while other visitors can read these thoughts, and add comments in response. The user journal is like a mini 'weblog' for each user.

Clicking the Journal link in the Your Account module brings up the main journal control panel:

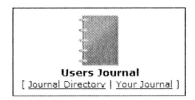

Users Journal
[Journal Directory | Your Journal]

From here, you can view a list of other users' journals (Journal Directory), or the entries in your own journal.

Your Journal Entries

Let's start with your journal. Clicking on the Your Journal link brings up three links:

Journal for testuser
[Add New Entry | Your Last 20 Entries | List All Your Entries]

When you have added some journal entries, a list of your journal entries is displayed under this panel.

Adding a Journal Entry

Clicking the Add New Entry links brings you to a simple panel for adding your entry:

Title:	Another Windows XP 64 Bit Incompatibility
Body:	Today I discovered that my printer driver does not work with Windows XP 64 bit edition. According to the manufacturer's website, they have no plans to create a 64-bit driver.

HTML code isn't allowed. Please use the editor functions instead.

Graphic:
(optional)

Public: Yes

Add New Entry

(Did you test it for typos?)

You set the Title for the entry, its main content goes in the Body field (with the usual restrictions on the use of HTML), and a Graphic element. This element actually goes at the start of your journal entry, to encapsulate, in some way, the mood of your entry.

You decide if the body of the entry can be read by other visitors with the Public drop-down box. Note that if you set Public to No, other people will still be able to see the title of the entry, but will not be able to read the entry itself.

Clicking the Add New Entry button records your entry in the journal.

Viewing your Journal Entries

You can view a list of your journal entries from the Your Journal page, and you will see your twenty most recent journal entries. Clicking the List All Your Entries link will display all of your entries, more or less ordered by the date of their entry.

Last 20 Journal Entries for testuser

Date	Time	Title (click to view)	Public	Edit	Delete
10-05-2005	08:07 pm	Another Windows XP 64 Bit Incompatibility — — 0 comments	Yes		

The listing shows the date and time each journal entry was added along with its title, and some buttons to edit or delete the post. Of course, only the owner of the journal entry is able to modify or delete a journal entry, and not just any passing visitor. The Public column in the table indicates if the content of the entry can be viewed by other visitors. Clicking on the Title of a journal entry brings you to its content, and comments if there are any.

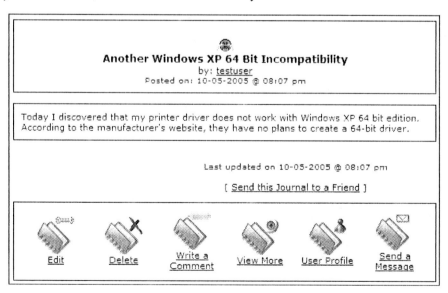

From this view, you can edit or delete your entry, or add comments to the entry. The View More link actually takes you back to the list of the journal entries by this user (that's you here), rather than showing you more of the entry (there is no more). The User Profile link doesn't really do much here, since you are clicking on a link to show information about yourself, and it simply returns you to the Your Account homepage. When viewing the journal entries of others, this link will take you to some information about that user, including their most recent posts. Also when viewing the journal entries of another user, the Send a Message link can be used to send a private message to that user.

As the owner of the journal entry, you are also able to delete any comments attached to your entry, even if you are not the author of the comment. This is one way of keeping dissenting views about your opinions in check!

Peeking into the Journals of Others

Clicking the Journal Directory link from the Journal homepage displays a list of other user's journals. You will see the list of the twenty users who have most recently added an entry to their journal, or you can click the List All Journals link to see every user who has a journal. Although not a problem at this point, if you visit another PHP-Nuke site with many users and view all the journals, this can be a very long list.

The rather gruesome sounding Search a Member link allows you to search for some text in other posts. You can search for your text in the user's name, the title or body of the entry, or the comments for each entry. A list of all journal entries matching your text is returned.

When viewing the list of users with journals, clicking either the name of the user or the icon in the View Journal column brings up the list of that user's journals. Clicking the icon in the Member's Profile column brings up some information about that user, which comes from the Your Account module, and includes such things as a history of their recent stories and comments made, and their online status.

As mentioned earlier, logged-in users are able to add comments to any public journal entry. The form for entering comments is very simple, consisting of a single box and a button to submit the comment. The comments for an entry are displayed in a line and it is not as rich in features as the one for story comments as you will find out in the next chapter. Since you have to be a logged-in user to post a comment to a journal entry, there is no anonymous posting and the username of the poster is displayed along with the comment.

Rewarding the User

Users who interact with the site can be awarded points. With enough points accumulated, a user becomes a member of a particular **user group**. You can restrict access to certain modules to registered users only; but you can take this even further, and allow only members of a particular user group access to the module. In this way, you can reward users who frequently participate in your community with extra modules or content that only they can view.

Although user groups and subscribed users seem similar in the sense that you can restrict module access exclusively for them, there are a number of key differences:

- Anyone can join a particular user group by participating in enough prize-winning activities on the site. Users can only be subscribed through the action of the super user.

- Conversely, without going into PHP-Nuke's database, the super user cannot put a particular user into a user group; this is something that the user has to *earn*.

Currently in PHP-Nuke we can restrict access only to an entire module; there is, in general, no way to restrict individual pieces of content within a module to specific user groups.

Points on Offer

By default, the following activities in PHP-Nuke qualify for points:

- Views: Viewing any page on the site.
- News: Getting a story published (namely submitting a story that then actually appears on the site, no points for just submitting a story!), posting a comment to a story, rating a story, or sending a story to a friend.
- Polls: Voting in polls or sending them to a friend.
- Downloads: Downloading a file, rating a download, or posting a comment about a download. There are also points available for similar activities in the Web Links module.
- Forums: Making a new post or replying to an existing post.
- Reviews: Posting a review in the Reviews section.
- Journal: Making a journal entry or commenting on someone else's entry.

There are also points for clicking on banners, broadcasting a public message, or recommending the site to a friend.

The number of points scored for each activity can be set up from the User Group Administration area. You are able to assign a different number of points to any of the activities, including, if you want to be sneaky, a negative number of points! By default, all the activities have 0 points.

The User Group Administration area is found by clicking on the User Groups icon in the Administration Menu:

This area shows you the currently created user groups, lets you to create a new user group, and lets you edit the number of points awarded for each activity.

Time For Action—Awarding Points for Viewing Pages

We will create a new user group, called PageViewers, to reward people for looking at the pages on our site. We will award one point for each page viewed, and membership to the group requires at least 20 points.

1. Make sure you are logged in as the super user If you are not in the User Group Administration area, click the User Groups icon in the Administration Menu.

2. In the Add New Users Group panel, enter the details of our group:

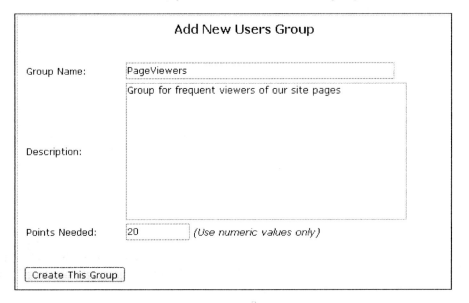

3. Click the Create This Group button.

4. When the page reloads, you can see your newly created PageViewers group in the list of user groups. The Edit or Delete links enable you to modify the details of the group or remove it completely should you require.

Users Groups

Name	Description	Points	Users Count	Functions
PageViewers	Group for frequent viewers of our site pages	20	0	[Edit	Delete]

5. Scroll down the screen to the Points System panel, and continue to do so until you see **Page View** in the left-hand column of the table. Enter the number 1 into the third column:

Page View	Get points for each page view generated by the user. Valid for any page of the site	1	Update

6. Click the **Update** button at the end of that row in the table. If you click the **Update** button of another row, your changes will not be saved!

7. Now view some pages; just click on a couple of the links in the Modules block, and then click the **Your Account** link. The points you have accumulated by viewing the pages can be seen in the middle of the page:

Actual User Status: **Online**
You're not subscribed to our Newsletter
Points you have by participating on the site's content: **7**

What Just Happened?

We just created a user group. The user group was called **PageViewers**, and we set a value of twenty points for the user to qualify as a member.

The only activity that we assigned points to was **Page View**. Every time the user visits a page on the PHP-Nuke site they will score one point; we only assigned one point to each page view. The number of points the user has accumulated can be seen in the **Your Account** module page, but any group to which they currently belong isn't displayed.

Restricting Module Access to User Groups

After you have created at least one user group, the option to restrict module access will appear in the Module Administration area. To restrict module access to a specific user group (and it can only be at most one user group) the module has to be first restricted to registered visitors only.

Time For Action—Restricting the Statistics Module to Frequent Page Viewers

1. Click on the Modules icon in the Modules Administration area.

2. Find the Statistics module in the list of modules, and click on the Edit icon in its Functions column.

3. Select Registered Users Only from the Who can View This? drop-down box.

4. Select PageViewers from the Users Group drop-down box:

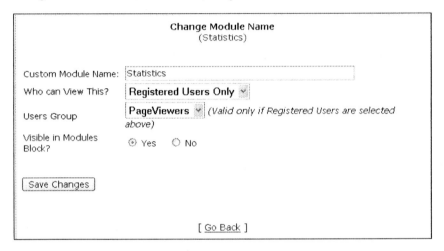

5. Click the Save Changes button.

6. When the page reloads, make sure the Statistics module is active by clicking the Activate link in the Functions column if necessary.

What Just Happened?

We restricted the Statistics module to members of the PageViewers group only. We had to select Registered Users Only for who can view the module; after all, the members of the PageViewers group are a subset of all the registered visitors. Finally, we made certain the Statistics module was activated.

However, when you click the Statistics module, it is possible that you will still be able to see it, although you do have not enough points—the module should only be viewable to people with at least 20 points. This problem arises because of a bug in the file modules.php. We first need to correct this bug in the following manner:

1. Open the file modules.php in a text editor (WordPad will do fine.)

2. Find the following line (reformatted here for readability):
```
}else if ($view == 1 AND (is_user($user) OR is_group($user, $name))
OR is_admin($admin)) {
```

And replace with the following:

```
}else if ($view == 1 AND (is_user($user) AND is_group($user, $name))
OR is_admin($admin)) {
```

Note that all we have done here is replace the first OR with an AND.

3. Save the file.

Now you will not be permitted to view the Statistics module. You will first have to visit some other pages to rack up your page view score (up to more than 20), and only then will you be allowed to view the module.

Managing Other Administrators

The super user account that you have been working with has complete control over the entire site. As your site grows, it is possible that you may wish to get other people to help you out with some administration of the site, such as moderating news stories, or monitoring downloads, but you don't want them to have full super user power.

PHP-Nuke provides a secondary type of administrator account, with privileges for certain modules. These accounts are the solution to the above problem. These other administrator accounts are also known as **authors** in various parts of PHP-Nuke. Users of these accounts also log in at the admin.php page as the super user does. The author accounts are not ordinary user accounts that have been 'promoted'; they are a 'genuine' administration account.

Authors versus the Super User

Specialist administrators (authors) can be created with power over any of the default modules (Content, Downloads, Encyclopedia, FAQ, News, Reviews, Surveys, Topics, Web Links, and Your Account modules), and these privileges can extend to more than one module. In fact, any module (default or third-party) that appears in the Modules Administration menu can have privileges set for it. Whether that module makes use of the privileges or not is another matter.

The difference between author accounts (administrators) and the super user account is that the authors only have access to module administration. They do not have access to core 'system' functionality as we saw in Chapter 4. For example, you cannot create an author account that has privileges for the News module, and also privileges to configure Blocks. The only way to achieve this is to give that account full super user power; it is possible to assign the super user power to an author account.

We saw that the Administration Area was divided into two menus of icons, the Administration Menu and the Modules Administration Menu. An author account will only have the Modules Administration Menu displayed to the author in the administration area. We will see this in a moment after we create an example author account.

Consequently, without the core system abilities, an author account cannot create another author account. This can only be done through an account with super user power.

Creating an Author

To create a new author, click the Edit Admins icon in the Administration Menu:

This brings up the Author's Administration page, which includes a panel for editing the details of an existing administrator account, including the super user account, or deleting a previously created administrator account:

The super user account is called the God account here.

Underneath this panel you will see a form to Add a New Administrator account:

Add a New Administrator		

Add a New Administrator

Name: _____ (required, can't be changed later)
Nickname: _____ (required)
Email: _____ (required)
URL: _____
Permissions:
☐ Advertising ☐ Content ☐ Downloads
☐ Encyclopedia ☐ FAQ ☐ Forums
☐ News ☐ Reviews ☐ Surveys
☐ Topics ☐ Web Links ☐ Your Account

☐ **Super User**
WARNING: If Super User is checked, the user will get full access!
Password: [***] (required)
[Add Author]

You need to provide a Name for the account—this is different from the Nickname of the account, which is used to log the administrator in. Also required is an email address for this administrator, and of course a password.

The Permissions field contains a list of modules with a checkbox for each. By checking these boxes, you are able to endow this administrator with privileges for that module. By clicking the Super User box, the account will have the same privileges as the super user account. However, this account can be deleted, unlike the original 'God' super user account that we created when we first set up the site.

Once the permissions are set up, and the account details entered, click Add Author to create this administrator account. This account is now valid from the administrator login (admin.php). Note that there is no additional 'normal' user account option available as was the case with the 'God' account.

> If you use this form to change your super user account password, you will find yourself logged out and you will have to log in again with the new password.

Once an administrator account is set up like this, when the administrator logs in they will be met with a limited set of options in the administrator menu. The following screenshot shows an administrator account with permissions for the News, Surveys / Polls, Topics, and Users modules:

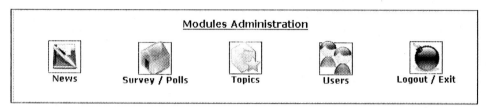

If this administrator attempts to bypass this menu and enter the URL of some of the other administrator pages directly, PHP-Nuke will still prevent access.

Summary

In this chapter we have seen how to add users to your site and how users are able to register themselves on your site, and have explored the personal area for each user provided by the Your Account module. Within the Your Account module each user is able to create their own Journal, which can be used to record their opinions, and can be viewed and commented on by other visitors to the site.

We also saw aspects of how to manage the users of your site, such as creating a subscription for a particular user. Subscriptions are typically used to restrict module access only to fee-paying customers. We also looked at user groups, and saw how PHP-Nuke can award points to users when they participate in site activities. When a user collects enough points, they can become a member of a user group, and possibly earn themselves access to restricted modules.

Finally, we looked at creating other administrator accounts that are less powerful than the super user account. These administrators, or authors as they are known in PHP-Nuke, can have permissions for specific modules, and allow you as the site administrator to put the management of these modules into the hands of others.

6
Story Management with PHP-Nuke

So far our PHP-Nuke site is pretty empty. Sure, we've got to grips with the administration area, moved blocks around the page, configured modules and site preferences, even added a new message to the homepage. However, the middle bit of our site still seems pretty empty. It feels like there is something missing... that's right, the content.

PHP-Nuke does not summon content from the darkest regions of the universe to appear on your site by magic (I'm sorry to disappoint you there). In this chapter, we will begin the journey of managing content with PHP-Nuke, or, in other words, getting stuff up on the site.

Here we're going to look at the fundamental type of PHP-Nuke content, the **story**. Stories in PHP-Nuke are the most versatile type of content, and have probably the richest set of features of all PHP-Nuke's content types. In fact, there are so many features it can make you dizzy. That is what this chapter is for. No—not making you dizzy, but helping you avoid the dizziness by guiding you through all the features of PHP-Nuke story management.

In this chapter, we will cover the following, paying attention to both the administrator and visitor points of view when required:

- An overview of stories and the story publication process
- Organizing stories into topics and categories
- Adding and editing stories
- Understanding comment moderation
- Managing stories
- The different modules that let you access stories
- Creating polls and surveys
- Syndicating your news with the backend.php file

The Story Story

In PHP-Nuke, a **story** is a general-purpose, piece of content. Maybe the story is an announcement, a press release or news item, or a piece of commentary or opinion, or maybe a tutorial article. The possibilities are almost endless!

With PHP-Nuke driving your site, the stories that appear on your site are not restricted to ones written by you. Users of the site—either registered or unregistered visitors, or other administrators—can write and submit stories to your site. The process of a story appearing on the site is known as publishing the story.

Of course this does not mean that your site is a free-for-all—stories submitted by users and others do not necessarily get published automatically—they are submitted for moderation by an administrator, and once approved, appear on your site. In this way, the content on your site grows itself through your community, but always (if you want) under your control. PHP-Nuke keeps track of such things as the author of the story, the date when the story first appeared on the site, and the number of times the story has been read, and also allows users to vote on the quality of the story. An impressive feature of PHP-Nuke stories is that users can comment on a posted story to build an open, topical discussion within your site.

You will see community-contributed stories when you visit any typical PHP-Nuke site; for example, on phpnuke.org itself, PHP-Nuke users and developers submit stories describing their latest PHP-Nuke add-on, or drawing attention to the latest theme that they've designed.

The 'story' engine in PHP-Nuke is provided by the News module. The total story functionality is actually spread across a number of modules, including Submit News, Stories Archive, Search, Topics, Your Account, and Surveys. We will explore all of these in this chapter.

The Story Publication Process

The path taken by a story from writing to publication depends upon who submits the story. The super user or an administrator with permissions for the News module can post a story through the administration area of the site. In this case, the publication process is simple, and the story appears on the site immediately, or can be scheduled for publication on a particular date.

Since the super user and any other administrators with the appropriate privileges are trusted (they have full power over stories, so they had better be trustworthy), there is no need to moderate or approve the text in the story, and the story is ready to go.

Registered and unregistered visitors can post stories through the Submit News module. When a story is submitted through this route, the publication process is lengthier.

1. The visitor enters the story through a form in the Submit News module.
2. The story administrator is notified that a new story has been submitted.
3. The story administrator checks over the story, editing, rejecting (deleting), or approving it. The administrator is also able to add notes to the story.
4. If the story is rejected, that is the end of the process, and the story is not published.
5. If the story is approved, it is either published to the site immediately, or can be scheduled for publication on a particular date.

Once the story is published to the site, the administrator can edit it further if needed. For a visitor, once they submit their story to the site they have no more control over the story.

Finding and Interacting with Stories

Stories on the site can be accessed in a number of ways, from a number of different places on the site. A limited number of stories can appear on the homepage, with older stories gradually moving down the list as newer stories are posted.

Stories can be retrieved by date from the Stories Archive module. The text in the story is also searchable from the Search module, so that specific stories can be located easily. Stories are organized into topics, and by browsing the list of topics from the Topics module stories can be tracked down.

Stories are not the end of content, they are actually the beginning. Comments can be posted about stories, and comments can be posted to these comments creating a discussion about the story. The quality of submitted comments can be assessed by users of the site and rated accordingly.

The quality or value of the story itself can be voted on by users, links to related stories can be created, and you can view a special printer-friendly version of the story for printing, or even send the story to a friend.

So many features... did I mention that you can also attach a poll to the story so that readers can participate in a survey related to the content of the story? So many features...

Organizing Stories

When you have even a reasonable number of stories on your PHP-Nuke site (and you will have—that's why you're reading this book!), you will be in need of some organization for this content.

PHP-Nuke provides two ways of organizing story content:

- Topics: what it's about
- Categories: what type of story it is

Topics

Topics define what a story is about. By organizing your stories into topics, stories about similar subjects will be grouped together for easy browsing and reading, and also to make it easier for people to contribute their stories to the right place.

When you're reading through a number of dinosaur-related stories, the sudden appearance of a story about cars would be rather off-putting (unless it was actually about fossil fuels or dinosaurs eating/driving cars).

PHP-Nuke does indeed offer organization of stories into **topics**, and before we can think of adding stories, we need to set up some topics for our stories.

A topic has an associated image that is displayed on the site whenever you view a story that belongs to that topic, or whenever you are browsing the list of topics. The image overleaf shows a 'teaser' of a story displayed on our site; the topic image is shown to the right-hand side of the story:

the Dinosaur Portal is Alive!

Since the beginning of time, man and dinosaur have wrestled for supremacy of the world we all inhabit. Finally, this site, the Dinosaur Portal, chronicles and informs of this struggle.

Posted by <u>admin</u> on Wednesday, August 10 @ GMT Daylight Time (0 reads)
(Read More... | 487 bytes more | comments? | Score: 0)

The Read More... link will take the visitor to the remainder of the story.

> Note that this arrangement of the story text and the topic image appearing to the right of the story is just the default layout due to the basic theme. When we come to look at creating our own themes, we will see how the topic image can be made to appear elsewhere relative to the story text.

By default, there is a single topic called PHP-Nuke. This has its own image, which should only be used for the PHP-Nuke topic.

Categories

As topics define what a story is about, categories define the 'type' of story. A category could be something like a weblog entry, a security announcement, or a press release.

There is one category defined by default, Article. This category has the following properties:

- You cannot change this category's name or delete it.
- Any story of type Article automatically appears on the homepage.
- Users can only submit stories of type Article.

Compared to topics, categories do not have particularly extensive support in PHP-Nuke.

Planning the Dinosaur Portal Topics and Categories

Before we move on to looking at managing topics and categories, we'll quickly discuss the kind of topics and categories that we would like for organizing our stories on the Dinosaur Portal. These are not set in stone, and after we create them, we can edit or delete them, or even add new ones.

First of all, there will probably be stories about the Dinosaur Portal itself that will contain general information about the site, such as new features that have been added to it, or warnings about planned site downtime (or apologies about unplanned site downtime!).

We will also have stories about dinosaurs, fossils, and dinosaur hunting; these can be the other topics on the site. What types of story will we have? In addition to the standard article, we can have new theories, technologies, or discoveries, maybe even tutorials (for example, how to identify fossils, or how to avoid being eaten when dinosaur hunting). There will also be stories about Project Chimera, but we can't reveal what that is just yet.

Thus a story about a controversial new dinosaur extinction theory could be given the 'dinosaur' topic, and the 'new theory' category.

This isn't an exhaustive list, but it is enough to give an idea of the topic-category split.

Topic Management

Before we do anything else, we'll create our topics. For each topic, we'll add the images first. After we create our topics, we'll look at how to modify them, and the consequences of deleting topics.

Before we get started creating our topics, we will add the topic images. To do this, you will need to copy all the files from the `topics` folder in the `ch06` folder of the code download to the `images/topics/` folder in the root of your PHP-Nuke installation.

You should have these files: `thedinosaurportal.gif`, `dinosaurs.gif`, `fossils.gif`, and `dinosaurhunting.gif`, in addition to files called `index.html`, `phpnuke.gif`, and `AllTopics.gif`, which were already present in the folder.

The `images/topics` folder is the place where PHP-Nuke will look for the topic icons. When adding image files to the `images/topics` folder, ensure that only alphanumeric characters or the underscore are used in your filename, or else PHP-Nuke will fail to pick up the filename when displaying the list of topic images.

> Note also that the total length of the filename and its extension must not exceed twenty characters, or PHP-Nuke will truncate the name when it stores a record of the filename. In this case, your topic image will not be displayed, because PHP-Nuke has not stored the correct name of the file. Also, if your image has an extension of more than three characters (such as `jpeg`) then it will be missed by PHP-Nuke.

The `AllTopics.gif` file in the `images/topics` folder does not correspond to a single topic, but is the image used when displaying the lists of topics. This file can be replaced by an image of your own.

Time For Action—Creating New Topics

1. Log in to your site as the administrator.
2. From the Modules Administration menu, click on the Topics icon:

3. You will come to the Topics Manager area. Scroll down to the Add a New Topic panel.

4. The first topic we create will be Dinosaur Hunting. Enter the text dinosaurhunting in the Topic Name field, enter Dinosaur Hunting into the Topic Text field, and select the file dinosaurhunting.gif from the Topic Image drop-down box:

Add a New Topic

Topic Name:
(just a name without spaces - max: 20 characters)
(for example: gamesandhobbies)

dinosaurhunting

Topic Text:
(the full topic text or description - max: 40 characters)
(for example: Games and Hobbies)

Dinosaur Hunting

Topic Image:
dinosaurhunting.gif

Add Topic

5. Click the Add Topic button.

6. When the screen refreshes, the newly created topic will be displayed in the Current Active Topics panel:

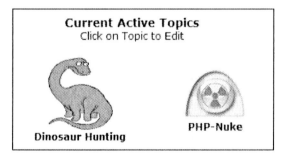

Current Active Topics
Click on Topic to Edit

Dinosaur Hunting   **PHP-Nuke**

This process can be repeated for our other topics:

Topic Text	Topic Name	Topic Image
Fossils	fossils	fossils.gif
Dinosaurs	dinosaurs	dinosaurs.gif

What Just Happened?

The Topics Manager, reached through the Topics icon in the administration menu, is the area from where we can add, edit, or delete topics.

The Topics Manager has two panels, one showing the Current Active Topics, and the other being the Add a New Topic panel.

A topic requires three pieces of data:

- A topic name, which is a short piece of text with no spaces. This is mostly used internally by PHP-Nuke. The topic name is usually the same as the topic text, but in lower case and with no spaces.

- The topic text, which is the title of the topic.

- The topic image. The name of the topic image is selected from the list of files in the images/topics folder. You can use the same image for more than one topic if you choose.

Once you have saved a topic, clicking on its image in the Current Active Topics panel takes you to the Edit Topic area, from where you can edit or delete your topic.

You may have noted that we haven't created the Dinosaur Portal topic. We'll do that now by editing the existing default topic, since we would like this to be the default topic for the portal anyway.

Time For Action—Editing Topics

We will edit the default topic to get the Dinosaur Portal topic:

1. In the Topic Manager area, click on the PHP-Nuke topic icon in the list of Current Active Topics.

2. When the page loads, enter the details as shown below:

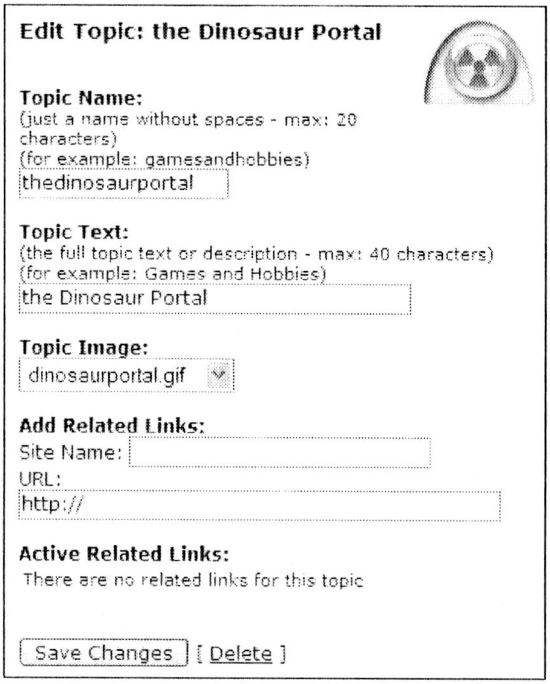

Edit Topic: the Dinosaur Portal

Topic Name:
(just a name without spaces - max: 20 characters)
(for example: gamesandhobbies)
`thedinosaurportal`

Topic Text:
(the full topic text or description - max: 40 characters)
(for example: Games and Hobbies)
`the Dinosaur Portal`

Topic Image:
`dinosaurportal.gif`

Add Related Links:
Site Name:
URL:
`http://`

Active Related Links:
There are no related links for this topic

[Save Changes] [Delete]

3. Click the Save Changes button to complete your editing.

4. When the page reloads, you will need to click the Topics icon again to return to the Topic Manager area, since you will be returned to the page for editing the topic.

What Just Happened?

We just edited the properties of an already existing topic. To get at a topic's properties, you click on its icon in the list of Current Active Topics in the Topic Manager area. The possible topic icons are again picked from the images/topics folder and displayed in a drop-down list for you to choose. Once you are done making changes to the topic, clicking the Save Changes button updates the topic.

Note that there is no cancel button, and if you decide to make no changes here, you can click the Topics icon in the Modules Administration menu to return to the Topic Manager area, or use the back button on your browser.

Deleting a Topic

It is possible to delete topics by clicking the Delete link next to the Save Changes button. However, deleting a topic will delete all the stories that belong to that topic. Fortunately, there is a confirmation screen before the topic is deleted:

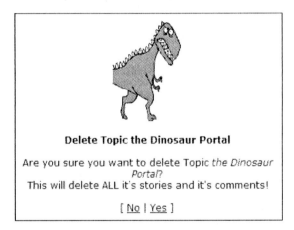

Delete Topic the Dinosaur Portal

Are you sure you want to delete Topic *the Dinosaur Portal?*
This will delete ALL it's stories and it's comments!

[No | Yes]

Since the Delete link is positioned so close to Save Changes, it's probably good that there is this screen. There is no turning back after you click Yes on this screen. Your topic is gone, and so are all the stories, and any comments attached to those stories. Note that the image associated with the topic is not deleted, and it still remains on the server, and can be used for another topic if wished.

Adding Stories

With the topic list set up as desired, we can now begin to add stories to our site. Our first story will be about the launch of our new site.

Time For Action—Adding a New Story

1. From the administration menu, click the News icon (in versions of PHP-Nuke before 7.5, this icon is titled Add Story):

2. You are now in the Article/Stories Administration area. At the top of the Add New Article panel, enter the following into the Title field:

   the Dinosaur Portal is Alive!

3. Select the Dinosaur Portal from the Topics drop-down box.

4. Don't select any of the Associated Topics.

5. Leave Article selected in the Categories drop-down box.

6. Skip over the Publish in Home? and Activate Comments for this Story? fields, they are already set to our required values.

7. Enter the following into the Story Text field.

   Since the beginning of time, man and dinosaur have wrestled for supremacy of the world we all inhabit. Finally, this site, the Dinosaur Portal, chronicles and informs of this struggle.

8. Enter the following into the Extended Text field:

   At the Dinosaur Portal, we believe that just because you haven't seen a dinosaur, doesn't mean that they've all died out.

   As such, this site has been specially created to address the needs of those who think likewise, and provide specific content targetted for this enthusiastic and unusual audience.

9. Leave the Do you want to program this story? field set to No.

10. Click the Ok! button next to the Preview Story drop-down box.

11. When the page reloads, a preview of the story is displayed:

Preview Story

the Dinosaur Portal is Alive!

Since the beginning of time, man and dinosaur have wrestled for supremacy of the world we all inhabit. Finally, this site, the Dinosaur Portal, chronicles and informs of this struggle.

At the Dinosaur Portal, we believe that just because you haven't seen a dinosaur, doesn't mean that they've all died out. As such, this site has been specially created to address the needs of those who think likewise, and provide specific content targetted for this enthusiastic and unusual audience.

---

12. Scroll down to the bottom of the story details, and select Post Story from the drop-down box next to the Ok! button:

13. Click the Ok! button, and your story is posted.

What Just Happened?

We just posted a story. First we went to the Add New Article panel in the Article/Story Administration area. Here, we went via the News icon in the Modules Administration menu. There is an alternative route; the NEW Story link in the Administration block takes you to this place as well:

We began by entering the story's title into the Title field, followed by selecting its topic from the Topic drop-down box. It is possible to forget to assign a topic to the story; PHP-Nuke will not warn you about this, although when you preview the story before posting, the absence of the topic image should be a clue that something has gone wrong. You can assign a new topic to a story when editing the story after it has been created.

You are able to choose a number of related topics for this story, and links to these topics are displayed under the story, allowing people to browse these other topics for similar stories.

Next it's time to select a category from the Category drop-down box. At the moment we only have one category, the default Article category. We'll look at managing categories in a moment.

The next field we encountered was Publish in Home?. Any story in the Article category is published to the homepage (in other words, displayed on the homepage of the site) regardless of this value. Stories from any other category can be set to appear on the homepage by selecting this option, although Yes is the default value.

The next field is Activate Comments for this Story? We'll spend a lot of time talking about comments in a moment. We left the value at its default, which is Yes.

We did a lot of typing next; we entered the Story Text and then the Extended Text. The Story Text is a summary or introduction to the story, a teaser if you like, and the main part of the story goes into the Extended Text. The Story Text is to introduce the story to the reader, and should only really contain enough to get the reader interested in wanting to read the full story.

When visitors begin submitting stories to your site, and you, as the administrator, begin the process of approving these stories for publication on your site, you may find yourself having to split up the submission of the visitor into a more balanced Story Text and Extended Story division.

Back to our current situation... the next thing we did was to select No for Do you want to program this story? By doing this, the story appears on the site immediately after we have posted it. By selecting Yes, and then entering a date through the various date options, you can schedule the story to be published at the time you choose:

Selecting a date for the publication of the story without selecting Yes for the Do you want to program this story? will not set a date for the story, and the story will be published immediately. Once a story is programmed, its schedule is set and there is no feature to alter the schedule.

With all the story details in place, all that remains is to preview the story (selecting Preview Story from the drop-down box next to Ok!) before posting it. If it looks OK, we can post the story by selecting Post Story from the drop-down box. If we felt bold, we could select Post Story without previewing the story first, and begin the publishing process.

Underneath the Add New Article panel is a panel for attaching a poll to the story. We will discuss polls and surveys later in the chapter.

Category Management

We saw the Category drop-down box in the Add New Article panel; it has three icons next to it for managing categories:

If you click any of these icons to go off and do a bit of category management, you will lose any text you've entered into the story at that point, so do any category management before you get too far into your story!

These icons are the only means of managing categories. If the category that you want for the story does not exist when you create the story, you can always create the category after creating the story and then change the story's details.

Adding a new category simply requires you to define a name for it. We'll add a few new categories to the Dinosaur Portal; New Theory, Technology, and Tutorial.

```
┌─────────────────────────────────────────────────────────┐
│              Categories Administration                    │
│  ┌─────────────────────────────────────────────────────┐ │
│  │              Add a New Category                       │ │
│  │                                                       │ │
│  │  Category Name: │New Theory          │  │ Save │     │ │
│  │                                                       │ │
│  └─────────────────────────────────────────────────────┘ │
└─────────────────────────────────────────────────────────┘
```

Note that after adding a category, there is no link to go back to the Add New Article panel, and if you use the Back button to go back there, you will have to refresh the browser for the new category to be displayed in the list of categories.

Editing a category allows you to change the name of the category. Note that another list of categories is displayed, and you have to select the category from that list; you will not be editing the category selected in the Category drop-down box of the Add New Article panel.

Deleting a category is more interesting. Clicking the Delete link next to the Category drop-down box brings up another list of the categories, from which we choose the one we want to delete and click a Delete button. If there are any stories in the category, we are presented with a warning screen. If there are no stories in the category, the category is simply deleted. Deleting a category will delete all the stories in that category, and so PHP-Nuke gives us a lifeline:

```
┌─────────────────────────────────────────────────────────┐
│                    Delete Category                        │
│                                                           │
│     Warning: The Category Category2 has 1 stories inside  │
│   You can Delete this Category and ALL its stories and    │
│            comments                                       │
│     or you can Move ALL the stories to a New Category.     │
│                                                           │
│                 What do you want to do?                   │
│                                                           │
│       [ Yes! Delete ALL! | No! Move my Stories ]          │
└─────────────────────────────────────────────────────────┘
```

If you click No! Move My Stories, you are able to select a category into which all the stories of your about-to-be deleted category will move. The stories are moved, and the category is deleted—the option No is rather misleading here, since the end result is still the removal of a category.

If you have changed your mind and do not wish to delete the category, click the Back button in your browser or click on one of the other icons in the Administration Menu to continue with your administration, rather than selecting one of the two Delete Category options.

Deleting a category contrasts with deleting a topic; there we saw that deleting a topic removes all the stories within that topic and there was no opportunity to move them as a group.

The Visitor View of a Story

Let's have a look at how the story will look to the visitor. Click the Home link in the Modules block to return to the homepage of the site. There, in the middle of the page, you will see the story you just entered.

the Dinosaur Portal is Alive!

Since the beginning of time, man and dinosaur have wrestled for supremacy of the world we all inhabit. Finally, this site, the Dinosaur Portal, chronicles and informs of this struggle.

Posted by <u>admin</u> on Wednesday, August 10 @ GMT Daylight Time (0 reads)
(**Read More...** | 487 bytes more | comments? | Score: 0)

This view shows the introduction to the story, the story text, along with some further details:

- Who posted the story to the site
- When was the story posted
- The number of times the story has been read
- The number of comments (if any) made on the story
- The remaining amount of text in the story (in bytes, which is more or less characters)
- A link to view the remainder of the story

The creator of the story is usually different from the person who posts (approves) the story to the site. The person who publishes the story is almost always one of the site administrators. This current view of the story can give a misleading impression, and have you believe that this story is written by admin.

Click on the Read More... link, and we will see the story's Extended Text.

the Dinosaur Portal is Alive!

Since the beginning of time, man and dinosaur have wrestled for supremacy of the world we all inhabit. Finally, this site, the Dinosaur Portal, chronicles and informs of this struggle.

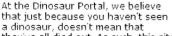

At the Dinosaur Portal, we believe that just because you haven't seen a dinosaur, doesn't mean that they've all died out. As such, this site has been specially created to address the needs of those who think likewise, and provide specific content targetted for this enthusiastic and unusual audience.

Note the extended text of the story is displayed along with the 'story text' of the story. To the right of the story text, the visitor will see a few blocks. If the visitor is not currently logged in, they will see four blocks. Otherwise, a visitor will see three blocks to the right of the extended story text. The extra block for the visitor who isn't logged in is a Login block, inviting the visitor to login or create an account if they don't have one. Apart from that, the other three blocks are the same if you are logged in or not.

These blocks guide the reader towards related content, allow the reader to rate the story, and allow the reader to view the story in a form more suitable for printing or pass it on to a friend.

Related Links, Scoring, and Friends

The Related Links block shows a link to other stories from the same topic as the current story, other stories from the author of the current story (in this case the author is admin), and the most viewed story from the same topic:

There isn't much competition for the most viewed story at this point!

Underneath the Related Links block is the Article Rating block:

This block allows visitor to score or rate the story, from one star (very bad) to five stars (very good). The result of the rating so far is displayed at the top of the panel—the average rating and the total number of votes cast. The score of the article was shown, if you recall, on the summary view of the story on the homepage.

Let's exercise our rights, and select five stars, and then click Cast my Vote! We will receive a message thanking us for voting:

Thanks for voting for this article!

[Back to Article's Page]

When the page reloads, the article tally has updated:

Let's abuse our right, and continue to vote. This time, select one star (boo), and click Cast my Vote! Fortunately, PHP-Nuke has seen through our villainy:

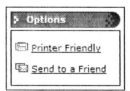

PHP-Nuke is able to detect that you have already voted from a cookie it stores on your machine. In fact, PHP-Nuke won't let somebody else from the same IP address vote in the poll again.

The block underneath the Article Rating block is the Options block:

Options

🖨 Printer Friendly

📧 Send to a Friend

For ordinary visitors, this block shows a link to a printer-friendly version of the page, and an opportunity to email details of the page to a friend.

When logged in as the administrator, extra icons are displayed, allowing you to modify the story being viewed. We'll look at this activity later in the chapter.

The printer-friendly page displays a 'clean' version of only the story and its content:

the Dinosaur Portal is Alive!
Date: Tuesday, October 04 @ GMT Daylight Time
Topic: The Dinosaur Portal

Since the beginning of time, man and dinosaur have wrestled for supremacy of the world we all inhabit. Finally, this site, the Dinosaur Portal, chronicles and informs of this struggle.

At the Dinosaur Portal, we believe that just because you haven't seen a dinosaur, doesn't mean that they've all died out. As such, this site has been specially created to address the needs of those who think likewise, and provide specific content targetted for this enthusiastic and unusual audience.

The image stamped at the top of the printer-friendly page is the image specified as the Site Logo in the site preferences. If you are particularly observant, you may have noticed that on the Site Preferences page, the Site Logo had the following text next to its field:

```
must be in /images/ directory. Valid only for AvantGo module
```

That statement turns out to be not entirely true; the image displayed at the top of the printer-friendly page (which is part of the News module) is also determined by the Site Logo field.

The other link in the Options block allows the visitor to send a link to the story to someone via email. Here is the email received by my friend Count Dracula about our first story:

```
Hello Count Dracula:

Your Friend Testuser considered the following article interesting and wanted
to send it to you.

the Dinosaur Portal is Alive!
(Date: 2005-08-09 11:22:13)
Topic: the Dinosaur Portal

URL: http://thedinosaurportal.com/modules.php?name=News&file=article&sid=1

You can read interesting articles at theDinosaurPortal
http://thedinosaurportal.com
```

By clicking on the URL after URL:, my friend, Count Dracula, will be able to read the story in full. And then probably email me asking why I thought it was interesting to him.

You will note that the full domain name of your site is included in the email; this is taken from the Site URL property of the Web Site Configuration menu. If you haven't set this properly, then the link will point to the wrong site! (It will be phpnuke.org if you haven't set the Site URL property.)

The subject of the email consists of the text Interesting Article at followed by your site name, which is the Site Name property of the Web Site Configuration menu. You will want to make sure you have set that property as well. For all of this, you must also have your site's mail server working.

Everyone Has an Opinion... Comments

Comments can be posted on stories, allowing readers to express their own carefully formulated opinion of the story content. Comments can be posted directly to the story (top-level comments), or they can be posted as replies to existing comments. In this way, 'threads' of discussion can be created related to the story, or at least, related to the comment they are replying to. Comments are 'owned by the poster'. This means that no one can edit the comments, not even the super user.

Time For Action—Posting a Comment

1. Log out of the administrator account if you are still logged in.

2. We're going to work as the `testuser` user, so log in as the `testuser` with password `testuser`.

3. Click the Home link in the Modules block to return to the homepage of the site.

4. The story that we entered in the *Adding Articles* section will be displayed in the middle of the homepage. Click its comments link.

5. Underneath the extended story text you will see the comments bar. Click the Post Comment button:

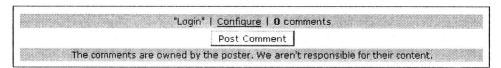

6. When the page reloads, the extended story text is displayed again, and underneath is the panel for entering your comment:

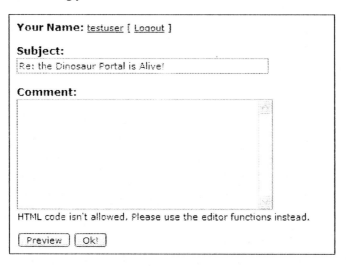

7. Let's enter some text for the comment into the Comment field:

   I am really excited by this prospect. It is the answer to so many of my needs.

8.   Click the Preview button.

9.   When the page reloads, you can indeed see a preview of your comment, with the comment editing panel underneath:

Comment Post Preview

Re: the Dinosaur Portal is Alive!
by testuser on...

I am really excited by this prospect. It is the answer to so many of my needs.

---

10.   We are satisfied with the look of our comment, so let's click the Ok! button at the bottom of the comment editing panel to submit our comment.

11.   When the page reloads, the story is displayed again, our newly posted comment is shown underneath, and the comment count in the comments bar has been updated:

"Login" | Configure | **1** comment | Search Discussion

Post Comment

The comments are owned by the poster. We aren't responsible for their content.

Re: the Dinosaur Portal is Alive! (Score: 1)
by testuser on Wednesday, August 10 @ GMT Daylight Time
(User Info | Send a Message | Journal)

I am really excited by this prospect. It is the answer to so many of my needs.

[Reply to This]

What Just Happened?

We just posted a comment to a story. The posting process itself was straightforward. To get a view of the comments, we chose to click the comments? link, although the Read More... link on the story text takes us to the same page.

Once we clicked Post Comment, it was simply a case of entering the text into the Comment field, which forms the body of the content. A subject was already provided for us in the Subject field (Re: followed by the title of the story), although we could have edited this field if we wanted. We chose to preview the story before posting (which is always wise).

Clicking the Ok! button on the comment edit panel posted the story to the site, and we were presented with the story along with the comment we just posted.

The comment panel is made up of two boxes (as seen in the last screenshot):

- The top box is the comments bar, and is used by the user to work with comments. Through the comments bar, the user can customize their view of the comments, search the current discussion, or post a comment (if this is allowed).

- The lower box is a posted comment. It shows the title of the comment, the comment's score, the name of the user who posted the comment and at what time they posted it, the text of the comment, a link to reply to the comment, and some further links about the user.

Time For Action—Replying to a Comment

It may seem rather sad replying to our own comments, but that is what we are about to do. You can pretend you are a different user if you like, or you could even create a new user account and log in as that user to complete the masquerade.

Following on directly from the last task, you should have a view of the comment you just posted (if not, click the comments (1) link of our story to return to the comments view). Click the Reply to This link.

You will be taken to a page with the comment you are replying to, followed by the comment edit panel for you to enter your response. Let's enter the text I second that! into the Comment field and click the Ok! button.

When the page reloads, our new reply is shown:

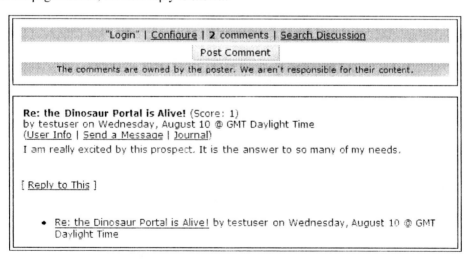

What Just Happened?

We just replied to a comment. Like posting comments, the replying process is straightforward. The subject of the comment is provided; this time it is the same subject as the comment you are replying to, but you are able to edit from the comment editing screen as you enter the text of your comment.

Seeing Your Comments

You can view a list of your ten most recent comments from the Your Account module. Click the Your Account module link and scroll down the screen to see them:

Last 10 Comments by testuser:
- Re: the Dinosaur Portal is Alive!
- Re: the Dinosaur Portal is Alive!

Clicking on one of these links will take you to the story with that comment, and will even have automatically moved you to the part of the page where the comment is displayed, so you do not have to scroll through all the comments to find it. With these links, the comment display is different from the view we saw earlier. All the comments are displayed in a long list with the full text of the comment visible. This is different from the 'thread' view we saw earlier, where only the comment subject was shown for replies. We'll see more about comment views later.

Controlling Comment Posting

However, the possibility of posting comments to stories does not mean anarchy on your site. There are a number of actions you can take as the administrator to control the posting of comments.

- You can allow/disallow comments to be posted for an individual story.
- You can allow only registered users to post comments.
- You can remove comments.
- The comments of certain users can be checked.
- The comments can be 'moderated' by other visitors.

Allowing Comments

First of all, you have to allow comments to be posted for the story in question. This is controlled by the Activate Comments for this Story? option when the story is created or edited:

Activate Comments for this Story? ⦿ Yes ◯ No

By default, this option is set to Yes, so that comments can be posted for the story. If you wished to disable comment posting for a particular story, you would set this option to No.

Disallowing Comments

To turn off comment posting for every story, there is an option in the Web Site Configuration menu of the site preferences. The Miscelaneous Options panel in the Web Site Configuration menu has the following option:

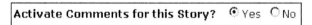

Activate Comments in Articles?   ⦿ Yes ◯ No

The default value of this option is Yes, so comments are activated for articles (the first type of story). Any story that has the Activate Comments for this Story? option set to No will override this value and not allow the posting of comments.

If the Activate Comments in Articles? option is set to No, then comments cannot be posted for any article, regardless of the value of the Activate Comments for this Story? option set for that story.

In general, disabling comment posting does not disable the display of comments. If comments have already been posted and you disable posting, then comments already posted will still be displayed. The options we have just discussed handle comment posting, not display.

Restricting Comment Posting to Registered Visitors

The next safety feature is to stop anyone other than registered visitors from posting comments on a story. This feature is controlled in the General Site Info panel (top bit) of the Web Site Configuration menu:

Recall that an Anonymous user is an unregistered user. Setting this option to No means that only registered visitors can post comments. Anonymous users will still be able to read the comments; they simply will not be able to participate in the discussion unless they register on the site. By default, this option is set to No.

Thus the default comment posting settings for a particular story are:

- Comments are enabled.
- Only registered visitors can post comments.

Therefore, without doing any extra configuration, any story posted to our site can be commented on only by registered visitors.

By default, an anonymous comment post is said to have been posted by Anonymous. You can change this from the Comments Option panel further down the Web Site Configuration menu:

Comments Option	
Comments Limit in Bytes:	4096
Anonymous Default Name:	Anonymous

Here you can restrict the size of a posted comment with the Comment Limit in Bytes (this is a count of all the characters used in the comment, including any HTML tags). You can also change the name of the anonymous poster from the Anonymous Default Name field. As ever, when working with site preferences remember to save your changes with the Save Changes button at the bottom of the Web Site Configuration menu.

Administrator Removal of Comments

When you are logged in as the administrator, a Delete link appears on each comment:

Re: the Dinosaur Portal is Alive! (Score: 1)
by testuser on Wednesday, August 10 @ GMT Daylight Time
(<u>User Info</u> | <u>Send a Message</u> | <u>Journal</u>)
(IP: 127.0.0.1) Bad Karma
I am really excited by this prospect. It is the answer to so many of my needs.

[<u>Reply to This</u> | <u>Delete</u>]

• <u>Re: the Dinosaur Portal is Alive!</u> by testuser on Wednesday, August 10 @ GMT Daylight Time

By clicking this link and confirming, you can remove the comment. Since the comment discussion is 'threaded', there could possibly be replies to that comment; in this case, all the replies to that comment will also be deleted. Also, all the replies to those replies will be deleted as well, and so on. This is the only way to remove comments from a particular story.

You may want to delete a comment if it is particularly offensive, or is just basically nonsense. This brings us onto a rather delicate topic...

Filth Filter

Some people have a rather 'colorful' vocabulary, and may feel the need to emphasize their point with bad language. I don't mean poor grammar, I mean BAD language. To prevent your site being filled with rude words from visitor-submitted content, PHP-Nuke has a built-in filter for obscenities, words that I'd rather not put on this page.

This filter is controlled from the panel called Censure Options of the Web Site Configuration menu (it's right at the bottom, you will have to scroll all the way down):

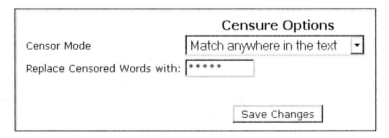

PHP-Nuke has a list of words (stored in the file config.php, if you really must look) that it will scan text for, depending on the value specified in the Censor Mode option. These options allow you to decide how the bad words should be matched.

You can choose one of the following options (let's pretend love is a bad word for the sake of argument here):

- No filtering: This option allows any kind of language in the comments. This turns the 'filth filter' off.

- Exact match: This option only matches exact occurrences of the bad words in your text. It will match the word love in the text this is love I think, but will not match in I think it is lovely.

- Match word at the beginning: This option will match occurrences of the bad words when they are the start of words. It will match the word love in the text I think it is lovely, but not in I am wearing a glove.

- Match anywhere in the text: This option will match bad words wherever they appear; at the start of words, or the middle of words, it will hunt them down and match them. With this setting, the word love will be matched in all the previous examples. This setting is the default value.

Once a bad word is found, it is replaced with the text specified in the Replace Censored Words with field.

Note that filtering happens before the text is stored in the database, but after any previewing. Thus if a bad word is found in the text with filtering turned on, that word is immediately replaced by the censor text, and the bad word is gone forever. If you change the settings of the filth filter later, then the bad word will not reappear; only the censored text remains. And another thing—turning on the filth filter will not 'retrospectively' filter text. If you have bad words in comments, they will not be censored automatically. You have been warned!

The filter does not apply to administrator-submitted stories. As the administrator, you are in a very trusted position, and you should always be careful what you write!

Karma and Comment Moderation

In an earlier screenshot of the comments, you may have caught sight of the poster's karma displayed next to their IP address:

```
(User Info | Send a Message)
(IP: 127.0.0.1) Bad Karma
```

The karma of the comment poster has consequences for the fate of their comments. Users who are marked with bad karma cannot post comments directly to the site. When they post a comment, they will be greeted with the following screen:

Comment Submitted - Approval Pending

Your comments has been submitted, but since you have
been marked by the administrator of this site as an user
with Bad Karma, your comment is subject to prior approval
by our staff. Please don't submit your comment twice or
your Karma may fall to the next level.

Our staff reserves the right to approve or delete your
comment at their sole discretion.

Return to Article's Page

The super user will have to approve the comment of a user marked with bad karma before it goes onto the site. If a user is marked with devil karma, then their comment is immediately rejected. This method of censorship isn't simply to keep dissenting or controversial opinions off your site; it is also to prevent people posting 'comment spam', which could be annoying adverts for other products or sites, or simply obscene and irrelevant comments.

We have just seen how PHP-Nuke handles obscene comments, but karma can be used to control situations where there seems to be a systematic abuse of your comment posting facility. After all, posting a comment is the easiest way for anyone to get their information up on your site, unopposed. Not everyone who registers with your site may be intending to use it as you imagine. If your site becomes successful, with good traffic, then people may view posting comments to stories on your site as an opportunity for free promotion, often for a product that is completely unrelated to your site, and often for something that you rather not have promoted on your site, if you take my drift....

If, as the super user, you find comments from a particular user that you do not feel belong on your site, then you can click the User Info link in the comment, and you will be taken to that user's Your Account module, and you will be able to see their current karma:

Administration Functions

Last user IP: **127.0.0.1**

[Ban This IP | Edit User]

User Karma: Bad Karma (Bad Karma)
(This user is bad and his comments are moderated)

Change Karma for User *testuser*

○ 🚩 😈

○	Default value. Users marked with *Good Karma* can post their comments without any restrictions.
🚩	Users marked with *Regular Karma* should be under observation. Consider this value a *flag* to have a eye on it.
Bad Karma	Users marked with *Bad Karma* can post comments but the administrator should approve/moderate them from the admin panel.
😈	Users marked with *Devil Karma* are very bad. This users are not allowed to post comments. All his content is just ignored and nothing will be published.

You can change the karma of that user by clicking on one of the images in the middle of the panel. The default value, good karma, allows users to freely post comments to new stories. If you feel the need to keep a user under observation, you can mark them with regular karma, but they can still post freely. Should they continue to misbehave with their comments, you can upgrade them to bad karma. This is when you have to approve their comments before they are accepted. If the comments continue to be unacceptable to you, marking them with devil karma prevents them from posting entirely.

Another alternative for dealing with systematic abuse of your system by a user is to disallow any access to the system from their IP address by clicking the Ban This IP link. This takes you to the Ban IP module. Banning IP addresses is a very drastic measure, especially since you may be banning an entire group of innocent people who may share the same IP address as the villain you are attempting to exclude. If people are accessing the Internet through a network or a proxy server then that will determine their IP address. Also, the villain may reconnect to the Internet and be assigned a new IP address by their ISP, in which case they will have avoided the ban.

After a marked user posts their comment, the super user can approve or reject their comment by first clicking the Moderation icon in the Administration Menu:

This will bring up the karma-moderation panel. This panel shows the number of comments that are waiting for you to approve, and also the number of marked users, if any.

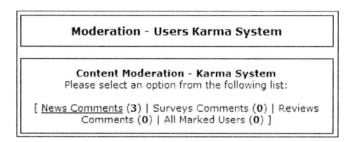

Clicking any of the Comments links will bring up a list of the comments waiting for you, a link to view the comment, and a pair of buttons to approve or reject these comments. You can't edit a comment, only approve or reject it. After approval, the comment will go onto the site as usual. You will note that this karma-approval system also applies to comments from some other modules, Surveys and Reviews.

You can click the All Marked Users link to bring up the list of users whose karma you have marked:

Clicking on the user name will take you to that user's Your Account module, from where you can modify their karma or ban their IP address as we discussed earlier.

This has been moderation by the super user. Now we turn our attention to another form of moderation; moderation by other users.

Comments in Moderation

We are now about to enter the arcane world of PHP-Nuke comment moderation by users. Moderation isn't quite the right word; nobody can alter another person's comment (apart from the administrator who can remove a comment entirely). First things first; we shall enable comment moderation from the Administration Menu.

Time For Action—Enabling Comment Moderation

1. Log in in as the administrator.
2. Go to the Web Site Configuration menu by clicking on the Preferences icon in the Administration Menu.
3. Scroll down the page until you see the Comments Moderation panel:

4. From the drop-down box, select Moderation by users.
5. Scroll further down the page, and click the Save Changes button.

What Just Happened?

Before we can use comment moderation, it needs to be enabled, and this is done through the Comments Moderation panel in the Web Site Configuration menu.

There are three options:

The default option, No Moderation means comments cannot be moderated. Moderation by Users allows registered visitors to moderate comments, and Moderation by Admin allows only administrators to moderate comments.

By selecting Moderation By Users we have chosen to allow any registered visitor to moderate the comments.

Users are able to 'rate' a comment with one of the following ratings:

1. As Is
2. Offtopic
3. Flamebait
4. Troll
5. Redundant
6. Insighful
7. Interesting
8. Informative
9. Funny
10. Overrated
11. Underrated

These ratings, rather than assigning a score to the comment, provide a description of the value of the comment. Some are straightforward; it's clear what Insightful, or Interesting means. Some, such as Flamebait or Troll are more steeped in the lore of discussion boards. Flamebait is a question or comment that people should really be able to find the answer about somewhere else easily. Marking a comment as Troll would indicate that you think it is making a provocative point just to start a heated argument. The poster looks like they're more interested in arguing than stating or learning sensible views.

Although the ratings do not directly assign a score, a comment does have a score and the type of rating does alter the comment's score.

When a comment is first posted, it is awarded a score of one (anonymous posts, if allowed, are awarded a score of zero).

When a user rates a comment, the score of the comment can change in one of the following ways:

*   No change: The user has chosen the As Is rating.
*   The score increases by one: The user has chosen a 'positive' rating. This is one of the Insightful, Interesting, Informative, Funny, or Underrated ratings.
*   The score decreases by one: The user has chosen a 'negative' rating. This is one of the OffTopic, Flamebait, Troll, Redundant, or Overrated ratings.

In this way the score of the comment changes as users rate the comment. The score can take a value from a minimum of -1 up to a maximum of 5. Note that the score of a comment has nothing to do with the score of the story that it is posted to; the score of a story is determined by user voting in the Article Rating block next to the story. We saw that earlier.

Now this is where the 'moderation' comes in. Every user has a 'comment score threshold', by default set to zero. The option to change the score is present on the Comments Configuration page (go there from the Comments link in Your Account or by clicking the Configure link in the comments bar). Any comment with a score less than this threshold value is not displayed to the user.

By adjusting their 'comment score threshold', the user can filter out comments that are not worth reading.

Other users who have read and rated the comment have made the judgment for you of whether a comment is worth reading.

That's the idea. Let's try it out.

Time For Action—Moderating Comments

1. Log out from the administrator account.

2. Click on the Home link in the Modules menu to return to your homepage.

3. In the Login block on the right-hand side of the page, log in as testuser (enter testuser as the Nickname and testuser as the Password, then click the Login button).

4. Once you are logged in, click on the Home link in the Modules menu to return to the site homepage.

5. Find our first story, and click the Read More... link

6. Scroll down the page to find our existing comment that we added earlier:

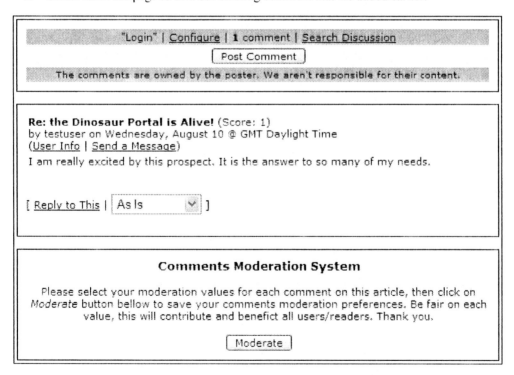

7. We really like this comment. Let's select Informative from the drop-down box.

8. Click the MODERATE! graphic. When the page reloads, you will see this:

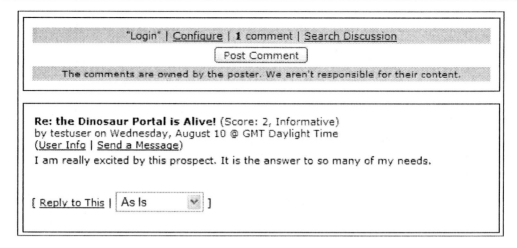

9. Actually, upon reading the comment again, I'm not that impressed. Select Offtopic from the drop-down list.

10. Click the MODERATE button.

11. When the page reloads, the comment should now look as in the first image above.

What Just Happened?

We just moderated a comment, twice in fact.

After logging out from the administrator account, and then logging back in as testuser, we had a look at the existing comment. We had seen this comment earlier (we added it!), but this time, the rating drop-down box has appeared.

First of all, we selected a 'positive' rating from the drop-down box—Informative. Clicking the MODERATE button got the moderation process underway, and when the page reloaded, the score of the comment had increased by one (to two if you must know).

Next, we chose a 'negative' rating—Offtopic, clicked the MODERATE! button and the score of the comment decreased by one.

Multiple Comment Moderation

It's worth noting that if there is more than one comment displayed on the page, then separate drop-down boxes will appear for each comment.

In cases like this, you can moderate several comments at once by selecting their rating from the relevant drop-down boxes. If you don't touch one of the comments, its rating will be submitted as As Is, and the score won't change.

Customizing the User View of Comments

Each individual user is able to customize their view of the displayed comments. This is done by clicking on the Configure link in the comments bar (shown enclosed in a box):

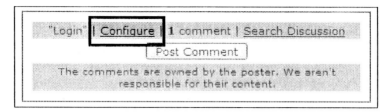

Clicking this link brings you to the Comments Configuration page of the Your Account module.

Another way to reach this page is to click the Comments link in the navigation bar of the Your Account module (shown below enclosed by a box):

Note that if the option Activate Comments in Articles? in the site preferences is set to No (so that comment posting is disabled for all articles), then the Comments link is not displayed in the Your Account menu, and the comments bar is not displayed under any stories. In this situation, no customization can be made by the user.

The Comment Configuration page has a number of options for customizing the display of comments:

Display Mode Thread

Sort Order Oldest First

Threshold Comments scored less than this setting will be ignored.

0: Almost Everything

Anonymous posts start at 0, logged in posts start at 1. Moderators add and subtract points.

☐ **Do Not Display Scores** (Hiddes score: They still apply, you just don't see them.)

Max Comment Length (Truncates long comments, and adds a Read More link. Set really big to disable)

4096 bytes (1024 bytes = 1K)

Save Changes

Do Not Display Scores is the most straightforward option, selecting this and clicking Save Changes causes the score of any comment to be not displayed. The scoring process still goes on, but the scores are never seen.

The Sort Order field allows you to order the list of comments by the date they were posted or by the score for the comments. The comments used in the sorting are only the top-level comments. If you have an old comment with a new reply, that is still viewed as an old comment from the sorting point of view.

You truncate the displayed length of any comment by putting a new value for Max Comment Length field. This does not prevent any comments being longer than that value; it simply abbreviates the display. Here we've set the Max Comment Length to 32 and are viewing our first comment:

A Read the rest of this comment... link has appeared, and clicking that link brings you to the full text of the comment:

Clicking the Root link takes you back to the list of all the top-level comments.

The Comment Configuration page allows you to choose from four ways of displaying comments. These options are available in the Display Mode drop-down box:

- No Comments
- Nested
- Flat
- Thread

The default value is Thread. This displays all the top-level comments, and any replies are shown indented, with only the title of the reply displayed. This is the view that we have been seeing on comments so far.

Choosing the No Comments option means comments will not be displayed to you, and the Flat option displays all the comments underneath each other, with no indentation, grouping a comment and all its replies together.

The Nested view is similar to the Thread view, in that it displays all the comments, grouping together a comment and its replies with indentation, but the text of any reply to a comment is displayed rather than just the title of the reply:

The final comment customization option for users is the 'comment-threshold value' that we mentioned earlier. You may recall that the point of this is to prevent any comments whose score is less than the 'comment-threshold value' from being shown. There are seven values for the 'comment-threshold value' selected from the Threshold dropdown:

- -1: Uncut and Raw
- 0: Almost Everything
- 1: Filter Most Anonymous
- +2: Score +2
- +3: Score +3
- +4: Score +4
- +5: Score +5

The default value is 0: Almost Everything. This means that majority of the comments will be displayed. The only comments that will not be displayed are those with score –1, which are comments considered to be poor by other users (or maybe even by you).

The value +1: Filter Most Anonymous value will filter out most of the anonymous postings made to the site; remember that an anonymous posting is assigned a score of zero by default. For an anonymous posting to be displayed with this setting means that it will have to have been 'moderated up' by other users.

The other values are quite straightforward; they will filter out any comments with value less than the score mentioned in the value. Thus choosing +5: Score +5 will mean that only the best 'quality' comments will be displayed to you.

Time For Action—Filtering out Comments

1. Make sure that you are logged in as the testuser user, and are on the Comments Configuration page (go there from the Comments link in Your Account or by clicking the Configure link in the comments bar).

2. Select +2: Score +2.

3. Click the Save Changes button.

4. When the page reloads, you will find yourself back in the Your Account module. Click the Home link in the Modules block to return to the homepage of your site.

5. Find our first story, and click the comments link.

6. When the story is displayed, the comments bar will be displayed underneath, but no comments can be seen! (that wouldn't make a very interesting screenshot).

What Just Happened?

We set the 'comment-threshold value' to a score of two in the Comment Configuration page. This meant any comment with a score of less than two is not displayed to us, in this case testuser. Our existing comment has a score of one (when we left it at the end of the last *Time For Action* moment it had). Thus it is not displayed to us. Visitors are able to moderate comments with impunity.

Story Management

For the administrator, story management begins on the homepage of the administration area. Scroll down the page and you will see the last 20 published stories:

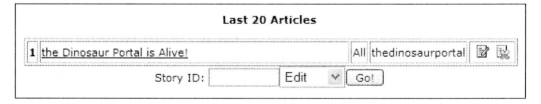

The story titles are displayed, along with their story ID (in the left-hand column of the table), the language they were entered in (All), the name of the topic (that short string with no spaces, remember that?), and then icons to edit or delete any of these published stories.

When a story is posted to your site and stored in PHP-Nuke, the story is assigned a story ID. The story ID is unique to each story, and is used to identify the story. For example, the URL of the extended text view of the story uses the story ID:

```
http://localhost/nuke/modules.php?name=News&file=article&sid=N
```

where N is the story ID.

Editing Stories

There are three ways to begin the editing process. One way is from the front end of the site, the other two are from the administration area:

1. From the extended text view of the story itself there is an Edit icon in the Options block:

2. If the story is displayed in the Last 20 Articles table on the administration homepage, it will have an Edit link.

3. By entering the story ID into the textbox under the list of Last 20 Articles, selecting Edit from the dropdown, and clicking the Go! button.

Each of these brings you to the Edit Article page.

The Edit Article page has almost the same fields as the Add New Article page. However, it is missing the ability to attach a poll to the story, and you cannot alter the schedule of a programmed story.

You can change the title of the story, the topic or category to which it belongs, and any related topics, and of course edit the story and extended text. The Publish in Home? and Activate Comments for this Story? fields are also there, on call to be changed if desired.

An additional field in the Edit Article page is the Notes field. This field allows the administrator to add notes about the story, for example to express the fact that the views of the story are not those of the site for a particularly contentious story.

Clicking the Save Changes button on the Edit Article page updates the story.

Deleting Stories

As with editing stories, there are the three same ways to delete a story.

1. From the extended text view of the story itself there is the Delete icon in the Options block:

2. If the story is displayed in the Last 20 Articles table on the administration homepage, it will have a Delete link.

3. By entering the story ID into the textbox under the list of Last 20 Articles, selecting Delete from the dropdown, and clicking the Go! button.

Each of these brings you to a screen asking you to confirm if you want to delete that story, and giving you the opportunity to back down. Deleting a story means deleting the story and all its comments.

User-Submitted Stories

So far we've been adding stories ourselves, as the site administrator. One of PHP-Nuke's coolest features is the ability for site visitors to submit their own stories for administrator approval and then, hopefully, publication to the site. In this section that's what we'll do.

Setting Up the Mail Notification

When a visitor submits a new story to your site it goes into a submissions queue, pending moderator approval. PHP-Nuke will email a notification of this to an administrator, alerting them to come and approve the story.

As we discussed in earlier chapters, using email in this way requires your site to have access to outbound mail functionality. We won't discuss that here, but leave that until we have deployed the live site. However, we will discuss the settings to form the notification email sent out.

The notification settings are set in the Web Site Configuration menu, in the Mail New Stories to Admin panel:

Mail New Stories to Admin	
Notify new submissions by email?	⊙ Yes ○ No
Email to send the message:	admin@thedinosaurportal.com
Email Subject:	New Story Submission
Email Message:	Hey there... You got a new submission for your site.
Email Account (From):	webmaster

Firstly, to get any email notifications at all, you need to select Yes in Notify new submissions by email?. The default value is No.

The Email to send the message: field is the email account of the person who will receive notification of the new submission. It is not the email account that sends the notification. In this field you will enter the email address of the administrator who is going to be responsible for approving the stories (that would be you!).

> If you need to specify more than one person to receive notifications, enter all the email addresses separated by semi-colons (;) into this field.

The Email subject: field holds the subject of the email notification. You can enter a short message for the receiving administrator into the Email message: field.

The Email Account (From): field specifies the account name from which the notification mail will be sent. You should not include the domain of the account in here; this is handled by the outbound mail server. Note that the account you specify here does not actually have to exist, since it is not actually 'sending' the mail, but only appears to be doing so to the sender.

Once you have set up these details, click the Save Changes button at the bottom of the Web Site Configuration menu and you're ready to receive notifications.

Visitor Story Submission

Users submit stories from the Submit News module. Stories can be posted by unregistered visitors. The Submit News module shows them a form similar to the Add New Article form, into which they type the title of their submission, select a topic, and then enter the story text and the extended text.

Users cannot select a category for the story, nor can they activate comments, nor program the story.

At the bottom of the form is a Preview button; once they have clicked that to see their story previewed, an Ok! button appears next to it for them to submit the story. Visitors cannot submit their stories without previewing them first. Whether they read the preview is another matter!

Once the visitor clicks Ok! and their story is submitted, their work is done. They are thanked for submitting their story, and told how many stories are waiting in the submission queue.

Approving Stories

Once the visitor has submitted their story, a notification is sent to the administrator. The email sent is of this form:

```
Hey there...
You got a new story submission for your site.


===========================================================
TITLE OF THE STORY

This is the story text

This is the extended text.

testuser
```

The message at the top of the email is from the Email Message field of the Mail New Stories to Admin panel of the Web Site Configuration menu, and the subject of the email is from the Email Subject field.

Underneath the top message is the story title, then the story text followed by the extended text, with the author's name at the bottom. The message is sent as a plain text email rather than in HTML form. Upon receipt of the email, the administrator will know that there is a new story waiting for them, and they will head off to the administration area of the site to check it out.

If there is no mail sent, or the administrator does not receive the mail for some reason, this does not alter the approval process. The administrator stills need to log into the administration area of the site, and the Waiting Content block will advise them of any submissions:

Clicking the Submissions link brings you to the Stories Submission Administration page, which lists the submitted stories that are still waiting approval:

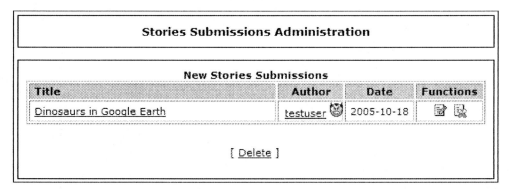

From this table, you can view the user profile of the submitting author by clicking on the author's name in the Author column. The user's karma is also displayed next to their username, so you can easily identify pests. If you wanted to delete the story without reading it, clicking the Delete icon allows you to do this. This removes the story entirely from the list of submissions.

The Delete link under the table clears the entire queue of submitted stories.

Clicking on the title of the story, or the Edit icon, brings you to a form similar to the one for adding a new story. Here you can edit any part of the story, add some notes to the story, or even change the topic or category if you desire. It is also possible to program this story or attach a poll. None of these things can be done by the user.

There is also a link to email the submitter directly, or send a Private Message. Possibly you want them to clarify something.

At the foot of the form is the familiar drop-down box to select previewing the story or posting it, an Ok! button for publishing the story, and a Delete link, which will delete the story from the list of waiting stories.

Once you click the Ok! button after selecting Post Story, the story will be posted to the site in the usual way, and the story is removed from the list of submissions.

If you post the story (accept it), there is no notification to the author that their story has been accepted. They will be able to see it on the site! If you delete the story (reject it), again there is no notification to the author. This is only a two-stage process—submission and approval. There is no real scope for sending comments about the story back to the author and having them resubmit, without having them type in the whole story again.

With users submitting their own stories, the content on your site will hopefully grow quickly, and users will have the satisfaction of contributing and participating in the community of your site.

Finding Stories

The visitor (and administrator) can access stories from a number of places on a PHP-Nuke site. These places are:

- The site homepage
- The Topics module
- The Search module
- The Story Archive module
- The Categories Menu block

In this section, we will run through how these places gain you access to particular stories.

From the Homepage

On the homepage of your site, provided the News module is selected as the Home module, the most recently published stories are listed. The number of stories displayed in this list is controlled by the Stories Number in Home option of the Web Site Configuration options. By default, the value is 10.

Clicking the Read More... link will take you to the extended text view of the story.

From the Topics module

The Topics module displays the list of topics and their associated images, along with the titles of the ten most recent stories posted on that topic.

Clicking on any of the story titles will take you to the standard, extended view of the story.

From the Search module

The Search module allows the visitor to search most of the content stored in PHP-Nuke (there are some other modules whose content is searchable from this module; we'll see them in the next chapter).

Of particular relevance to stories is that you can choose to refine your search like this:

- Search all topics or a single topic.
- Search stories in all categories or a single category.
- Search stories by all authors or a particular author. Note that here author means the user who posted the story to the site (usually the administrator), not the original author of the story.
- Search only stories posted within the last week, last two weeks, or up to three months ago.

These options are chosen from the drop-down box in the Search module:

If any results are found, the titles of the stories and information like the author of the story is displayed. Clicking on the title of a story will take you to the extended text view of the story.

From the Story Archive

The Story Archive module first displays a list of months for which stories were posted, and clicking on any of the months will bring up all the stories posted that month:

```
                    Stories Archive

              the Dinosaur Portal: August 2005

  Articles                      comments  reads  Score    Date     Actions
  • the Dinosaur Portal is Alive!    2       39      5    2005-08-10   ▭ ▣

  Please select the month you want to see:

      • August, 2005


                   [                    ] [ Search ]
              [ Stories Archive Index | Show ALL Stories ]
```

From this table, you can click on the story title to view the extended text of the story, or jump straight to the printer-friendly view of the page or send the story to a friend using the icons on the right-hand side of the table.

From the Categories Menu Block

There is no built-in module for displaying the list of story categories. However, the Categories Menu block is included with the PHP-Nuke installation, and this block gives you a display of all the story categories that actually have stories assigned to them.

This block is already loaded into PHP-Nuke but is not activated. It is also set up as a right-hand block by default.

Each of the category titles displayed in the block is a link to the page displaying the most recent stories in that category. The page containing the most recent stories in a category has a URL of this form:

```
http://localhost/nuke/modules.php?name=News&file=categories&op=newindex&catid=1
```

where catid is known as the category ID, with 0 being the Article category.

The category that you are currently viewing is indicated in the Categories Menu block in bold, and is not a clickable link. This can be quite frustrating if you click on a story in that category, read it, and then want to return to the list of stories in the category. You will have to use the Back button in your browser since the link to the category in the Category Menu block is not a link at all.

Special Administrator

For working with stories, a special administrator account can be created with privileges for only the News module.

This administrator is created in the usual way from the Edit Admins link in the Administration Menu. Here we are creating an administrator with News privileges:

Add a New Administrator

Name: StoryDude (required, can't be changed later)

Nickname: storydude (required)

Email: storydude@thedinosaurportal.com (required)

URL:

Permissions:
- ☐ Content   ☐ Downloads   ☐ Encyclopedia
- ☐ FAQ   ☐ Forums   ☑ News
- ☐ Reviews   ☐ Surveys   ☐ Topics
- ☐ Web Links   ☐ Your Account

☐ **Super User**

WARNING: If Super User is checked, the user will get full access!

Password ******** (required)

[Add Author]

When logging into the administration area with this account, the administration menu looks desolate with only two icons displayed in the Modules Administration menu, and there is no sign of the Administration Menu, since this administrator does not have the permissions to access the core administration operations, only News operations:

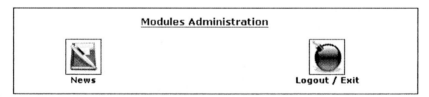

We can still create, edit, and manage stories with this account, but we cannot do anything outside the confines of the News module. We cannot for example, disable comment posting from the Web Site Configuration menu with this account; we do not have those privileges.

There is also a Surveys privilege in the administrator account menu. If you have News privileges but not Surveys privileges then you can fill in the details to attach a new poll to a story, but the poll itself will not be created.

If you create a News administrator without access to the Topics module, then they cannot create or edit topics. They can create manage categories, but not topics.

If you wish to use the email address of the News-only administrator to receive email notifications of user-submitted stories, then the site super user must set this from the Web Site Configuration menu. Just because an administrator has News privileges does not mean they will receive the notification emails.

Points and Prizes

There are a lot of opportunities for visitors to interact with stories, and as such, there are many opportunities for them to collect points:

- Submitting a story from the Submit News module that is actually published by the administrator
- Posting comments
- Sending a story to a friend
- Rating a story
- Voting in a survey
- Commenting on a survey

The points for these activities are, as usual, determined from the User Groups area of the administration area.

Sharing your News

In an earlier chapter, we saw the RSS/RDF block. This block was able to pull headlines from another site via RSS and display them in the block. With PHP-Nuke it is possible to have your stories 'exposed' in a similar way.

Browse to the `http://localhost/nuke/backend.php` file in your browser, and you should see something like this in your browser window:

```
<?xml version="1.0" encoding="ISO-8859-1"?>
<!DOCTYPE rss PUBLIC "-//Netscape Communications//DTD RSS 0.91//EN"
 "http://my.netscape.com/publish/formats/rss-0.91.dtd">
<rss version="0.91">
 <channel>
  <title>the Dinosaur Portal</title>
  <link>http://localhost/nuke</link>
  <description>
    Just because you haven&#039;t seen a dinosaur, doesn&#039;t mean
    they&#039;ve all died out!
  </description>
  <language>en-us</language>
  <item>
   <title>the Dinosaur Portal is Alive!</title>
   <link>http://localhost/nuke/modules.php?name=News&amp;
        file=article&amp;sid=1
   </link>
  </item>

 </channel>
</rss>
```

That's clearly not a standard HTML webpage, and it's not supposed to be. It's a specially structured file, an XML file in fact, with the story titles and a link to them. This is the format of the RSS news feed, and can be consumed by RSS readers, such as your own RSS/RDF blocks that we saw in previous chapters.

The description and language elements are set from the Backend Configuration panel in the Web Site Configuration menu:

A maximum of ten stories can be included in the output of the backend.php file. Adding a cat parameter to the URL, say http://localhost/nuke/backend.php?cat=1 will display the stories in the category corresponding to the category ID specified by the cat parameter. We discussed the category ID earlier in the *From the Categories Menu Block* section. There is nothing else that you need to do to prepare your stories for RSS syndication.

Polls and the Surveys Module

As we mentioned earlier, when a story is created there is the option to associate a poll with the story. This can only be done at the time of story creation; you cannot add a poll to the story later. A poll attached to a story can be thought of as a survey related to the story's content.

Although you can't add a poll to a story after the story has been created, you can create a survey independently of a story from the Surveys module. If you want your poll/survey to appear in the Survey block (like the What do you think of this site? poll) then you must create it as a survey.

First we'll look at adding a poll to a story.

Attaching a Poll to a Story

As the administrator, you get the option to attach a poll to the story before you post a story to the site. Underneath the Add New Article panel is the Attach a Poll to this article panel. To create a new poll you simply enter the question into the Poll Title field, and then enter the options below:

Attach a Poll to this article
(Leave blank to post the article without any attached Poll)
(NOTE: Automated/Programmed news can't have attached Polls)

Poll Title: [Which is the most fearsome dinosaur?]

Please enter each available option into a single field
Option 1: [Allosaurus]
Option 2: [Tyrannosaurus Rex]
Option 3: [Gorgosaurus]
Option 4: [Notasaurus]

There is no need to click any more buttons. When the story is posted, provided there is some text in the Poll Title field, the new poll will be created and attached to the story.

The poll is displayed to the right of the extended view of the story:

Note that the Article Rating poll is still there as well, but pushed further down the page.

By selecting one of the options and clicking the Vote button, you can participate in this poll—the same voting restrictions apply as seen earlier with the Article Rating poll. After your vote is registered, the current results of the poll are shown. This is all happening in the Surveys module.

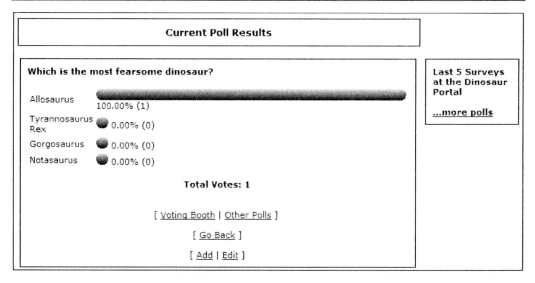

Here you can see the total number of votes cast in the poll, and the percentage split of the votes. This is also the view you will get by clicking the Results link in the poll block itself. It is also possible to post comments for an individual poll. The comments are displayed underneath the poll as they are with stories.

The image above actually shows the administrator view of the results, with the extra Add and Edit links that are not visible to the standard visitor. As administrator, you can change the options of the poll by clicking the Edit link. The Add link allows you to create a new survey.

Curiously, when creating a new poll from the Add link, you are actually able to attach a story to the poll, for announcing the poll if you like. However, the poll will not be displayed alongside the story in the way that a poll attached to a story is. If you want to include a link to the poll from the story announcement, the link will be of the form

```
http://localhost/nuke/modules.php?name=Surveys&pollID=NNN
```

However, you won't know the pollID until the poll has been created, so you will have to edit the story after creating the poll to correct the link.

The Surveys Module

Voting and seeing the result of polls takes place in the Surveys module. When you click on the Surveys link in the Modules block and go to the homepage of the Surveys module, you are shown the list of surveys and any surveys attached to articles.

Past Surveys

• What do you think about this site? (Results - 0 votes - Edit)

Surveys Attached to Articles

• Which is the most fearsome dinosaur? (Results - 1 votes - Edit)
- Attached to article: An article to have a poll

The What do you think about this site? survey is added to the site by default. From here you can vote in the survey by clicking on the title of the survey, or view the results from the Results link. Administrators are able to edit the story options by clicking the Edit link (shown in the image above).

Survey Management

In addition to this front-end way of managing surveys through the various Edit and Add links, there is also functionality in the Modules Administration area for managing surveys.

First of all, if you scroll down the screen on the administration menu page you will see the title of the current poll (the most recently created poll that is not attached to an article) displayed:

Current Poll: What do you think about this site? [Edit | Add]

You can use the links there to edit the options of that poll, or create a new one.

In the Modules Administration menu of the Administration Menu page is the Surveys icon:

Surveys/Polls

Clicking on this icon brings you to the Polls/Surveys Administration area. In this area you can add new polls and edit existing polls as we have seen already, but you can also delete polls.

Clicking the Delete Polls link in the Polls/Survey Administration area brings up a list of the current polls. Selecting the poll to remove and clicking the Delete button removes the poll. There is no confirmation screen, it goes straight away.

Summary

This chapter gave us an overview of stories and the story publication process. We saw the way stories on our site are organized; stories are classified into topics and categories. We also added our own stories and saw how to edit and manage them.

One of PHP-Nuke's great features with its handling of stories is the number of opportunities for visitors to contribute. We saw how visitors can post their own stories, and the process the administrator follows to approve these stories for publication on the site.

Comments are an important part of any community-driven site and we had an in-depth look at these. We also saw how comments are moderated, both by the administrator and by the users of the site.

7

Content Management Modules

In the last chapter, we had a really good look at story management, and in this chapter we'll look at the other PHP-Nuke modules for handling content. We will see how each of them works, how you add content with them, and what features they possess.

We will cover these modules:

- Content
- FAQ
- Encyclopedia
- Web Links and Downloads
- Reviews

For each module, we will explore both the visitor and administrator experience, and see how to work with the types of content these modules handle.

Each of these modules handles a different type of content, as is hinted at by their name, and each offers a different amount of functionality for visitors to interact with the content. We will see all of this, and also see how each module organizes the content it manages.

Content

The Content module, as the name suggests, simply handles content. The Content module is handy for adding general pieces of information to your site, which are not particularly time-sensitive or intended to generate discussion.

The 'content' of the Content module is called a content page, and content pages may be organized into categories. Note that these categories have nothing to do with the categories created for news stories. In fact, several of the modules in this chapter will organize their content into 'categories', and there will be no relation between the categories of one module and the categories of another module.

A content page consists of some main page text, a **title**, a **subtitle**, a **header** and **footer**, and another field, called the **signature**. The display of a single content page may be split easily across several web pages, with PHP-Nuke providing Next and Previous page links automatically. Content pages are ideal for holding general pieces of HTML text that need to be organized into groups or categories. Using the Content module to handle such information means that you do not have to create a new module just to display things like site policy or privacy policy documents on your site.

Content pages are not searched by the Search module.

There are no comment features or ratings available for Content content, and only the administrator may add pages; there is no place for user-submitted content here.

In versions of PHP-Nuke prior to 7.5, there was a module called Sections, which was almost identical in functionality to Content, with the addition of an image for the categories. From PHP-Nuke 7.5, the Sections module is no longer shipped with the standard installation of PHP-Nuke, and we will not consider it any further.

Like the other modules, the Content module is not activated by default, but since we did activate this module in Chapter 4, we are ready to go. If you didn't activate the Content module then, do so now. Refer back to the *Managing Modules* section of Chapter 4 to refresh your memory if required.

Time For Action—Creating a Content Category

We are going to use the Content module to add site 'policy' documents, in this case a site Privacy Policy.

1. Log in as administrator.
2. To access the Content administration area, click on the Content link in the Administration block, or click on the Content icon in the Modules menu:

3. In the Add a New Category panel, enter the text Site Documents into the Title field.
4. Enter the following text into the Description field:
   Here you will find a collection of documents about the site.
5. Click the Add button.
6. When the page reloads, there isn't much evidence that your category has been entered, but if you scroll down the screen to the Edit Category panel, you will find the category in the Category drop-down box:

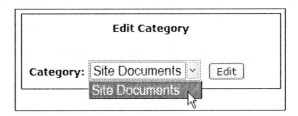

What Just Happened?

We just added a content category. They are added from the Content Manager area of the administration area. The disconcerting thing is that it's difficult to tell if your category has been added successfully; there is no list of the content categories displayed in the Content Manager area. You will have to look in the drop-down box in the Edit Category panel to confirm that your category has indeed been added.

Now we have a category, let's add some pages.

Time For Action—Adding a Content Page

1. In the Content Manager area of the administration area, scroll down to find the Add a New Page panel.

2. Enter the title of the page into the Title textbox. In our case, this page will be titled Privacy Policy.

3. Select Site Documents from the Category drop-down box.

4. Enter the Dinosaur Portal Privacy Policy into the Sub-Title field.

5. Next comes the Header Text. Enter the following into that field:

    ```
    This policy applies to all web sites and email services provided by the
    Dinosaur Portal. By using these web sites you consent to the general terms
    and conditions of usage and to the terms of this privacy policy.
    ```

6. The Page Text field contains the body of the page. We'll enter the following:

    ```
    <h2>Collection of your Personal Information</h2>
    <p>We will ask you when we need information that personally identifies you
    (personal information) or allows us to contact you. Generally, we request
    this information when you are registering before ordering products from
    theDinosaurPortal.com, downloading or viewing limited-access content,
    entering a contest, ordering email newsletters. In each circumstance we
    try to limit the information we request to the minimum required to deliver
    the service to you. We also use various standard technologies such as
    cookies to track user activity on our sites.</p>
    <!--pagebreak-->
    <h2>Use of your Personal Information</h2>
    <p>We use your personal information for the following purposes...</p>
    ```

7. There are two fields remaining, Footer Text and Signature. We'll enter this for the Footer Text:

    ```
    If you require any further assistance, please contact
    contact@thedinosaurportal.com
    ```

    and this for the Signature:

    ```
    the DINOSAUR PORTAL - Just because you've never seen one,  doesn't mean
    they've all died out...
    ```

8. Click the Send button.

9. When the page reloads, the details of our first page are visible in the Content Manager panel, confirming its creation:

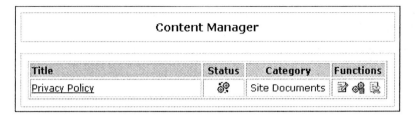

10. Now click on the Content link in the Modules block, or go straight to `http://localhost/nuke/modules.php?name=Content`. You will see the list of content categories:

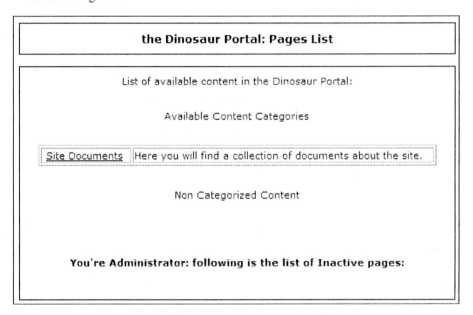

11. Click on the Site Documents link, and you will see the list of content pages in this category:

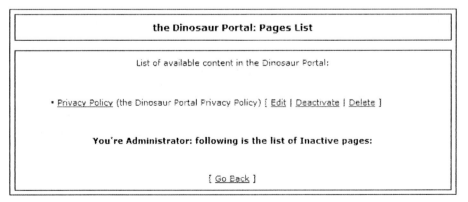

12. Clicking on the Privacy Policy link will take us to our document:

Privacy Policy
the Dinosaur Portal Privacy Policy

Page: 1/2

This policy applies to all web sites and email services provided by the Dinosaur Portal. By using these web sites you consent to the general terms and conditions of usage and to the terms of this privacy policy.

Collection of your Personal Information

We will ask you when we need information that personally identifies you (personal information) or allows us to contact you. Generally, we request this information when you are registering before ordering products from theDinosaurPortal.com, downloading or viewing limited-access content, entering a contest, ordering email newsletters. In each circumstance we try to limit the information we request to the minimum required to deliver the service to you. We also use various standard technologies such as cookies to track user activity on our sites.

Next Page (2/2) ⇨

---

13. Click the Next Page link to see the rest of the document:

Privacy Policy
the Dinosaur Portal Privacy Policy

Page: 2/2

Use of your Personal Information

We use your personal information for the following purposes...

If you require any further assistance, please contact contact@thedinosaurportal.com

⇦ Previous Page (1/2)

the DINOSAUR PORTAL – Just because you've never seen one, doesn't mean they've all died out...

Copyright © by the Dinosaur Portal All Right Reserved.

Published on: 2005-08-04 (1 reads)

[Go Back]

What Just Happened?

We just added a content page, and then viewed the page. We assigned the content page to the Site Documents category when we created the page. It is possible to create content pages that do not belong to any category. The current list of content pages is shown in a table in the Content Manager area; we saw this screenshot at the end of step 11.

When you visit the front page of the Content module, the list of categories is displayed. Only the categories that have content pages associated with them are displayed. Also, if there are any content pages not associated with a category, their titles will be listed here.

Clicking on a category takes you to a list of the content pages associated with that category. This list is ordered by the date on which the pages were entered; the content page created first is displayed at the top of the list and so on. For each content page, the text entered into its Title field is displayed in this list, along with the Sub-Title in brackets. Clicking on the title of a content page will take you to display of the page itself. The following diagram shows this navigation hierarchy:

Note that there is no direct link to go back from the content page to its 'parent' category. You will have to use the Back button of your browser to do this. You can get back to the list of all categories by clicking the Content link in the Modules block, but you will still need to click again on the category to display the list of content pages it contains.

Returning to our privacy content page, we see that our content page has been split into two pages. This is done by inserting the <!--pagebreak--> text into the Page Text field, which forces PHP-Nuke to break the page at that point. The contents of the Page Text field form the body of a content page, with the Title and Sub-Title always displayed at the top.

The Next Page pager is automatically provided by PHP-Nuke, and with that you can navigate through the pages of the content page. On the first page, the Header Text is displayed before the Page Text starts, and on the final page, the Footer Text is displayed at the end of the Page Text, followed by the Signature text. A copyright notice, including the site name, follows the Signature, and then there is the date the page was created, followed by the number of times the page has been read.

Since we were still logged in as an administrator, at each part of this journey there are panels allowing you to edit the details of either the category or the content pages. For example, there is a panel for altering the category on the page displaying that category's content pages, in addition to a 'content page editing' panel on each page of the content itself:

Any of these links can be used to change the object in question. Of course, these links are visible only to an administrator. No visitor will be able to see these links or access their functionality.

Deactivating a page makes it invisible to a visitor from the list of available content pages, and the page will not be displayed even if the visitor manages to enter the URL of the content page. The administrator will be able to see a list of deactivated pages on the front page of the Content module (`http://localhost/nuke/modules.php?name=Content`) or in the Content Manager area of the administration area.

Currently, our Privacy Policy document is at the URL `http://localhost/nuke/modules.php?name=Content&pa=showpage&pid=1`. To view this page, the visitor need not go through the entire Content 'hierarchy' if they are provided with a direct link. We could, for example, add a link to the Privacy Policy in the footer of our page, from the Web Site Configuration menu. The link would point to the above URL, and the reader would be taken directly to our document.

The `pid` value of the query string is the unique identifier for this piece of content in the same way as we saw the story ID when looking at stories. This value will not change with subsequent modifications of the content page, or even moving it to another category.

The Content Block

The Content block is part of the standard PHP-Nuke installation, but isn't loaded. You can load this block from Blocks area of the administration area by selecting Content from the Filename dropdown, and choosing a title for the block as usually done for file blocks.

Once the block is activated, it will display a list of the titles of all active content pages, with links to view each content page in full.

> Note that the Content block will still display the list of titles present in the content pages even if the user does not have read access to the Content module.

Managing Categories

Categories can be edited or deleted through the Edit Category panel in the Content Manager area. Simply select a category from the drop-down box and click the Edit button to go to the Edit Category page. Here you can edit the title and description of the category, or delete the category.

Note that deleting the category does not delete the content pages associated with that category. All pages in a deleted category are preserved, but no longer belong to any category (they belong to the None category!).

Special Administrator

You can create a special administrator with rights to only the Content module in the Edit Admins menu of the Administration Menu.

Restricting Access

Access to the Content module is done on a 'whole module' basis. The visitor either sees nothing or everything. You cannot configure individual categories or content pages to be viewed by certain user groups.

Points and Prizes

There are no activities in the Content module that contribute any points towards a user's point score.

FAQ

The FAQ (Frequently Asked Questions) module allows you to create categories of questions, with answers. This module contains a list of questions (and their answers) frequently asked by visitors.

Only an administrator may enter questions and answers, and by default, the text in neither the question nor the answer is searchable. However, if you provide suitably named categories it should not be difficult for a visitor to find the question they are after.

By default, the FAQ module is not activated.

Time For Action—Adding a FAQ Category

1. Log in as the administrator.

2. Click the FAQ icon in the Modules menu of the administration area:

3. We first need to create a new category. We will create a category called Dinosaur Survival Tips. This category will provide visitors with answers to common questions about what to do when confronted with some marauding dinosaur. Enter the text Dinosaur Survival Tips into the Categories field to create a new category with this name.

4. Click the Save button.

5. The title of our newly created FAQ category is displayed, along with links to add a question to that category, edit the title of the category, or delete the category:

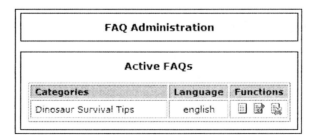

What Just Happened?

We visited the FAQ Administration area and created the new category. All that was required was for us to specify the category title. The current list of categories is displayed in a table, along with three icons for each category. The first icon is the Content icon, which allows you to add a FAQ to that category. The next icon is the Edit icon, which allows you to modify the category title. The final icon is the Delete icon, which removes the category.

Time For Action—Adding a FAQ

Now that we have a category, we can add a question (and answer) to it:

1. In the table of Active FAQs in the FAQ Administration area, find our Dinosaur Survival Tips category. (We only have one category—it shouldn't be too hard to find.)

2. Click the Content icon of the Dinosaur Survival Tips category to add a new question to that category. You will be taken to the Add a New Question panel. Enter the following text into the Question field:

   ```
   What do I do if a fearsome Allosaurus tries to bite me?
   ```
   and into the Answer field, type:

   ```
   Bite it. <br><br>
   The <b>Allosaurus</b> is actually rather timid, and a quick chomp
   will put him back in his place.
   ```

3. Click the Save button.

4. Our new question is now displayed, along with links to edit it further, or delete it. We are done here.

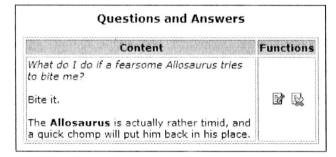

5. Let's see what the visitor will see. Click the FAQ link in the Modules block on the left-hand side of the screen to start the FAQ module:

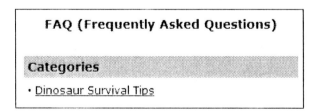

6. We have only one category, so click the Dinosaur Survival Tips category and the questions in that category will be displayed. Underneath the questions, the answers are displayed. Clicking on any of the questions will take you down to the part of the page containing the answer:

---

the Dinosaur Portal FAQ (Frequently Asked Questions)

Category: <u>Main</u> -> Dinosaur Survival Tips

Question

- <u>What do I do if a fearsome Allosaurus tries to bite me?</u>

Answer

- **What do I do if a fearsome Allosaurus tries to bite me?**

Bite it.

The **Allosaurus** is actually rather timid, and a quick chomp will put him back in his place.

[<u>Back to Top</u>]

[<u>Back to FAQ Index</u>]

---

7. Clicking the Back to Top link will take you back to the list of questions, and the Back to FAQ Index link takes you back to the list of FAQ categories.

What Just Happened?

We just added a FAQ. We selected the category to add the FAQ to (from the list of Active FAQs), and then provided the question and answer, and we were done.

Managing FAQs

From the list of FAQ categories shown in the Active FAQs panel of the FAQ Administration area, we can edit the category title, delete the category, or modify questions in that category.

Note that deleting a FAQ category will delete all the questions associated with that category. You should also be aware that there is no functionality to move questions from one category to another other than by manual copy and paste of the question and answer texts.

Editing a FAQ

Clicking the Content icon of a category in the FAQ Administration area brings up a list of entered questions for that category, and allows you to enter a new question, or edit an existing question. In the list of questions here and when presented to the visitor, the most recently entered FAQ is displayed first, and then the next most recent FAQ and so on. In other words, the list of FAQs is ordered by the date the FAQ was entered, in descending order.

The FAQ Block

There is no block shipped with PHP-Nuke for displaying the list of most recent FAQs or FAQ categories.

Special Administrator

You can create a special administrator with rights to only the FAQ module in the Edit Admins menu of the Administration area.

Restricting Access

Access to the FAQ module is done on a 'whole module' basis. The visitor either sees nothing or everything. You cannot configure individual categories or questions to be viewed by certain user groups.

Points and Prizes

There are no activities in the FAQ module that contribute any points towards a user's point score.

Encyclopedia

The Encyclopedia module provides sets of 'alphabetized' entries. As the name suggests, this module is used as a reference for terms or definitions. The collection of terms is known as an **encyclopedia**, and the Encyclopedia module allows you to create these, and then add terms or entries to each encyclopedia.

Only an administrator may enter encyclopedia entries or create a new encyclopedia. Entries are searchable from the Search module, but it is easy to retrieve an entry in an encyclopedia since the module offers a simple, alphabetical navigation menu.

By default, the Encyclopedia module is not activated.

We will make use of the Encyclopedia module to provide information about a range of dinosaurs. We can create different encyclopedias for the different periods during which dinosaurs existed (Triassic, Cretaceous, Jurassic, and so on).

Time For Action—Adding a new Encyclopedia

1. Log in as the administrator.

2. Click on the Encyclopedia icon in the Modules Administration area:

3. You are in the Encyclopedia Manager area; scroll down to find the Add a New Encyclopedia Panel, and enter The Jurassic Period into the Title field.

4. Enter the following for the Description:

   A collection of dinosaurs from the Jurassic period, which began some 210 million years ago, and lasted for about 70 million years.

5. Make sure that Activate this Page? is set to Yes.

6. Click the Save button.

7. When the page reloads, the title of your newly created encyclopedia is displayed in the list of existing encyclopedia:

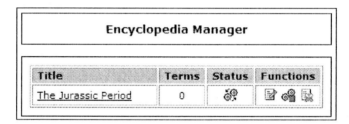

What Just Happened?

You just added a new encyclopedia; all that was required was a title and a description, and this was entered from the Encyclopedia Manager area of the administration area. A table of created encyclopedias is displayed in the Encyclopedia Manager area, along with icons for editing the titles and descriptions, activating or deactivating each encyclopedia, or deleting each encyclopedia entirely. Also displayed is a count of the number of terms currently entered for each encyclopedia, and whether that encyclopedia has currently been activated. Each of the icons is one of the familiar ones that we have seen much of before, and their meaning should be clear. Simply hover the mouse cursor over one of the icons to be reminded of its action.

Note that an encyclopedia has to be activated before it can be displayed to the visitor.

Time For Action—Adding a new Entry

Now that we have an encyclopedia, we can add our first definition to our encyclopedia.

1. In the Encyclopedia Manager area, scroll down to find the Add a New Encyclopedia Term panel.

2. The definition will require a title and some body text, and then needs to be assigned to an encyclopedia. Let's add the Title of Allosaurus.

3. In the Term Text field, we will enter the following:

```
The Allosaurus lived about 150 to 145 million years ago in the Late
Jurassic period. Allosaurus was a carnivore with big, curved teeth that
were grooved for extra sharpness, and was about 12m long and weighed up to
3 tonnes.
<center><img src="images/dinosaurs/allosaur.jpg"
             title="Allosaurus" border="1"></center>
```

4. Select The Jurassic Period from the Encyclopedia drop-down box.

5. Click the Add button.

6. When the page reloads, you can see from the count of terms that our encyclopedia now has an entry:

What Just Happened?

We just added an encyclopedia entry. Entries are added from the Add a New Encyclopedia Term panel below the Add a New Encyclopedia panel. You provide the title and text for the entry, and then you select the encyclopedia to add the entry to from a drop-down box. In the same way as you could with Content pages, you can create multi-page entries by inserting <!--pagebreak--> into your text, and the text will be broken at that point, with PHP-Nuke providing the Next and Previous page navigation for you.

Managing the Encyclopedia

Once an encyclopedia is created, you can edit its title to rename it, deactivate it, or delete it completely. This can be done from either the Encyclopedia Manager area, or from the visitor end of the site when logged is as the administrator:

If you choose to delete an encyclopedia, you will be prompted to confirm your choice before the encyclopedia is deleted.

Note that deleting an encyclopedia will delete all the entries associated with it. You should also be aware that there is no way to move entries from one encyclopedia to another other than by manual copy and paste of the entries.

Viewing the Encyclopedia

To get a proper visitor's view of the Encyclopedia, we'll log out by clicking the Logout link in the Administration block, or the Logout icons in the Administration Menu.

The list of active encyclopedias is found by clicking on the Encyclopedia link in the Modules block. The title of each encyclopedia along with its description is then shown:

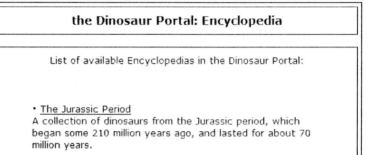

There are Edit, Deactivate, and Delete links that are only shown when you are logged in as the administrator; the administrator is also able to see any deactivated encyclopedia listed here. As mentioned above, these extra links take you to the Encyclopedia Manager area from where you can edit, deactivate, or delete that encyclopedia.

Clicking on the title of the encyclopedia will bring up the alphabetical navigation menu:

Entries are alphabetized by the first letter of their title, and any letters that actually have entries are shown underlined; this is because they are actually links to those entries. In our case, we only have one entry, Allosaurus, so only the A entry is underlined. By clicking on one of these underlined entries you can view all the entries corresponding to that letter (we click on A):

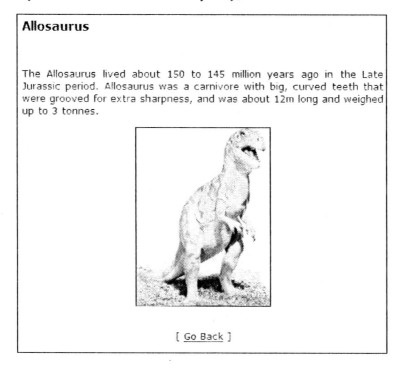

The entries will be arranged alphabetically by their titles. Clicking on any of the entries will display that entry's text. Here we click on our only entry, Allosaurus:

Allosaurus

The Allosaurus lived about 150 to 145 million years ago in the Late Jurassic period. Allosaurus was a carnivore with big, curved teeth that were grooved for extra sharpness, and was about 12m long and weighed up to 3 tonnes.

[Go Back]

(Note that you will only see the image if you have added it from the code download into the images/dinosaurs folder of your PHP-Nuke installation.)

In each of these screens, there is a Go Back link, which has the same effect as clicking Back in your browser; it does not necessarily take to you to the previous screen in the Encyclopedia navigation process unless that is where you have come from.

When logged in as the administrator, you will catch sight of an Edit link at the right-hand foot of the entry. Clicking this link takes you into the Encyclopedia Terms Edit panel in the Encyclopedia administration area. From this panel, you can edit the text of the entry, assign it to another encyclopedia if you like, or delete the entry entirely.

The Encyclopedia Block

There is an Encyclopedia block that ships with PHP-Nuke. (It is not displayed by default.) The Encyclopedia block simply displays a menu of the currently active encyclopedias, with links to view the entries in those encyclopedias.

Like the Content block, the Encyclopedia block will display the list of active encyclopedias even if the visitor does not have access to the Encyclopedia module to view the entries.

Special Administrator

An administrator for only the Encyclopedia module can be created from the Edit Admins area of the Administration Menu.

Restricting Access

Access to the Encyclopedia module is done on a 'whole module' basis. The visitor either sees nothing or everything. You cannot configure individual encyclopedias to be viewed only by certain user groups.

Points and Prizes

Since the visitor doesn't really do much with this module, there are no activities in the Encyclopedia module that contribute any points towards a user's score.

Web Links and Downloads

The Web Links module is an excellent piece of work; it provides directories of links to other websites. Visitors themselves are able to suggest sites and links to add to the collection, after administrator moderation.

The Web Links module has a 'sister' module, the Downloads module, with virtually identical functionality and use. One of the main differences between the modules is that while Web Links is used to manage links that will point at other *web pages* on other sites, Downloads is intended to manage links to *files* on other sites. When the visitor clicks on a download, they will download the file from the other site rather than viewing the page on that site. We won't spend much time covering the Downloads module here—you will be able to apply the Web Links expertise you gain here to that module.

Web Links works with links. For each link, you provide this information to PHP-Nuke:

- The title of the page the link points to
- A URL for the link
- A description of the content of the page or site the link is pointing to

The text contained in these details can be searched from the Search module.

When you visit the index of the Web Links module, either by clicking the Web Links link in the Modules block or going straight to the URL, `http://localhost/nuke/modules.php?name=Web_Links`, the top panel gives you an idea of the features you can expect from the Web Links module:

From here people can add their own links to the collection, view the newest links added, view the most popular (most clicked-on) links, or view the highest-rated web links. There is also an option to view a randomly-chosen link from the collection. All of this suggests that there is much that can be done with the Web Links module, for both administrator and visitor, so let's press on.

Links are organized into **categories**. Categories can be nested, so within one category you can have other categories. The top-level categories are called main categories.

For the Dinosaur Portal, we are going to add a Museums category. This will hold links to the websites of various Natural History and Dinosaur Museums around the world.

Time For Action—Creating a Web Link Category Structure

1. Ensure you are logged in as the administration, and go to the administration menu.

2. Click on the Web Links icon in the Modules Administration menu:

3. You will come to the Web Links administration area. We are going to add a main category, our Museums category.

4. Enter Museums in the Name field.

5. Enter the following text into the Description field:

   `Visit Natural History and Dinosaur Museums from all round the world.`

6. Click the Add button.

7. When the page reloads, you will see the Add a Main Category panel again. Scroll down to find the Add a SUB-Category panel that has just appeared.

8. In the Add a SUB-Category panel, enter North America into the Name field, and leave Museums selected in the drop-down box.

9. Enter the following text into the Description field:

   `Museums in North America.`

Add a SUB-Category

Name: North America   in Museums ▼
Description:
Museums in North America.

[Add]

10. Click the Add button.

What Just Happened?

We just added two new categories, Museums and North America. Museums is a main (top-level) category and North America a subcategory. The parent category has to be created first, and then the subcategory is created from the Add a SUB-Category panel and added to the parent category.

Time For Action—Adding a Web Link

Our first link will point to the website of the Fossil Halls at the American Museum of Natural History in New York. We will add it to the North America subcategory of Museums.

1. In the Web Links Administration page, under the Add a Main Category and Add a SUB-Category panel, you will find the Add a New Link panel.

2. In the Add a New Link panel, enter Fossil Halls: American Museum of Natural History into the Page Title field.

3. Enter the following URL into the Page URL field:

   `http://www.amnh.org/exhibitions/permanent/fossilhalls/?src=h_h`

4. Ensure that Museums/North America is selected from the Category drop-down box:

Add a New Link

Page Title: Fossil Halls: American Museum of Natural History

Page URL: http://www.amnh.org/exhibitions/permanent/foss

Category: Museums

    Museums

    Museums/North America

5. In the Description field, enter the following text:

   This museum is home to the world's largest collection of vertebrate
   fossils, totaling nearly one million specimens.

6. Enter your name into the Name field, and your email address into the Email field.

7. Click the Add this URL button. When the page reloads, you will see a message confirming the successful addition of your file to the collection.

8. Click the link to return to the Web Links administration page.

What Just Happened?

We just added our first web link. We provided a title for the link, the URL for the link, as well as a short description about the link. Note that the URL of the link can only appear once in the database; you cannot submit two different links pointing to the same URL. This will be refused by PHP-Nuke.

The link was assigned to the North America category by selecting it from the Category drop-down box. The 'full path' of the category shown in this drop-down box—Museums/North America—indicates that North America is a subcategory of Museums. If we were to go on to create a subcategory of North America, say MidWest, then it would appear as Museums/North America/MidWest in the drop-down box.

If you now click the Web Links link in the Modules block, or go straight to the URL `http://localhost/nuke/modules.php?name=Web_Links`, then you can see the list of web links. First, each of the main categories is displayed, followed by a list of its subcategories. At this point our web links database is rather bare:

Links Main Categories

• **Museums** ⬤⬤⬤
Visit natural history and dinosaur museums from all round the world.
North America

There are 1 Links and 2 Categories in our database

If you click the North America link, you will be taken to the list of web links within that category:

Category: Main/Museums/North America

Sort Links by: Title (A\D) Date (A\D) Rating (A\D) Popularity (A\D)
Sites currently sorted by: Title (A to Z)

Fossil Halls: American Museum of Natural History (new)
Description: This museum is home to the world's largest collection of vertebrate
fossils, totaling nearly one million specimens.
Added on: 21-Oct-2005 Hits: 0
Edit | Rate this Site | Report Broken Link

The new text next to the title of the link indicates that it has been added to the database recently.

The visitor is able to sort the list of links with the Sort Links by options. The links can be sorted in ascending or descending order, and by title, date of submission, rating, or popularity, which we will come to in a minute.

To follow the link itself, and visit its target site, you simply click its title. Note that this link does not actually point to the target of the web link; it actually points back to another part of the Web Links module on our PHP-Nuke site, and from there, you will be redirected to the target of the link.

The advantage of this approach is that PHP-Nuke is able to keep a count of the number of times the link has been clicked-through in the Web Links module; if clicking the title of the link took you straight to the target of the link, this would be impossible. You can see the number of times the link has been clicked-through in the Hits field under the Description in the screenshot above.

If you click the link now, you will be taken to the Fossil Halls of the American Museum of Natural History. While that site is interesting in its own right, we still have to continue our work with the Web Links module.

Since clicking the link takes you to its target, we're going to refer to this page as the 'exit page' of the link. This will help us in a moment.

A consequence of the way PHP-Nuke handles web links is that there isn't actually any record of the URL of the web link on any of your pages. The link of a web link points back to your site, from where you are redirected to the target. There is no <a> tag anywhere in the page that points to the target site. This means that the Web Links module isn't suitable for **link exchanges**, where you put a link to someone's site on your site, in return for them putting a link to your site on theirs.

Although the Web Links module allows visitors to move easily from your site to other sites that may be of interest to them, the point of a link exchange is to actually increase incoming links to each site. The physical presence of the link in the page is beneficial to the search ranking of the target site, and this is often a primary purpose of link exchanges.

Interacting with Web Links

Visitors are able to rate a web link and add comments by clicking Rate this Site. This brings them to a page where they can score the target site from 1 to 10, and, if they don't have a bad or devil karma, they can add comments:

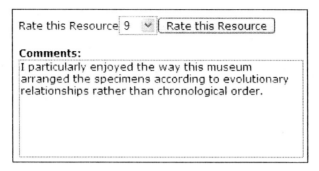

After selecting your rating from the Rate this Resource dropdown, entering your comment, and then clicking the Rate this Resource button, you are presented with a thank-you screen and some options:

Your vote is appreciated.
Thank you for taking the time to rate a site here at the Dinosaur Portal. Input from users such as yourself will help other visitors better decide which links to click on.

[Link Comments | Additional Details | Editor Review | Modify | Report Broken Link]

Note that Report Broken Link is only shown to registered users. When you are logged in, you can only vote once for any particular link. Unregistered users are checked by their IP address—there can be only one rating submitted from a given IP address in a particular day, or PHP-Nuke will reject the rating.

The results of visitor ratings can be seen by clicking the Additional Details link. This brings up the Link Profile page, which shows how people have rated the web link, breaking down the votes between registered users, unregistered users, and outside voters, and showing a distribution of the scores within each of these groups:

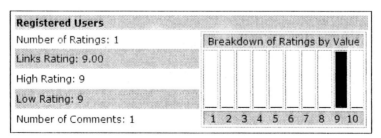

An outside vote is one where the rating has been done through an external website—the Is this your resource? <u>Allow other users to rate it from your web site!</u> link at the bottom of the Link Profile provides three options for website/resource owners to let visitors to their site vote in this poll.

Clicking on Link Comments at the top of the Links Profile area shows the comments left by visitors expressing what they thought of that link:

> **User: testuser**   **Rating: 9**
> User's Average Rating: 9.0   # of Ratings: 1
> I particularly enjoyed the way this museum arranged the specimens according to evolutionary relationships rather than chronological order.

Note that the Link Profile page can lead to some confusion since there is more than one route to the same feature. Once a rating has been logged for a web link, a Details link appears under the web link description:

> **Fossil Halls: American Museum of Natural History**
> Description: This museum is home to the world's largest collection of vertebrate fossils, totaling nearly one million specimens.
> Added on: 21-Oct-2005 Hits: 1 Rating: 9.0 (1 Vote)
> Edit | Rate this Site | Report Broken Link | Details | Comments (1)

The Details link takes you to the Link Profile page we saw above. Once on the Link Profile page, there is an Additional Details link, which again points to the Link Profile page.

Similarly, when comments have been entered for a web link, a Comments link appears under the description, showing how many comments have been added for that web link (in the same way as the number of comments is displayed for a story, as seen in the previous chapter). Clicking that Comments link will display the comments, and takes you to the same place as the Link Comments link from the Link Profile page.

Checking the Web Link

Visitors are also able to assist the administrator of the site by reporting if the details of the web link are incorrect, or if the link is broken. Broken means the file is no longer there; possibly the website isn't available at this time, or maybe the website has stopped its service or the page has been moved. In any case, having your visitors submit corrections to existing information makes the job of managing a large number of web links easier.

Modifying Web Link Details

First of all, the visitor can click the Modify link to bring up the details of the current web link:

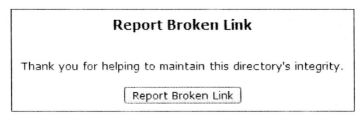

Request Link Modification
Link ID: **1**

Link Title:
Fossil Halls: American Museum of Natural History

URL:
http://www.amnh.org/exhibitions/permanent/fossilhalls

Description:
This museum is home to the world's largest collection of vertebrate fossils, totaling nearly one million specimens.

Category: Museums/North America ⌄

Send Request

The visitor is able to edit any of these fields, and click the Send Request button to notify the administrator that some of the details may need amending. We will see how to manage these modification requests in a moment.

Reporting Broken Links

When the visitor is a registered user and logged in, the other important way they can contribute to the Web Links module is to report broken links. This is done by clicking Report Broken Link under the web link description. This link is only visible to registered users.

Clicking this brings up a screen with a button to click to submit the broken link report:

Report Broken Link

Thank you for helping to maintain this directory's integrity.

Report Broken Link

When the user clicks the Report Broken Link button, this link is submitted, and the user's job is done!

Submitting Web Links

Visitors are able to submit their own web links to be included in the list. Clicking Add Link from the top menu of the Web Links module brings up the familiar web link details screen:

Add a New Link

Instructions:
- Submit a unique link only once.
- All links are posted pending verification.
- Username and IP are recorded, so please don't abuse the system.

Page Title: The Carnegie Museum of Natural History

Page URL: http://www.carnegiemuseums.org/cmnh/

Category: Museums/North America

Description: (255 characters max)

Featuring Dinosaurs in Their World, an exciting exhibit that reflects current scientific evidence of these colossal creatures and their environments.

Your Name: Douglas Paterson

Your Email:

[Add this URL] [Go Back]

The user enters the details of their web link and then clicks Add this URL. A confirmation that their submission has been received is displayed, and the user's part is done.

Note that the submitted link is not immediately added to the system; administrator action is required before that happens. That's what we will look at now.

Managing Web Links

Now that we've seen what the visitor can do with a web link, let's have a look at what the administrator is able to do. We'll see how to:

- Modify web link details
- Manage user web link submissions, modifications, and broken link reports
- Change the existing category structure and move web links from one category to another

Modifying Web Links

The details of a particular web link can be edited in one of two ways:

- From an Edit link that appears under the web link description when logged in as the administrator
- From the Modify a Link panel in the Web Link Administration area

Both of these methods take you to the same page for editing details. The first method is simple; when logged in as administrator, an Edit link appears for you on any given web link:

> **Fossil Halls: American Museum of Natural History** ⬤⬤⬤
> Description: This museum is home to the world's largest collection of vertebrate fossils, totaling nearly one million specimens.
> Added on: 21-Oct-2005 Hits: 1 Rating: 9.0 (1 Vote)
> [Edit] | Rate this Site | Report Broken Link | Details | Comments (1)

Clicking this will take you to the Modify a Link page in the administration area, which we will look at in a moment.

The other way to access the details of a web link is from the Web Links administration area. Scroll down to find the Modify a Link panel:

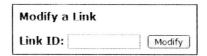

> **Modify a Link**
>
> **Link ID:** [   ]   [Modify]

You enter the link ID and click the Modify button. This ID is found from the front-end display of the web link itself. Hover your mouse cursor over the title of the link, and the URL it points to will appear in your browser status bar. This URL will be of the form:

```
http://localhost/nuke/modules.php?name=Web_Links&l_op=visit&lid=1
```

The link ID is got from looking at the lid value in the URL. Here, the value is 1, and this is the link ID that we enter into the Modify a Link panel to begin editing its details:

Clicking the Modify button brings us to the Modify a Link page. This is the same page that we arrive at when we click Edit from the web link description:

Modify a Link

Link ID: **1**
Page Title: Fossil Halls: American Museum of Natural History
Page URL: http://www.amnh.org/exhibitions/permanent/fossilhalls [Visit]
Description:
This museum is home to the world's largest collection of vertebrate
fossils, totaling nearly one million specimens.

Name: Douglas Paterson
Email:
Hits: 4
Category: Museums/North America ∨ [Modify] [Delete]

Here you can change any of the details of the web link, or reassign it a different category from the Category drop-down box. You click the Modify button to save your changes, or the Delete button to remove the web link from the database. Despite the fact these buttons are right next to the Category drop-down box, they do apply to the web link and are not ways to modify or delete categories. We'll come onto that in a moment.

Underneath the Modify a Link panel there is the Add Editorial panel.

This panel allows you to add some 'editorial' comments about the web link, and the presence of an editorial is indicated by an Editorial link that appears under the link description:

Fossil Halls: American Museum of Natural History
Description: This museum is home to the world's largest collection of vertebrate
fossils, totaling nearly one million specimens.
Added on: 04-Aug-2005 Hits: 4 Rating: 9 (1 Vote)
Edit | Rate this Site | Report Broken Link | Details | Comments (1) | Editorial

The editorial text can be viewed by clicking that link or by clicking the Editor Review link of the Link Profile page.

There is more underneath the Add Editorial panel when you edit web link details. You can find a list of all the comments and ratings that have been submitted for that web link:

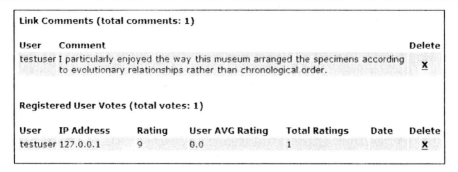

If you have a large number of ratings for your web link, this could be a very long list!

Each table has a Delete column, and clicking the X link in that column will remove the comment or the rating of the web link.

Managing User-Submitted Web Links

Earlier we saw ways for the visitor to submit information about web links—requesting modifications to details, reporting a broken link, and also submitting a new web link. We left that at the point of the visitor making their submission, and now we'll continue from there.

Firstly we'll look at handling web links submitted by users. After the submission, the administrator will know there is a link submission in the queue by looking at the Waiting Content administration block.

- Waiting Links: 1
- Mod. Links: 0
- Broken Links: 0

The number next to Links indicates the length of the queue for submitted web links. Clicking Waiting Links here brings you to the Links Waiting for Validation page:

Links Waiting for Validation

Link ID: 1

Submitter: testuser
Page Title: The Carnegie Museum of Natural History
Page URL: http://www.carnegiemuseums.org/cmnh/   [Visit]
Description:
Featuring Dinosaurs in Their World, an exciting exhibit that reflects current scientific evidence of these colossal creatures and their environments.

Name: _____   Email: _____
Category: Museums/North America ⌄ [Add] [Delete]

The Submitter field shows the name of the user who added the web link. After that, the details are the same as those that you worked with earlier while adding a web link through the administration area. Since these details were entered by another user, you will have to check through them carefully before deciding what to do with the web link.

You are able to edit and correct any of these details before clicking the Add button to accept the web link, or Delete to discard it. Clicking either of these will remove the web link from the queue.

Managing User-Submitted Modification Requests

Earlier we saw that a visitor is able to request changes to the web link details—possibly to point out an inaccuracy in it that needs to be corrected.

Once the visitor submits their change request, the Waiting Content administrator block notifies the administrator of it:

```
• Waiting Links: 0
• Mod. Links: 1
• Broken Links: 0
```

Again, the number next to Mod. Links indicates the length of the queue for web link modification requests. Clicking that link brings you to the User Link Modification Requests page. Each of the submitted requests is shown along with the original web link and options to Accept or Ignore the request. Choosing to Accept or Ignore the request removes it from the queue. Clicking Accept will replace the existing web link details with the requested details. Be certain to check these details carefully! Clicking Ignore simply discards the request.

Managing User-Submitted Broken Link Notifications

We also saw earlier that visitors are able to report 'broken' links. In the same way as modification requests, the Waiting Content administration block also notifies you of any broken links submitted:

```
• Waiting Links: 0
• Mod. Links: 0
• Broken Links: 1
```

Clicking Broken Links brings you to the User Reported Broken Links page, your control center for investigating these claims. All reports of broken links are listed here, along with options to Ignore (discard) the report, Delete the report and the web link that goes with it, or Edit the web link details to correct the link. The link itself is in the Link column—a click of that should confirm if your link is indeed broken.

User Reported Broken Links (1)

Ignore (Deletes all *requests* for a given link)
Delete (Deletes *broken link* and *requests* for a given link)

Link	Submitter	Link Owner	Edit	Ignore	Delete
Fossil Halls: American Museum of Natural History	testuser		X	X	X

If you click the Edit link, and then correct the link, you will still have to return to the User Reported Broken Links page to discard the report.

An alternative way to access these last two features is from a menu at the top of the Web Links administration page:

[Clean Links Votes | Broken Links Reports (1) | Link Modification Requests (0) | Validate Links]

This menu has links to web link modification request and broken link reports that we have just seen, along with the Clean Links Votes link, which tidies up the rating totals and averages, resetting all the votes to zero for each link.

Validating Links

Although visitors can report broken links, it would be good for you to periodically check on the status of all your links, without having to go through them individually and click on all the links. This is done by clicking the Validate Links link.

This brings you to a list of your categories:

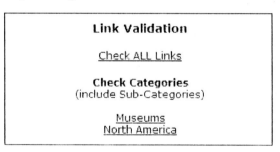

By clicking one of the category titles, each web link in that category will be checked (or every web link in the database if you click Check ALL Links). Once this is complete, you see the status report:

> **Validating Category (and all subcategories): NorthAmerica**
> (please be patient)
>
> | Status | Link Title | Functions |
> |--------|------------|-----------|
> | Ok! | Fossil Halls: American Museum of Natural History | None |
> | Ok! | The Carnegie Museum of Natural History | None |

'Checking the links' means that PHP-Nuke will be sending a request to the server hosting each of your web links, and then waiting for a response. As such, this process could take quite a while, depending on various network connection factors. The Status column reports whether the link is Ok! or if there was some problem with the link.

In fact, link validation doesn't actually check if there is a problem with the target page at all, it only checks if there is a response from the host site of the link. If the target page of the web link has been moved to a different location on the host server (or even if it is no longer on that server), then the Status will still be Ok!, although the link itself is no longer useful. If the host doesn't exist or is unavailable at the time, only then will PHP-Nuke report a problem.

If the Status does show as Failed!, then you will find links in the Functions column to edit the web link details, or delete the web link entirely.

Changing Category Structure

It is also possible to modify the web link category structure. We have already seen how to create new categories, and now we will see how to 'move' categories around to different points in the hierarchy, and how to transport their web links along with the category.

> The process that we describe here moves all the web links from one category to another. If you only want to move certain web links within a category, then you will have to do that on an individual basis by assigning them to a new category from the Modify a Link panel in the Web Links administration menu.

Time For Action—Moving Categories

We will add a subcategory of Museums called Fossils, and we will move our North America category along with its web links into that category.

1. From the Web Links administration area, we begin by creating a new subcategory, Fossils, to go in the Museums category. Enter the details as shown, and click the Add button:

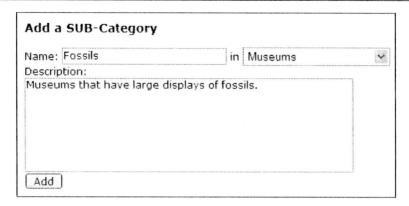

2. Next we create another subcategory called North America. This has the same description as the North America category we created earlier, but this time, the category is a subcategory of Museums/Fossils. We enter the details, and click Add to create the subcategory:

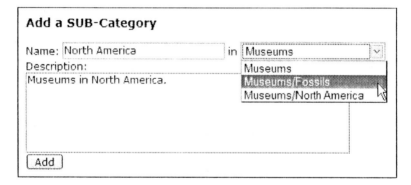

3. When the page reloads, scroll down the screen to find the Transfer all links from category panel. Select Museums/North America from the upper Category drop-down box:

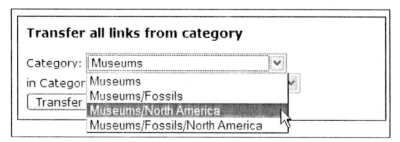

4. And now select Museums/Fossils/North America from the lower in Category drop-down box, and then click Transfer:

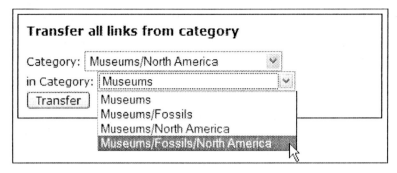

5. When the page reloads, scroll down to the find the Modify a Category panel. Select the Museums/North America category from the Category dropdown, and click Modify.

6. When the page reloads, you see the name and description of the category displayed; click the Delete button to delete this category:

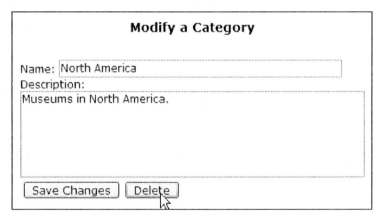

7. You will then be asked to confirm the deletion of this category, so click Yes.

8. Now when you revisit the index of your Web Links, you will see the Fossils subcategory:

Links Main Categories

• **Museums**
Visit natural history and dinosaur
museums from all round the world.
Fossils

There are 2 Links and 3 Categories in our
database

9. Clicking the Fossils link shows the new Fossils/North America category that we just created, in which can be found the web links copied from the original Museums/North America category.

What Just Happened?

We moved a set of web links from one category to another. In PHP-Nuke, you can change the name or description of a category, but you cannot actually move it to another parent category. What we performed above achieved the equivalent of this.

To obtain the effect of moving a category to a new parent category, you first have to create the new subcategory in the 'target' category. This was done in the first two steps by creating the Fossils subcategory of Museums, and then a North America subcategory of Fossils. The Museums/Fossils/North America category is our target category, and it will become the new home for the web links of the Museums/North America category.

With the target category in place, the next step is to move the web links from one category to the other. This is done through the Transfer all links from category panel. From the top drop-down box in that panel you select the category that you are moving the web links from, and in the bottom drop-down box you select the category you are moving the web links to. After selecting these categories, clicking the Transfer button moves the web links from one category to the other.

At the end of step 4, we had created a new Museums/Fossils/North America category and moved all the web links from the existing Museums/North America category to that category. The final piece of tidying up was to delete the original Museums/North America category; this is done from the Modify a Category panel.

In this panel, you first select the category and then click the Modify button. This brings you to a screen where you can edit the details of the category, or click the Delete button to remove the category. Note that deleting a category removes all its web links from the database, in addition to removing any subcategories.

Web Links Block

The Top10_Links block that ships with PHP-Nuke displays the ten most viewed links, along with a link to their details. Similarly, there is a Top10_Downloads block that displays the ten most popular downloads.

Like the other blocks mentioned in this chapter, these blocks still display the list of links or downloads even if the visitor has no access to the modules themselves.

Special Administrator

An administrator with privileges only for the Web Links module can be created from the Edit Admins menu of the administration area.

Restricting Access

You can restrict access to the Web Links module from the Modules administration area as you can for any other module.

The same holds for the Downloads module. However, restricting access in this way means that before the visitor has even had a chance to see what downloads you have on offer, they are presented with the 'NO ACCESS' screen, and told they need to register or login to proceed.

You might consider this as rather unfriendly to your visitors; people may be prepared to register in order to get at a particular download, but they're not prepared to register blindly without knowing what's on offer.

One way of giving people a taste of what is in your Downloads module is through the Top 10 module. This module displays a list of 10 pieces of content from a variety of modules. Like many of the module blocks we have seen in this chapter, the list will be displayed to the visitor even if they do not have permission to access the full content itself. However, the Top10 module does not display a list of the top 10 web links, so this strategy will fail for Web Links.

Points and Prizes

There are a number of activities in the Web Links module that can earn points for registered visitors. The administrator can allot points for clicking a web link, rating a web link, or commenting on a web link. Same goes for the sister module, Downloads.

Reviews

The Reviews module enables the creation of a collection of articles, ratings, and comments about particular products, or indeed, about anything.

Like Encyclopedia, the reviews are alphabetized, and this makes it easy for the visitor to find a review on something—they simply have to know the first letter of the subject of the review to find it.

The image below shows the welcome screen of the Reviews module; the alphabetical navigation menu is clear:

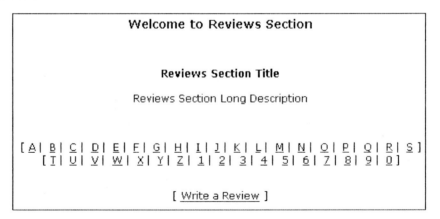

Clicking on any of the letters or digits brings up a list of the entered reviews whose titles begin with that letter:

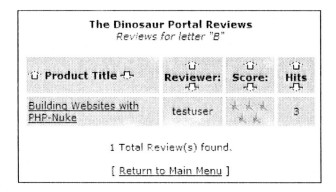

From the list of reviews, clicking the title of the review shows the review, and the list also shows the author of the review, the rating awarded in the review, and the number of views of that review. There are little arrows in the title bar of the list to sort the display by any of the columns.

Submitting Reviews

Reviews can be submitted by registered or unregistered visitors, and the submitted reviews need to be approved by the administrator before they are posted to the site. Administrator-submitted reviews go directly onto the site.

The review-submitting process begins by clicking the Write a Review link on the Reviews welcome page. This brings up a form for the details of the review; here is the top part:

Write a Review for the Dinosaur Portal

Please enter information according to the specifications

Product Title:

Building Websites with PHP-Nuke

Name of the Reviewed Product.

Review:

I found this book interesting. It was very helpful in setting up my dinosaur-based community site. Remarkably, the site created in the book was a dinosaur-based community site. That was quite a coincidence

If you want multiple pages you can write **<!--pagebreak-->** where you want to cut.

Your actual review. Please observe proper grammar! Make it at least 100 words, OK? You may also use HTML tags if you know how to use them.

You enter the Product Title followed by the text of the review into the Review textbox. The Product Title must be entered, and so must some text for the review, or the review will not be accepted. Underneath it you will find more fields:

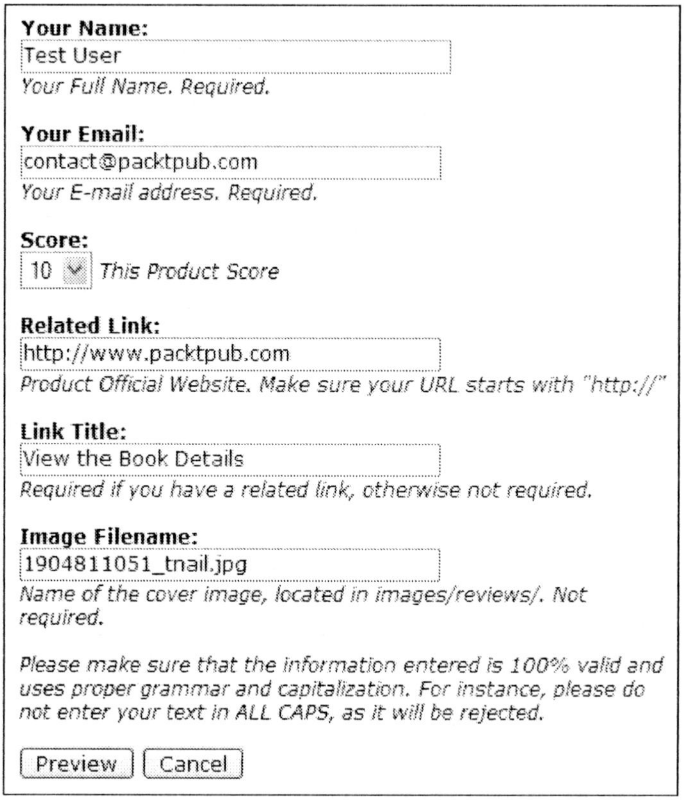

Your Name:

Test User

Your Full Name. Required.

Your Email:

contact@packtpub.com

Your E-mail address. Required.

Score:

10 ⌄ *This Product Score*

Related Link:

http://www.packtpub.com

Product Official Website. Make sure your URL starts with "http://"

Link Title:

View the Book Details

Required if you have a related link, otherwise not required.

Image Filename:

1904811051_tnail.jpg

Name of the cover image, located in images/reviews/. Not required.

Please make sure that the information entered is 100% valid and uses proper grammar and capitalization. For instance, please do not enter your text in ALL CAPS, as it will be rejected.

[Preview] [Cancel]

First of all are fields for your name and email address. If you are already logged in, these will be filled with the details from your user account. The name and email address must be provided or the review is not accepted. Under those fields is a drop-down box to select a Score from 1 to 10. After that are fields for adding a link to the product website, and a title to accompany that link—if you enter some text for one of these fields you must enter text for them both.

The Image Filename field only appears if you are the administrator. This is the name of an accompanying image that must be located in the /images/reviews/ folder. There is no facility to upload images to this location from within the module, so the image must be placed there by other means (such as FTP). This is why the field only appears for administrators; ordinary users should not be able to place images directly onto the server. If the image is missing from that folder, it will simply be displayed in the same way as any missing image is displayed on a web page.

To proceed, you must click the Preview button, or click Cancel to discard your review:

Building Websites with PHP-Nuke

I found this book interesting. It was very helpful in setting up my dinosaur-based community site. Remarkably, the site created in the book was a dinosaur-based community site. That was quite a coincidence

Added: August 4th 2005
Reviewer: Test User
Score: ★ ★ ★ ★ ★
Related Link: View the Book Details

Does this looks right? [Yes] [No]

Note: Currently logged in as admin... this review will be immediately added.

Clicking the Yes button submits the review, or No goes back to the previous page to amend the details.

When logged in as the administrator, the review is immediately posted to the site, and can be seen in the list of recent reviews on the Reviews welcome page:

10 most popular reviews	10 most recent reviews
1) Building Websites with PHP-Nuke	1) Building Websites with PHP-Nuke
2)	2)
3)	3)
4)	4)
5)	5)
6)	6)
7)	7)
8)	8)
9)	9)
10)	10)
There are 1 Reviews in the Database	

Clicking the review title in this list will display the review immediately. If the review is submitted by an ordinary visitor, it goes into the reviews queue, and the length of the queue can be seen by the administrator in the Waiting Content administrator block:

- Submissions: 0
- Waiting Reviews: 1
- Waiting Links: 0

Clicking the Waiting Reviews link brings you to a page showing the Reviews Waiting for Validation panel, which—in the same way as you saw with the Web Link checking—displays the details of the review, and allows you to add or discard the review.

Interacting with Reviews

Visitors are able to post comments to submitted reviews. There is a Post Comment link on the review itself from where visitors can add their own opinion about the product, and their own rating. On each comment there is a Delete link for the administrator to remove the comment if required.

Managing Reviews

The administrator interface of the Reviews module is limited, since the power to edit and delete reviews is accessed from the review display itself. When logged in as administrator, there are Edit and Delete links embedded in the text of the review:

Admin: [Edit | Delete]

These links give you power to manage the reviews in the database. Clicking the Edit link brings up a form that allows you edit the details of the review. After making your changes, you can preview your changes as you did earlier, and click Yes to accept them. Note that only the administrator can edit reviews in this way; the original submitter of the review cannot do so.

Customizing the Reviews Welcome Page

Clicking the Reviews icon in the Modules Administration menu brings you to the Reviews Administration page:

The Reviews Administration page really has only one feature—the ability to change the text that is displayed on the reviews welcome page:

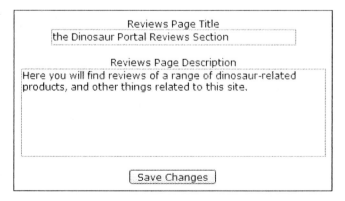

Reviews Page Title
the Dinosaur Portal Reviews Section

Reviews Page Description
Here you will find reviews of a range of dinosaur-related products, and other things related to this site.

Save Changes

Changing the text in these fields and clicking the Save Changes button gives your Reviews module a new-look front page:

```
┌─────────────────────────────────────────┐
│        Welcome to Reviews Section         │
│                                           │
│     the Dinosaur Portal Reviews Section   │
│                                           │
│      Here you will find reviews of a range of │
│    dinosaur-related products, and other things │
│            related to this site.          │
└─────────────────────────────────────────┘
```

The Reviews Block

There is a Reviews block that ships with PHP-Nuke, but is not displayed by default. This block simply displays the titles of the ten most-recently entered reviews, with a link to read each review.

Special Administrator

You can create a special administrator with rights to only the Reviews module in the Edit Admins menu of the administration area. This administrator has the ability to approve or remove submitted reviews, in addition to posting their own.

Restricting Access

Access to the Reviews module is done on a 'whole module' basis. The visitor either sees nothing or everything. You cannot configure individual reviews to be viewed by certain user groups.

Points and Prizes

Posting a review is strangely not worth any points, but posting a comment to a review is eligible for earning user points.

Module Feature Comparison

We've now seen the major content types of PHP-Nuke. In an attempt to help you remember what you have seen, here is a table listing the content types for you to quickly compare the features they have:

Feature	Stories	Content	Web Links / Downloads	FAQ	Encyclopedia
Searchable	Yes	No	Yes	No	Yes
Categorized	Yes	Yes	Yes	Yes	Yes
Hierarchical (nested)	No	No	Yes	No	No

Feature	Stories	Content	Web Links / Downloads	FAQ	Encyclopedia
Ordered By	Category Topics Date of Publication	Category	Category Subcategory	Category	Encyclopedia
User Submitted Content	Yes	No	Yes	No	No
Ratings	Yes	No	Yes	No	No
Comments	Yes	No	No	No	No
Polls	Yes	No	No	No	No
Points Awarded	Yes	No	Yes	No	No
Special Administrator	Yes	Yes	Yes	Yes	Yes
Block Available	No	Yes	Yes	No	Yes

Summary

In this chapter we have had a tour of the other default modules that ship with PHP-Nuke, and seen the types of content they manage.

We looked at the Content, FAQ, Encyclopedia, Web Links and Downloads, and Reviews modules.

Each of these modules handles different types of content, but there are similarities. Each module organizes the content into hierarchical structures, and most allow their content to be searched from the Search module.

We saw that the Web Links and Downloads modules (which are very similar) have the most features among the modules in this chapter. These two modules allow users to submit their own links, rate or comment on existing links, and also help out the administrator by notifying the administrator of any broken link or download.

For each module, we looked at both the visitor and the administrator experience, seeing how to add, edit, and manage the content these modules work with. We also looked at the existence of blocks that come with PHP-Nuke that can be used to display lists of content from the module, as well as which module activities let the user earn points.

8
Managing the Discussion Forums

PHP-Nuke has an awesome discussion board module, the Forums module, which is a complete application. phpBB—the leading free, open-source discussion board application—has been 'refitted' as a PHP-Nuke module, providing integration with the PHP-Nuke user accounts.

In this chapter, we will begin to explore the PHP-Nuke Forums module. You will:

- Learn about the structure of a discussion board
- Learn how to create categories and forums, and make postings
- Create groups, and set simple permissions for forums
- See how to moderate forum content

Forum Structure

Rather than having a single discussion area, with topics intermingling with other topics, themes of conversation are organized into a number of different containers, rather like the folder and file structure of your hard disk.

The top-level of organization is the **category**. Note that the categories here are different from the categories we have met in the other modules!

Within categories, the next level of organization is into **forums**. Forums consist of **topics**, and finally, users are able to creating **postings** on these topics. Thus categories, forums, and topics act like folders, with postings being analogous to the files, to continue the file system analogy.

Only forum administrators can create categories and forums. Topics (and obviously postings, since they are the real body of a discussion area) can be added by users of the forum. A topic is essentially a 'first' posting, with subsequent postings on that topic being replies to the topic subject.

Here is a diagram of the forums hierarchy:

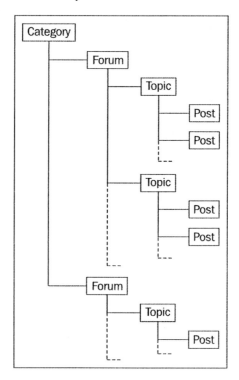

Although a forum is contained in a category, the term 'forum' is generally used informally to refer to the whole discussion environment, covering categories, forums, topics, and postings. When you 'post to a forum', you are actually posting to a topic in a particular forum of a certain category! The general term 'board' or 'discussion board' is usually used to refer to the whole forum experience.

Access to categories and forums can be restricted to groups of users. These restricted categories and forums can also be made invisible to those unable to access them. This is in contrast with other modules in PHP-Nuke where you restrict access to the entire module. In general, visitors either see all the contents of the module or none of it. The Forums module enables a set of 'mini-administrators', forum moderators, who are able to control who is able to post what, and where. We'll see more about that later.

The Forums Administration Area

The Forums administration area is accessed through the PHP-Nuke Administration area, in the same way as for any other module.

This brings you to an area very different from the other PHP-Nuke module administration areas. This is the phpBB administration area, and is the nerve center of your phpBB forums.

The page has a frame-based layout, with the left-hand frame being the navigation panel, giving you links to the various phpBB administration tasks. The right-hand frame holds the main page content.

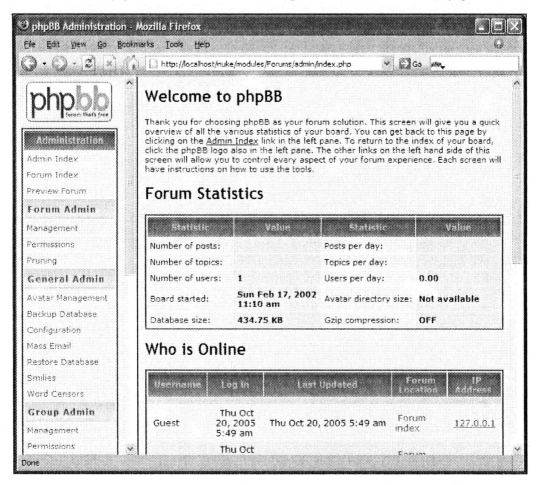

This screen shows you some statistics about your board, and the details of current, online visitors. Clicking the Admin Index link will return you to this page, with the Forum Index link taking you into your forums. The Preview Forum link also takes you to your forums, but opens them up in the right-hand frame of the browser, retaining the phpBB administration navigation in the left-hand frame, so you can continue to work in the phpBB administration area if you need to.

phpBB is truly awesome. It is arguably one of the most impressive free, open-source PHP web applications available, and we can only scratch the surface of its true power here. phpBB is worthy of a book by itself, and there is one: *Building Online Communities with phpBB 2* by Stoyan Stefanov, Jeremy Rogers, and Mike Lothar from Packt Publishing (ISBN 1-904811-13-2).

Here we will step through the tasks of creating the structure to allow users to make postings, follow the posting process, and also see how to make some basic configuration changes.

Forum Configuration

Just as with PHP-Nuke where we began by making changes to PHP-Nuke's site configuration, here too, we begin with some global configuration settings for phpBB. Clicking the Configuration link in the General Admin part of the left-hand panel takes you to the phpBB configuration area. There are many options; only some of the top ones are shown here:

General Configuration

The form below will allow you to customize all the general board options. For User and Forum configurations use the related links on the left hand side.

General Board Settings	
Domain Name	theDinosaurPortal.com
Server Port The port your server is running on, usually 80. Only change if different	80
Script path The path where phpBB2 is located relative to the domain name	/modules/Forums/
Site name	the Dinosaur Portal
Site description	Just because you haven't seen a dinosaur,
Disable board This will make the board unavailable to users. Administrators are able to access the Administration Panel while the board is disabled.	○ Yes ⊙ No
Enable account activation	⊙ None ○ User ○ Admin
User email via board Users send email to each other via this board	○ Enabled ⊙ Disabled
Flood Interval Number of seconds a user must wait between posts	15
Topics Per Page	50
Posts Per Page	15
Posts for Popular Threshold	25
Default Style	subSilver ▾

The Domain Name, Site name, and Site description fields are similar to the Site URL, Site Name, and Slogan fields of the PHP-Nuke preferences. The Domain Name field holds the domain name of your site, and we'll set the Site name and Site description fields to match those in our PHP-Nuke site configuration.

We will also set the Cookie Domain to our site domain name, and the Cookie name to dinoportalforum. Note that if you change these settings after your site has gone live with people having visited the forums and logged in, then they won't be able to log in automatically since the Forums module will be looking for a different cookie from the one they have stored in their browser.

PHP-Nuke generally uses the PHP mail() function to send its emails, but the Forums module offers the option to use an SMTP server to send mail. If you know the details of an SMTP server that you can use (possibly your Internet Service Provider has given you access to an SMTP server), then you can enter the settings for this in the Email Settings panel. If you don't have access to an SMTP server, then the default action of the Forums module is to use the PHP mail() function, as PHP-Nuke would normally do.

Scrolling down the screen you will find a Submit button that will save your changes.

Creating a Category

Click the Management link in the Forum Admin panel to begin creating the forum structure. First, you will need to create a category:

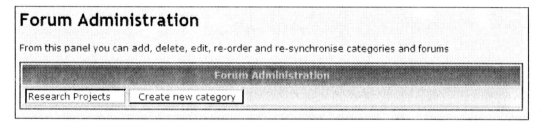

Once you enter the name for the category into the box and click the Create new category button, you have a category.

Creating a Forum

When the page reloads after creating the category, you are presented with a screen confirming the creation of your forum, and a Click Here to return to Forum Administration link. Clicking this link brings you to a page with the list of current categories displayed, along with links to edit, delete, or change their ordering in the list. You are also able to continue creating new categories.

Immediately underneath our new category is a box for entering the name of a new forum for that category, and clicking the Create new forum button will create a forum of that name:

Forum Administration

From this panel you can add, delete, edit, re-order and re-synchronise categories and forums

Forum Administration			
Research Projects	Edit	Delete	Move up Move down
Project Chimera	Create new forum		
	Create new category		

When the page reloads, you will be given a screen into which you can enter a description of the forum, and set some properties for it. You can assign the forum to another category from the Category dropdown, or you can set the Forum Status. The Forum Status is Locked or Unlocked. An Unlocked forum is free for all to view and contribute to; a Locked forum requires the user to have specific access to write or post to it.

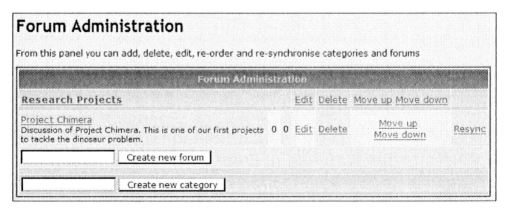

There are also 'pruning' options available for removing topics that haven't seen enough activity in the forum. These options will be useful for keeping your 'board' clean over time.

Clicking the Create new forum button creates the forum:

Forum Administration

From this panel you can add, delete, edit, re-order and re-synchronise categories and forums

Forum Administration					
Research Projects		Edit	Delete	Move up Move down	
Project Chimera Discussion of Project Chimera. This is one of our first projects to tackle the dinosaur problem.	0 0	Edit	Delete	Move up Move down	Resync

Create new forum

Create new category

Now we have forums, we are ready for topics. It is only a matter of time before we are posting!

The Visitor Experience

Open a new browser window, visit your PHP-Nuke site, and click the Forums link. The visitor is welcomed to the Forums module with a list of the categories:

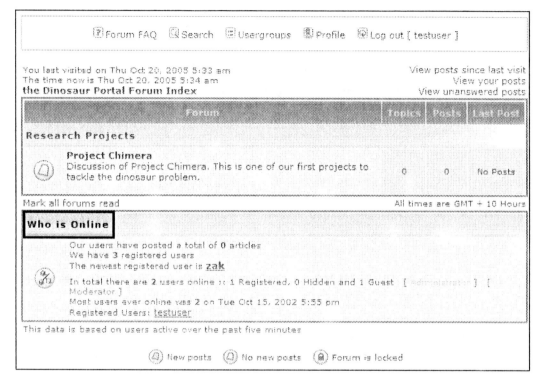

Clicking the Who is Online link presents you with a list of people who are currently viewing the forum, and where they are in the forum.

Clicking on one of the forums takes you to the list of topics in that forum. At the moment, our forum is empty.

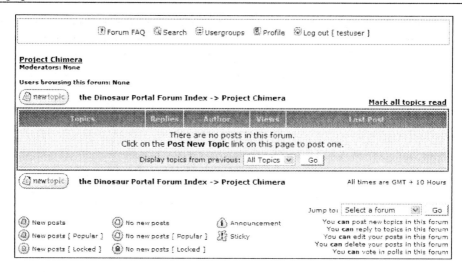

As the screen is encouraging us to do, we can click on the new topic button to post a new topic to the forum. We do not have to be an administrator to do this, but we do have to be a registered user of the PHP-Nuke site.

Posting a Topic

The form for posting a new topic is rather exciting:

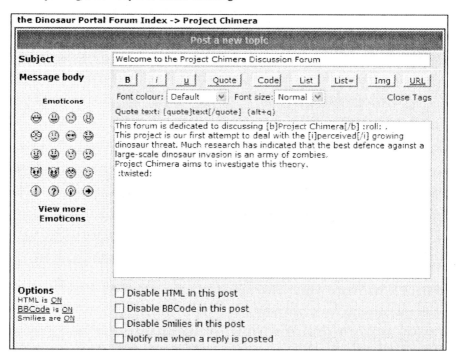

You can enter the Subject of your topic, and enter the body of the topic in the Message body box. You are able to use a range of formatting effects within the body of your posting, including inserting those the little emoticons by clicking on them to add them to your text.

Before posting your topic, it is worth taking a moment to preview it by clicking the Preview Post button:

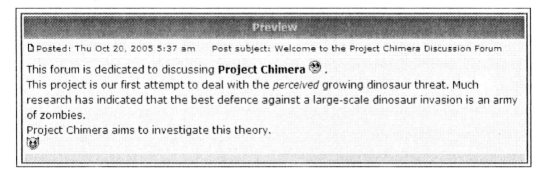

If you are happy with the posting as it is, click the Submit button and the posting is submitted. Your new topic is displayed in the forum's topic list:

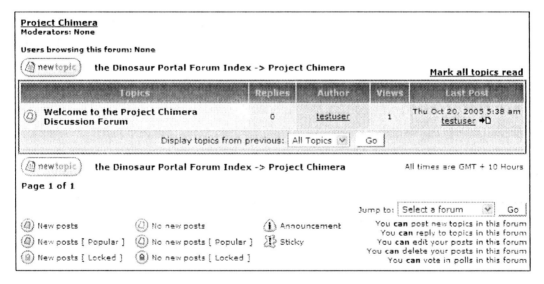

Clicking the topic title brings up the submitted postings for that topic. At this point, we have only one—the topic posting:

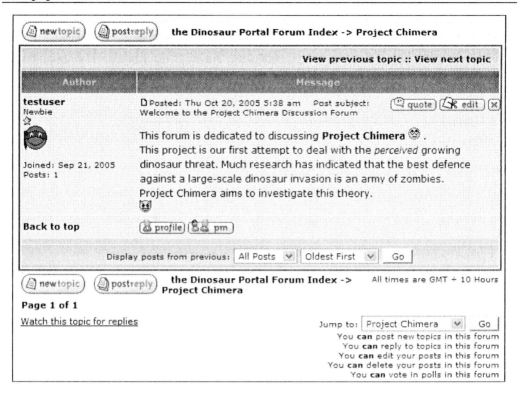

Users can now continue the discussion by posting a reply to this post. The author of the post is able to reply to, edit, or delete his or her own post with the aid of the three icons in the top right-hand corner of the post before any replies have been posted to the posting.

Forum Permissions

Access to particular forums can be restricted to groups of users. Going one step further, forums can be made invisible to anyone outside the group.

Before we set up permissions, we will create a group of users who will have access to our Project Chimera forum. The moderator of this group will be our `testuser` account, and that user will have the responsibility of approving membership to the group.

Creating Groups

We return to the Forum Administration area, and click the Management link in the Group Admin section of the left-hand navigation pane:

We are presented with the Group Administration page, where we begin the process of configuring group permissions by selecting the group from the dropdown. At this point, we need to create a group, so we click the Create New Group button instead:

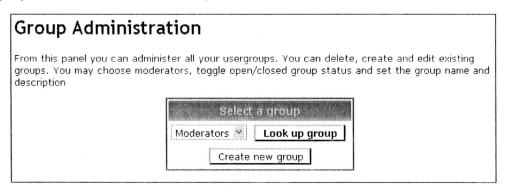

This brings us to a form for entering our group's details:

We provide the group name, a description, and also enter the username of a group moderator. (The Find a username button opens a dialog that allows you to search the list of users to find your moderator if you have forgotten their full username.) You must specify a moderator for the group; you won't be allowed to create the group without one.

The Group status works like this:

- Anyone can apply to join an **open group**, and the moderator approves or denies their membership. Alternatively, the moderator can add them directly to the group.

- For a **closed group**, there is no application process, and the moderator has to add the user directly to the group.

- **Hidden groups** work in the same way as closed groups, except they are invisible to non-members.

We select testuser as our moderator and Open group for the group status.

Once our details are complete, we click the Submit button and our group is created.

Setting Forum Permissions

To begin the process of restricting permissions, we return to the Forum Administration area, and click the Permissions link in the left-hand navigation frame:

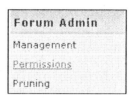

This takes you to the Forum Permissions Control interface. From here you select a forum; click the Look up Forum button and then you can set the permissions for that forum:

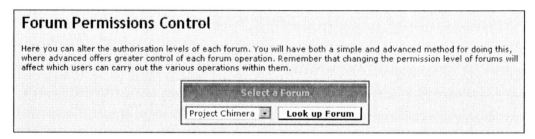

The next screen presents you a dropdown for selecting the access mode of the forum. There is a Simple Mode of assigning phpBB privileges and, for finer control over your forum privileges, there's also a link to the Advanced Mode. Discussion of that is beyond our scope here; suffice it to say that this allows control over what users can do within a particular forum. This level of permissions is reflected by the text at the right-hand foot of the forum area:

> You **can** post new topics in this forum
> You **can** reply to topics in this forum
> You **can** edit your posts in this forum
> You **can** delete your posts in this forum
> You **can** vote in polls in this forum

We will select Private from the dropdown, so that only authorized users will be able to see the forum. The authorized users will be members of the Project Chimera team.

After selecting Private, we click the Submit button, and our forum's permissions are updated.

Now, if you return to the Forums homepage and attempt to view the Project Chimera forum, you will receive a 'no entry' message:

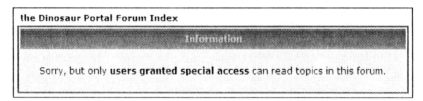

Although you are still logged in as testuser, and that user is the moderator of the Project Chimera Team group, that group itself has no access to the forum. Thus we will need to add that in order to continue.

Setting Group Permissions

Click the Permissions link in the Group Admin section of the left-hand navigation frame:

You find yourself in the Group Permissions Control page. From here we can select a group and move on to manage its permissions. We select Project Chimera Team from the dropdown and click Look up Group:

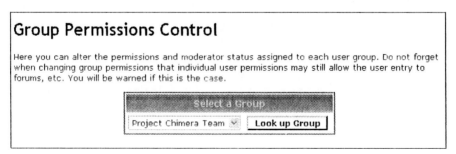

Now we are able to allow the members of the Project Chimera Team to view their forum by selecting Allowed Access from the Simple Permissions dropdown. Again, there is an Advanced Mode, but that is beyond the scope of our discussion here. Clicking the Submit button saves our permissions:

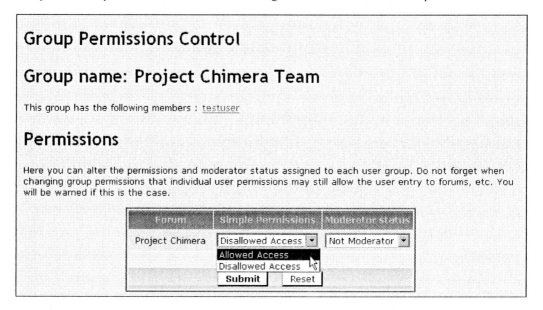

Now, when you return to the Forums homepage you will be able to view the Project Chimera forum, when logged in as testuser.

Joining Groups

We've created another user for the PHP-Nuke site, called Zak. As a member of the ill-fated Project Chimera team, he wants to add himself to the Project Chimera Team group so that he is able to view the forum, and find out what's going on.

Zak does this by going to the Forums module, and clicking the Usergroups link:

This brings you to a page with group membership details. In the list of Non-member groups, we can see the groups that can be joined. Zak can select one from the dropdown, and then click its View Information button:

On clicking the button, Zak is presented with details of the group, including the group description that we entered when we created the group, a button to join the group, and a list of the group members:

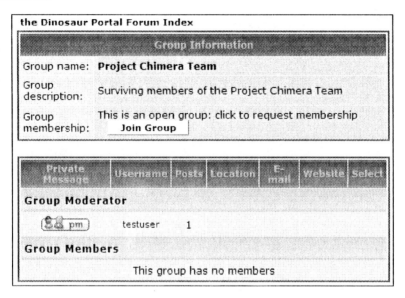

Clicking the Join Group button begins the process of Zak joining the Project Chimera Team group. To be fully accepted into the group, the application has to be approved by a moderator of the group, as can be seen below when Zak views the group's information:

Group membership:	Your membership of this group is pending	Unsubscribe

Approving the Membership Application

Now it is up to the moderator, testuser, to approve Zak's membership. This process begins by testuser clicking on the Usergroups link, selecting the Project Chimera Team group from the Group Membership Details, and clicking the View Information button.

The moderator's view of the group information is different from that of the standard user. In addition to seeing the list of group members, there are buttons to remove members from the group, and also an opportunity to add a new member without the need for the approval stage.

At the foot of the display is a list of pending memberships:

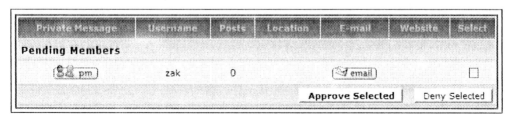

By checking the box next to zak's name, and clicking the Approve Selected button, zak is admitted to the group.

Now zak is free to read the Project Chimera forum, and post to his heart's content.

Underneath the list of pending members is a textbox to add members directly to the group:

By entering the username into the textbox and clicking the Add Member button, that user is added to the group. For closed or hidden groups, there will be no list of pending members since applications are not accepted, and you add members through this textbox.

Moderating the Forum

Although testuser is the Project Chimera Team group moderator, that user is not the moderator of the forum itself. In order to make testuser the forum moderator, so that they can edit or delete posts to that forum, we need to set this permission explicitly.

Setting a Forum Moderator

We start by clicking the Permissions link in the User Admin portion of the left-hand navigation frame:

This brings us to the User Permission Control page, where we first have to enter the username of the user whose permissions we wish to modify:

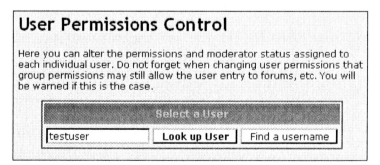

Clicking the Look up User button brings us to the details of this user's permissions. At the top of the page is information about the level of that user (Administrator or User), and the groups that they are members of:

Underneath that is the information about the user-to-forum permissions:

Although the Simple Permissions column of the Project Chimera forum shows Disallowed Access, this is overridden by testuser's membership of the Project Chimera Team group, and they are able to access that forum. However, to allow Zak and the other members of the Project Chimera Team to view the forum, it needs to be set to Allowed Access.

To make testuser a moderator of the forum, select Is Moderator from the Moderator status dropdown, and click the Submit button.

Now that testuser is a moderator of the Project Chimera forum, on their next visit they will notice an extra 'toolbar' that is added to the top right-hand of each of the posts:

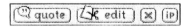

The buttons on this toolbar allow testuser to edit the post, delete the post, or view the IP address of the poster.

Clicking the edit button allows you to modify the post, maybe removing or disclaiming some statement in the text. Click the delete button (the cross icon) and confirm that you want that post deleted to remove it from the topic.

Summary

As we mentioned earlier, we can only hope to scratch the surface of phpBB's awesome power in this single chapter. However, we have covered the basics of working with PHP-Nuke's Forums module.

We covered the basic structure of a discussion board, and saw how categories, forums, and postings relate to each other.

We then moved on to create some categories and forums, and make postings to the forum. Restricting forums to particular groups of users was our next stop, creating groups, setting the permissions for those groups, and then seeing how users can be assigned to those groups. We finished off with a quick look at moderation, how to set up a user as a forum moderator, and saw the extra information visible to the moderator that appeared in each post. Also, we finally saw exactly what Project Chimera is.

9

Customizing Layout with Themes

In this chapter, we are going to transform the look of the Dinosaur Portal with the help of a new PHP-Nuke theme. A PHP-Nuke theme is a collection of HTML files, CSS styles, images, and PHP code that defines the layout and appearance of your pages, and hence, the look and feel of your site. Through the use of themes, without having to touch the inner workings of PHP-Nuke, you can create a new look for your site, enforced throughout the site. There is even the possibility of allowing the user to choose a personal theme.

Creating a PHP-Nuke theme gives your site its own special look, distinguishing it from other PHP-Nuke-created sites and offers an effective outlet for your creative talents. Creating a theme requires some knowledge of HTML, confidence in working with CSS and PHP, but most important is some imagination and creativity!

Unlike the tasks we have tackled in previous chapters, where we have been working exclusively through a web browser to control and configure PHP-Nuke, working with themes is the start of a new era in your PHP-Nuke skills; editing the code files of PHP-Nuke itself. Fortunately, the design of PHP-Nuke means that our theme work won't be tampering with the inner workings of PHP-Nuke. However, becoming confident in handling the mixture of HTML and PHP code that is a PHP-Nuke theme will prepare you for the more advanced work ahead, when we really get to grips with PHP-Nuke at the code level.

In this chapter, we will look at:

- Theme management
- Templates in themes
- Changing the page header
- Working with the stylesheet
- Changing blocks
- Changing the format of stories

What Does a Theme Control?

Despite the fact that we say 'themes control the look and feel of your site', a theme does not determine every aspect of the page output. PHP-Nuke is an incredibly versatile application, but it cannot produce every website imaginable.

Appearance

First of all, the appearance of the page can be controlled through the use of colors, fonts, font sizes, weights, and so on. This can either be done through the use of CSS styles or HTML. You can also add JavaScript for fancier effects, or even Flash animations, Java applets, or sounds—anything that you can add to a standard HTML page.

Graphical aspects of the page such as the site banner, background images, and so on, are under the care of the theme. There are also some modules that allow their standard graphical icons to be overridden with images from a theme.

Page Layout

Roughly speaking, a PHP-Nuke page consists of three parts; the top bit, the bit in the middle, and the bit at the bottom! The top bit—the header—usually contains a site logo and such things as a horizontal navigation bar for going directly to important parts of your site. The bottom bit—the footer—contains the copyright message.

In between the header and the footer, the output is usually divided into three columns. The left-hand column typically contains blocks, displayed one of top each other, the middle column contains the module output, and the right-hand column contains more blocks. The layout of these columns (their width for example) is controlled by the theme. You may have noticed that the right-hand column is generally only displayed on the homepage of a PHP-Nuke site; this too, is something that is controlled by the theme.

The appearance of the blocks is controlled by the theme; PHP-Nuke provides the title of the block and its content, and the theme will generally 'frame' these to produce the familiar block look.

The theme also determines how the description of stories appears on the homepage. In addition, the theme determines how the full text of the story, its extended text, is displayed.

We've talked about how the theme controls the 'look' of things. The theme also allows you to add other site-related data to your page; for example the name of the site can appear, and the site slogan, and you can even add such things as the user's name with a friendly welcome message.

Theme Management

Basically, a theme is a folder that sits inside the themes folder in your PHP-Nuke installation. Different themes correspond to different folders in the themes folder, and adding or removing a theme is as straightforward as adding or removing the relevant folder from the themes folder.

By default, you will find around 14 themes in a standard PHP-Nuke installation. DeepBlue is the default theme.

Themes can be chosen in one of two ways:

- **By the administrator**: You can simply select the required theme from the General Site Info panel of the Site Preferences administration menu and save the changes. The theme selected by the administrator is the default theme for the site and will be seen by all users of the site, registered or unregistered.

- **By the user**: Users can override the default theme set by the administrator from the Themes option of the Your Account module. This sets a new, personal, theme that will be displayed to that user. Note that this isn't a theme especially customized for that user; it is just one chosen from the list of standard themes installed on your site.

Unregistered visitors do not have an option to choose a theme; they have to become registered users.

Theme File Structure

Let's start with the default theme, DeepBlue. If you open up the DeepBlue folder within the themes folder in the root of your PHP-Nuke installation, you will find three folders and two files. The three folders are:

- forums: This folder contains the theme for the Forums module. This is not strictly a requirement of a PHP-Nuke theme, and not every PHP-Nuke theme has a forums theme. The Forums module (otherwise known as phpBB) has its own theme 'engine'. The purpose of including a theme for the forums is that you have consistency between the rest of your PHP-Nuke display and the phpBB display.

- images: This folder contains the image files used by your theme. These include the site logo, background images, and graphics for blocks among others. As mentioned earlier, within this folder can be other folders containing images to override the standard icons.

- style: This folder contains the CSS files for your theme. Usually, there is one CSS file in the style folder, style.css. Each theme will make use of its style.css file, and this is the file into which we will add our style definitions when the time comes.

Of the two files, index.html is simply there to prevent people browsing to your themes folder and seeing what it contains; visiting this page in a browser simply produces a blank page. It is a very simple security measure.

The themes.php file is a PHP code file, and is where all the action happens. This file must always exist within a theme folder. We will concentrate on this file later when we customize the theme.

In other themes you will find more files; we will look at these later.

Installing a New Theme

Installing and uninstalling themes comes down to adding or removing folders from the themes folder, and whenever a list of available themes is presented, either in the Site Preferences menu or the Your Accounts module, PHP-Nuke refreshes this list by getting the names of the folders in the themes folder.

You will find a huge range of themes on the Web. For example, there is a gallery of themes at:

```
http://nukecops.com/modules.php?set_albumName=packs&op=modload&name=Gallery&
file=index&include=view_album.php
```

Many of these are themes written for older versions of PHP-Nuke, but most are still compatible with the newer releases.

There is also a live demonstration of some themes at:

```
http://www.portedmods.com/styles/
```

On this page you can select the new theme and see it applied immediately, before you download it.

Removing an Existing Theme

To remove a theme from your PHP-Nuke site you simply remove the corresponding folder from the themes folder, and it will no longer be available to PHP-Nuke.

However, you should be careful when removing themes—what if somebody is actually using that theme?

- If a user has that theme selected as their personal theme, and you remove that theme, then that user's personal theme will revert to the default theme selected in Site Preferences.
- If you remove the site's default theme, then you will break your site!

Deleting the site's default theme will produce either a blank screen or messages like the following when you attempt to view your site.

```
Warning: head(themes/NonExistentTheme/theme.php)
[function.head]: failed to create stream:
No such file or directory in c:\nuke\html\header.php on line 31
```

The only people who can continue to use your site in this situation are those who have selected a personal theme for themselves—and only if that theme is still installed.

To correct such a faux pas, make a copy of one of the other themes in your themes folder (unless you happen to have a copy of the theme you just deleted elsewhere), and rename it to the name of the theme you just deleted.

In conclusion, removing themes should only be a problem if you somehow manage to remove your site's default theme. For users who have selected the theme you just removed, their theme will revert to the default theme and life goes on for them.

A final caveat about the names of theme folders; do not use spaces in the names of the folders in the themes folder—this can lead to strange behavior when the list of themes is displayed in the drop-down menus for users to select from.

From an Existing Theme to a New Theme

We'll create a new theme for the Dinosaur Portal by making changes to an existing theme. This will not only make you feel like the theme master, but it will also serve to illustrate the nature of the theme-customization problem. We'll be making changes all over the place—adding and replacing things in HTML and PHP files—but it will be worth it. Another thing to bear in mind is that we're creating a completely different looking site without making any changes to the inner parts of PHP-Nuke. At this point, all we are changing is the theme definition.

The theme for the Dinosaur Portal will have a warm, tropical feel to it to evoke the atmosphere of a steaming, tropical, prehistoric jungle, and will use lots of orange color on the page.

First of all, we need a theme on which to conduct our experiments. We'll work on the 3D-Fantasy theme.

Starting Off

The first thing we will do is to create a new theme folder, which will be a copy of the 3D-Fantasy theme.

Open up the themes folder in your file explorer, and create a copy of the 3D-Fantasy folder. Rename this copy as TheDinosaurPortal.

Now log into your site as testuser, and from the Your Account module, select TheDinosaurPortal as the theme. Your site will immediately switch to this theme, but it will look exactly like 3D-Fantasy, because, at the moment, it is!

You will also need some images from the code download for this chapter; you will find them in the siteImages folder of this chapter's code.

Replacing Traces of the Old Theme

The theme that we are about to work on has many occurrences of 3D-Fantasy in a number of files, such as references to images. We will have to remove these first of all, or else our new theme will be looking in the wrong folder for images and other resources.

Open each of the files below in your text editor, and replace every occurrence of 3D-Fantasy with TheDinosaurPortal in a text editor, we'll use Wordpad. "You can use the replace functionality of your editor to do this. For example, in Wordpad, select Edit | Replace; enter the text to be replaced, and then click Replace All to replace all the occurrences in the open file. After making all the changes, save each file:

- blocks.html
- footer.html
- header.html
- story_home.html
- story_page.html
- theme.php
- tables.php

Templates and PHP Files

We've just encountered two types of file in the theme folder—PHP code files (`theme.php` and `tables.php`) and HTML files (`blocks.html`, `footer.html`, and so on). Before we go any further, we need to have a quick discussion of what roles these types of file play in the theme construction.

PHP Files

The PHP files do the main work of the theme. These files contain the definitions of some functions that handle the display of the page header and how an individual block or article is formatted, among other tasks. These functions are called from other parts of PHP-Nuke when required. We'll talk about them when they are required later in the chapter. Part of our customization work will be to make some changes to these functions and have them act in a different way when called.

Historically, the code for a PHP-Nuke theme consisted of a single PHP file, `theme.php`. One major drawback of this was the difficulty you would have in editing this file in the 'design' view of an HTML editor. Instead of seeing the HTML that you wished to edit, you probably wouldn't see anything in the 'design' view of most HTML editors, since the HTML was inextricably intertwined with the PHP code. This made creating a new theme, or even editing an existing theme, not something for the faint-hearted—you had to be confident with your PHP coding to make sure you were changing the right places, and in the right way.

The `theme.php` file consists of a number of functions that are called from other parts of PHP-Nuke when required. These functions are how the theme does its work.

One of the neat appearances in recent versions of PHP-Nuke is the use of a 'mini-templating' engine for themes. Not all themes make use of this method (DeepBlue is one theme that doesn't), and that is one of the reasons we are working with 3D-Fantasy as our base theme, since it does follow the 'templating' model.

Templates

The HTML files that we modified above are the theme templates. They consist of HTML, without any PHP code. Each template is responsible for a particular part of the page, and is called into action by the functions of the theme when required.

One advantage of using these templates is that they can be easily edited in visual HTML editors, such as Macromedia's Dreamweaver, without any PHP code to interfere with the page design.

Another advantage of using these templates is to separate logic from presentation. The idea of a template is that it should determine how something is displayed (its presentation). The template makes use of some data supplied to it, but acquiring and choosing this data (the logic) is not done in the template. The template is processed or evaluated by the 'template engine', and output is generated. The template engine in this case is the `theme.php` file.

To see how the template and PHP-Nuke 'communicate', let's look at an extract from the `header.html` file in the 3D-Fantasy folder:

```
<a href="index.php">
    <img src="themes/3D-Fantasy/images/logo.gif" border="0"
        alt="Welcome to $sitename" align="left">
</a>
```

The $sitename text (shown highlighted) is an example of what we'll call a **placeholder**. There is a correspondence between these placeholders and PHP variables that have the same name as the placeholder text. Themes that make use of this templating process more or less replace any text beginning with $ in the template by the value of the corresponding PHP variable.

This means that you can make use of variables from PHP-Nuke itself in your themes; these could be the name of your site ($sitename), your site slogan, or even information about the user. In fact, you can add your own PHP code to create a new variable, which you can then display from within one of the templates.

To complete the discussion, we will look at how the templates are processed in PHP-Nuke. The code below is a snippet from one of the themeheader() function in the theme.php file. This particular snippet is taken from the 3D-Fantasy theme.

```
function themeheader()
{
    global $user, $banners, $sitename, $slogan, $cookie, $prefix,
        $anonymous, $db;
    ... code continues ....

    $tmpl_file = "themes/3D-Fantasy/header.html";
    $thefile = implode("", file($tmpl_file));
    $thefile = addslashes($thefile);
    $thefile = "\$r_file=\"".$thefile."\";";
    eval($thefile);
    print $r_file;
    ... code continues ....
```

The processing starts with the line where the $tmpl_file variable is defined. This variable is set to the file name of the template to be processed, in this case header.html. The next line grabs the content of the file as a string. Let's suppose the header.html file contained the text You're welcomed to $sitename, thanks for coming!. Then, continuing in the code above, the $thefile variable would eventually hold this:

```
\$r_file = \" You\'re welcomed to $sitename, thanks for coming!\";
```

This looks very much like a PHP statement, and that is exactly what PHP-Nuke is attempting to create. The eval() function executes the statement; it defines the variable $r_file as above. This is equivalent to putting this line straight into the code:

```
$r_file = " You\'re welcomed to $sitename, thanks for coming!";
```

If this line were in the PHP code, the value of the $sitename variable will be inserted into the string, and this is exactly how the placeholders in the templates are replaced with the values of the corresponding PHP variables.

This means that the placeholders in templates can only use variables accessible at the point in the code where the template is processed with the eval() function. This means any parameters passed to the function at the time—global variables that have been announced with the global statement or any variables local to the function that have been defined before the line with the eval() function. This does mean that you will have to study the function processing the template to see what variables are available. In the examples in this chapter we'll look at the most relevant variables.

The templates do not allow for any form of 'computation' within them; you cannot use loops or call PHP functions. You do your computations 'outside' the template in the theme.php file, and the results are 'pulled' into the template and displayed from there.

Now that we're familiar with what we're going to be working with, let's get started.

Changing the Page Header

The first port of call will be creating a new version of the page header. We will make these customizations:

- Changing the site logo graphic
- Changing the layout of the page header
- Adding a welcome message to the user, and displaying the user's avatar
- Adding a drop-down list of topics to the header
- Creating a navigation bar

Time For Action—Changing the Site Logo Graphic

1. Grab the logo.gif file from the SiteImages folder in the code download.
2. Copy it to the themes/TheDinosaurPortal/images folder, overwriting the existing logo.gif file.
3. Refresh the page in your browser. The logo will have changed!

What Just Happened?

The logo.gif file in the images folder is the site logo. We replaced it with a new banner, and immediately the change came into effect.

Time For Action—Changing the Site Header Layout

1. In the theme folder is a file called header.html. Open up this file in a text editor, we'll use Wordpad.
2. Replace all the code in this file with the following:

```
<!-- Time For Action-Changing the Site Header Layout -->
<table border="0" cellspacing="0" cellpadding="6" width="100%"
       bgcolor="#FFCC33">
 <tr valign="middle">
  <td width="60%" align="right" rowspan="2">
  <a href="index.php"><img src="themes/$GLOBALS[ThemeSel]/images/logo.gif"
                     border="1" alt="Welcome to $sitename">
  </a></td>
```

```
        <td width="40%" colspan="2">
          <p align="center"><b>WELCOME TO $sitename!</b></td>
      </tr>
      <tr>
          <td width="20%">GAP</td>
          <td width="20%">GAP</td>
      </tr>
    </table>
    <!-- End of Time for Action -->
    $public_msg<br>
    <table cellpadding="0" cellspacing="0" width="99%" border="0"
          align="center" bgcolor="#ffffff">
    <tr><td bgcolor="#ffffff" valign="top">
```

3. Save the `header.html` file.

4. Refresh your browser. The site header now looks like this:

What Just Happened?

The `header.html` file is the template responsible for formatting the site header. Changing this file will change the format of your site header.

We simply created a table that displays the site logo in the left-hand column, a welcome message in the right-hand column, and under that, two GAPs that we will add more to in a moment. We set the background color of the table to an orange color (#FFCC33). We used the `$sitename` placeholder to display the name of the site from the template.

Note that everything after the line:

```
<!-- End of Time for Action -->
```

in our new `header.html` file is from the original file. (The `<!-- ... -->` characters here denote an HTML comment that is not displayed in the browser). This is because the end of the `header.html` file starts a new table that will continue in other templates. If we had removed these lines, the page output would have been broken.

There was another interesting thing we used in the template, the `$GLOBALS[ThemeSel]` placeholder:

```
<a href="index.php"><img src="themes/$GLOBALS[ThemeSel]/images/logo.gif"
```

`ThemeSel` is a global variable that holds the name of the current theme—it's either the default site theme or the user's chosen theme. Although it's a global variable, using just `$ThemeSel` in the template would give a blank, this is because it has not been declared as global by the function in PHP-Nuke that consumes the `header.html` template. However, all the global variables can be accessed through the `$GLOBALS` array, and using `$GLOBALS[ThemeSel]` accesses this particular global variable. Note that this syntax is different from the way you may usually access elements of the `$GLOBALS` array in PHP. You might use `$GLOBALS['ThemeSel']` or `$GLOBALS["ThemeSel"]`. Neither of these work in the template so we have to use the form without the ' or ".

Time For Action—Fixing and Adding the Topics List

Next we'll add the list of topics as a drop-down box to the page header. The visitor will be able to select one of the topics from the box, and then the list of stories from that topic will be displayed to them through the News module. Also, the current topic will be selected in the drop-down box to avoid confusion.

This task involves fixing some bugs in the current version of the 3D-Fantasy theme.

1. First of all, open the `theme.php` file and find the following line in the `themeheader()` function definition:

   ```
   $topics_list = "<select name=\"topic\" onChange='submit()'>\n";
   ```

2. Replace this line with these two lines:

   ```
   global $new_topic;
   $topics_list = "<select name=\"new_topic\" onChange='submit()'>\n";
   ```

3. If you move a few lines down in the `themeheader()` function, you will find this line:

   ```
   if ($topicid==$topic) { $sel = "selected "; }
   ```

4. Replace $topic with $new_topic in this line to get:

   ```
   if ($topicid==$new_topic) { $sel = "selected "; }
   ```

5. Save the `theme.php` file.

6. Open the `header.html` file in your text editor, and where the second GAP is, make the modifications as shown below:

   ```
   <td width="20%">GAP</td>
     <td width="20%"><form action="modules.php?name=News&new_topic"
     method="post">
     Select a Topic:<br>$topics_list</select></form></td>
   </tr>
   </table>
   <!-- End of Time for Action -->
   ```

7. Save the `header.html` file.

8. Refresh your browser. You will see the new drop-down box in your page header:

What just Happened?

The `themeheader()` function is the function in `theme.php` responsible for processing the `header.html` template, and outputting the page header.

The `$topics_list` variable has already been created for us in the `themeheader()` function, and can be used from the `header.html` template. It is a string of HTML that defines an HTML `select` drop-down list consisting of the topic titles.

However, the first few steps require us to make a change to the $topics_list variable, correcting the name of the select element and also using the correct variable to ensure the current topic (if any) is selected in the drop-down box. The select element needs to have the name of new_topic, so that the News module is able to identify which topic we're after.

This is all done with the changes to the theme.php file. First, we add the global statement to access the $new_topic variable, before correcting the name of the select element:

```
global $new_topic;
$topics_list = "<select name=\"new_topic\" onChange='submit()'>\n";
```

The next change we made is to make sure we are looking for the $new_topic variable, not the $topic variable, which isn't even defined:

```
if ($topicid==$new_topic) { $sel = "selected "; }
```

Now the $topics_list variable is corrected, all we have to do is add a placeholder for this variable to the header.html template, and some more HTML around it. We added the placeholder for $topics_list to display the drop-down list, and a message to go with it encouraging the reader to select a topic into one of the GAP table cells we created in the new-look header.

The list of topics will be contained in a form tag, and when the user selects a topic, the form will be posted back to the server to the News module, and the stories in the selected topic will be displayed. (The extra HTML that handles submitting the form is contained with the $topics_list variable.)

```
<form action="modules.php?name=News" method="post">
Select a Topic:<br>$topics_list
```

All that remains now is to close the select tag—the tag was opened in the $topics_list variable but not closed—and then close the form tag:

```
</select></form>
```

When the page is displayed, this is the HTML that PHP-Nuke produces for the topics drop-down list:

```
<form action="modules.php?name=News&new_topic" method="post">
Select a Topic:<br><select name="topic" onChange='submit()'>
<option value="">All Topics</option>
<option  value="1">The Dinosaur Portal</option>
<option  value="2">Dinosuar Hunting</option>
</select></form>
```

Time For Action—Adding a Welcome Message to the User

We will add some more information the page header; a friendly message to salute our visitors:

1. Open the theme.php file in your text editor, and inside the themeheader() function definition, find the following line:

    ```
    $theuser = "  Welcome $username!";
    ```

2. Change that line to the following:

    ```
    $theuser = "  Hi $username!, how you doing?";
    ```

3. Save the theme.php file.

4. Open the header.html file, and modify the remaining GAP as shown below:

    ```
    <td width="20%">$theuser</td>
        <td width="20%"><form action="modules.php?name=News"
    ```

```
                                method="post">
Select a Topic:<br>$topics_list</select></form></td>
</tr></table>
</div>
    <!-- End of Time for Action -->
```

5. Save the `header.html` file.

6. Refresh the browser. A polite welcome is displayed to the user:

What Just Happened?

The `$theuser` variable already contained a message of the form Welcome <username>! However, we wanted a friendlier greeting, so we edited the definition of the `$theuser` variable in `theme.php`. The `$username` variable, used to define `$theuser`, holds the name of the user, and had been set up earlier in the `themeheader()` function definition.

After that was done, all we had to do was add a placeholder for the `$theuser` variable into our template, and we were away.

The introductory Hi was added to the `$theuser` string because if the user is not logged in, a link to Create an Account is displayed instead. If we had put Hi in the template instead of the variable, it would say Hi Create An Account to a new visitor, which could be rather confusing.

Time For Action—Adding the User Avatar

We've said hello to our user, now let's show the user their face—well, their avatar at least. We will display their avatar underneath the welcome message:

1. In the `theme.php` file, add the following code immediately after the line we just modified (shown highlighted—it's in the `themeheader()` function definition if you have lost track):

```
$theuser = "Hi $username!, how you doing?";
$profile = getusrinfo($user);
$avatar = $profile['user_avatar'];
if ($avatar)
{
    $theuser .= "<br><center>
            <img src=\"modules/Forums/images/avatars/$avatar\"
        alt=\"Your Face!\"></center>\n";
}
```

2. Save the `theme.php` file.

3. Refresh your browser to see the avatar.

What Just Happened?

Extended information about the user is obtained through a call to the `getusrinfo()` function, passing in the `$user` variable. The `$user` global variable holds a limited amount of information about the user, including the username and password, which is used to identify the user and retrieve their profile. This is all done in the `getusrinfo()` function in the `mainfile.php` file. This function returns an array of data to us, which we store in an array we call `$profile`.

The exciting bit of data for us is the avatar entry in our `$profile` array (accessed through `$profile['avatar']`). This contains the filename of the user avatar image, and all we have to do is add the path to the avatar images in the Forums module and we have a picture.

If the user isn't logged in, this bit of code won't even be executed, so there is no need to worry about not finding an avatar image for a non-existent user.

Time For Action—Adding a Horizontal Navigation Bar

Now we'll take the first steps towards adding a horizontal navigation bar. These first steps will not produce a very exciting result; we will put the finishing touches to this when we use CSS in the next section.

1. Open the `header.html` file, and add the highlighted code as shown below:

    ```
    Select a Topic:<br>$topics_list</select></form></td>
    </tr>
    <tr>
        <td colspan="3" >
        <div id="navBar">
          <a href="index.php">Home</a>
          <a href="modules.php?name=Downloads">Downloads</a>
          <a href="modules.php?name=Encyclopedia">Encyclopedia</a>
          <a href="modules.php?name=Your_Account">Your Account</a>
          <a href="modules.php?name=Submit_News">Submit News</a>
        </div>
        </td>
    </tr>
    </table>
    <!-- End of Time for Action -->
    ```

2. Save the file.

3. Refresh your browser, and your navigation bar will be there:

    Home Downloads Encyclopedia Your Account Submit News

What Just Happened?

All that we did here was to insert an extra row into the page header table, and then add a couple of links to that row. We had to set the `colspan` for the `td` element to 3, since there are three columns in the table, and our row was to have only one column that spans the entire width of the table.

Time For Action—Changing Some Background Colors

There are a couple of global variables defined by the theme that can be used by various modules of PHP-Nuke. Two of these are `$bgcolor1` and `$bgcolor2`. These define background colors, and are used, for example, by the comments navigation bar:

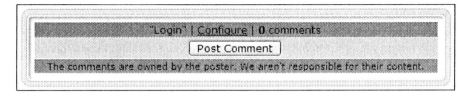

1. Open the theme.php file in your text editor.

2. Find the definition of the $bgcolor1 and $bgcolor2 variables:

```
$bgcolor1 = "#d5d5d5";
$bgcolor2 = "#7b91ac";
```

3. Change them to the following:

```
$bgcolor1 = "#FFCC33";
$bgcolor2 = "#FFCC99";
```

4. Save the theme.php file.

Now view one of the stories on your site, and have a look at the comments navigation bar; the dark and light shades of blue have been replaced by dark and light shades of orange:

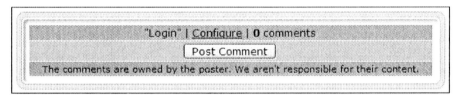

What Just Happened?

We set new values for the $bgcolor1 and $bgcolor2 global variables. We set $bgcolor2 to a dark orange and $bgcolor1 to a lighter orange. After making the change, we had a look at the comments navigation bar, which is one place where these background colors are actually used. These variables are also used in the Downloads, News, Statistics, and Web Links modules among others, and are used to control the 'shading' or background color of a number of elements.

Working with the Stylesheet

Now it's time to start making changes to the theme's Cascading Style Sheet (CSS) file, the stylesheet. Using the stylesheet will allow us to move formatting details out of the theme's HTML templates (and PHP code).

However, to prepare the way for using the stylesheet we will sometimes find ourselves having to remove some hardcoded HTML attributes from the templates (or PHP code). We will need to do this because these HTML attributes will override our settings in the CSS file, and our changes to the stylesheet won't be seen. We will also find that, as we move the formatting from the templates and PHP code into the stylesheet, we get greater control over the formatting of our elements. As we make further customizations to our theme in this chapter, we will move the formatting responsibility to the stylesheet and out of the templates.

Time For Action—Background Image with Style

The first thing we're going to do is set the background image of the page from the CSS file.

1. Grab the `background.jpg` file from the `siteImages` folder in the code download, and copy it to the `themes/TheDinosaurPortal/images` folder.

2. Open the `theme.php` file in your text editor.

3. Inside the `themeheader()` function definition, find the following line:

```
echo "<body bgcolor=\"#ffffff\" text=\"#000000\" link=\"#363636\"
      vlink=\"#363636\" alink=\"#d5ae83\"><br>\n\n\n";
```

4. Remove all the attributes after <body, and then remove the <br>, to produce the following:

```
echo "<body>\n\n\n";
```

5. Save the file.

6. In the `style` folder of the theme you will find the `style.css` file; open this file in your text editor.

7. Delete the following line:

```
BODY        {FONT-FAMILY: Verdana,Helvetica; FONT-SIZE: 10px}
```

8. Move your cursor to the end of this file (you may have to move to the right-hand end of the last line in the file and press *Enter* to create a new line).

9. Enter the following into the file:

```
body {
   color:#000000;
   background-image:  url(../images/background.jpg);
   font-family: arial, helvetica, sans-serif;
   font-size: 1em;
   }
```

10. Save the `style.css` file.

11. Refresh your browser—nothing should have changed!

What Just Happened?

The first three steps were preparing the way for using CSS—we removed the hardcoded HTML attributes from the body tag. We could have set the background image from the line in the `themeheader()` function with the background attribute of the body tag, but controlling the format of the body tag from the stylesheet will offer us greater flexibility.

Every theme has its own stylesheet, `style.css`, located in the `style` subfolder of its folder. To add any CSS information, we make changes there. That's what the remainder of the steps do.

Once we are in `style.css`, we remove the existing style information for the body tag (step 4). This leaves us a clean slate for creating new style information for this tag.

The new style information—known as properties in CSS parlance—is added in step 9. First of all, we added properties for the body tag:

```
body {
  color:#000000;
  background-image:  url(../images/background.jpg);
  font-family: arial, helvetica, sans-serif;
  font-size: 1em;
  }
```

The `color` property specifies the color of the text used in the body of the document—here we've gone for black (#000000). The `background-image` property specifies the image used for the body background. The `font-family` and `font-size` properties are simple enough. The font-size has been specified using the em units, setting the font-size in relative units.

The path to the `background-image` property is interesting:

```
url(../images/background.jpg)
```

This path is *relative to the stylesheet*, unlike the path to images used from the templates in the theme, which are relative to the root of our PHP-Nuke installation (like `/themes/TheDinosaurPortal/images/logo.gif` for example).

To get from the stylesheet (in `TheDinosaurPortal/style/style.css`) you have to go up a folder (`../`) bringing you to the `TheDinosuarPortal` folder, and then into the `images` folder. Specifying background images using CSS in this way means that you bypass the need for including the name of the theme.

When you view the new page, you will see that much of our background image is obscured by large blocks of white on the page. We need to look into the `header.html` to find what is responsible for this. In the last few lines of the `header.html` file you will find:

```
<table cellpadding="0" cellspacing="0" width="99%" border="0"
       align="center"
       bgcolor="#ffffff">
<tr><td bgcolor="#ffffff" valign="top">
```

We need to remove the two bgcolor="#fffff" instances to get:

```
<table cellpadding="0" cellspacing="0" width="99%" border="0"
       align="center" >
<tr><td  valign="top">
```

Then we can resave the `header.html` file. When you refresh your browser, the background image should be more clearly visible. The bgcolor="#ffffff" attributes we just removed were setting the background color of the main part of the page to white. The table starting at the end of `header.html` contains the block and module output, and the background image was being hidden by the white background color of this table, which will fill up most of the page when the page is finished.

Time For Action—Changing the Links

In the last task we also removed the definitions for displaying links from the body tag. Now we will add these to the stylesheet:

1. Open the `style.css` file in your text editor.

2. Delete the following four lines (only the first line is shown in full, the other lines contain the same text between the braces):

222

```
A:link          {BACKGROUND: none; COLOR: #000000; FONT-SIZE: 11px; FONT-
FAMILY: Verdana, Helvetica; TEXT-DECORATION: underline}
A:active        {...}
A:visited       {...}
A:hover         {...}
```

3. Move your cursor to the end of this file, and add these lines:

    ```
    a {text-decoration:none; color:red; font-weight:bold;}
    ```

4. Save the `style.css` file, and refresh your browser.

What Just Happened?

We specified a new definition for links in the CSS stylesheet. We removed the line under the link with the `text-decoration:none` setting, and set the color of a link to red, and made it bold.

Note that we removed four link definitions and replaced them with one. The color of a standard link is defined by `a:link`, and `a:visited` takes care of links that have been visited. The behavior of a link as you click on it is determined by `a:active`. These settings correspond to the values of the `link`, `alink`, and `vlink` HTML attributes we removed from the body tag in `theme.php`.

The `a:hover` definition comes into play when you move your mouse cursor over a link and takes care of that link's format. We will make use of that in a moment. For our settings here, we have simply set all links to look the same—using a in the stylesheet rather than `a:link`, `a:active`, and so on, means the definition will apply to all links, regardless of whether the visitor is hovering their mouse cursor over the link, or if they have already clicked on that link.

Time For Action—Changing the OpenTable() Function

The `OpenTable()` and `CloseTable()` functions defined in `tables.php` are used to enclose elements on the page, and they are used throughout PHP-Nuke.

1. In the `TheDinosaurPortal` folder is a file called `tables.php`. Open it in your text editor.

2. Select all the text in this file and delete it.

3. Add the following text to this file:

    ```php
    <?php
    function OpenTable()
    {
       echo "\n<table class=\"openTable\"
                    cellspacing=\"0\" cellpadding=\"0\" width=\"100%\">
             <tr>
               <td>";
    }

    function CloseTable()
    {
       echo "\n</td>
           </tr></table>
           <br>";
    }

    function OpenTable2()
    {
       echo "\n<table class=\"openTable\"
                    cellspacing=\"0\" cellpadding=\"0\" width=\"100%\">
             <tr>
               <td>";
    }
    ```

```
function CloseTable2()
{
  echo "\n</td>
      </tr></table>
      <br>";
}
?>
```

4. Save the `tables.php` file.

5. Open the `style.css` file and add the following to the end of the file:

```
table.openTable {
   border:1px black solid;
   background-color:white;
   padding-top:8px;padding-bottom:8px;
   padding-left:4px;padding-right:4px;
   }
```

6. Save the `style.css` file, view the homepage of your site, and have a look at the message at the top of the middle column:

Welcome to theDinosaurPortal

Welcome to **theDinosaurPortal**. This site is founded on the premise that...

Just because you haven't seen a dinosaur, doesn't mean they've all died out....

What Just Happened?

The `OpenTable()` and `CloseTable()` functions are used throughout PHP-Nuke to define how elements in the main body of the page are enclosed. The `OpenTable()` function starts the element, usually a table, and the `CloseTable()` function finishes it. For our example here, we simply removed all the existing code and started from scratch with the definitions; all we had to do was to define these functions, as well as `OpenTable2()` and `CloseTable2()`, which are used less frequently but still need a definition. Note that we have just used the same code for the definition of this pair of functions as we did for the first pair.

`OpenTable()` starts a new table. This table only needs one column because of its simple design; the table will just hold content; it won't do anything fancy since we already have enough striking elements on our page.

```
function OpenTable()
{
    echo "\n<table class=\"openTable\"
                   cellspacing=\"0\" cellpadding=\"0\" width=\"100%\">
               <tr>
                 <td>";
}
```

We mark the table with the `openTable` class, which we will define in the stylesheet, so we can basically forget about these functions now. We begin the output with a newline \n character, to aid readability of the HTML source.

The `CloseTable()` function is simple—all it has to do is close the single `td` element, and then close off the table:

```
function CloseTable()
{
    echo "\n</td>
            </tr></table>
            <br>";
}
```

The final step is to create the `openTable` class in the stylesheet:

```
table.openTable {
    border:1px black solid;
    background-color:white;
    padding-top:8px;padding-bottom:8px;
    padding-left:4px;padding-right:4px;
}
```

We specified a thin border for the table, (a one-pixel solid-black border), some padding to move the text away from the edge of the table, and a background color of white for the element. Note that specifying the border like this in the stylesheet, rather than using the `border` attribute of the `table` tag, gives us a border only around the outside of the table, rather than borders around the cells of the table.

Time For Action—Styling the Navigation Bar

Now we can make our navigation bar actually look good. So far, it just looks like a group of links. A few additions to the stylesheet and it will be transformed.

1. Open the `style.css` file in your text editor.

2. Add the following to the end of the file:

```
div#navBar {
    text-align:center; margin:4px;
    font-family:Arial; font-weight:bold;
}

div#navBar a {
    color:#000000;
    padding: 5px 4px 5px 5px;
    border: 2px solid #808080;
    background: #cccccc;
    text-decoration: none;
}

div#navBar  a:hover {
    border-color: #000000;
    color: #ffffff;
    background: #336699;
}
```

3. Save the file, and refresh your browser. The image below shows the mouse being hovered over the Encyclopedia link:

4. Open the `header.html` file in your text editor, and make the highlighted change shown below:

```
<td colspan="3"
    class="navBarRow">
<div id="navBar">
```

5. Save the `header.html` file, open the `style.css` file again, and add this to the end:

```
td.navBarRow {
   padding: 6px;
   background-color: #2F5376;
   color: #FFFFFF;
   font-size:14pt;
   font-weight:bold;
   font-family:arial, helvetica, sans-serif;
   margin-left:8px;
   margin-right:8px;
   line-height: 1.5em;
   }
```

6. Save the file and refresh your browser.

What Just Happened?

You may recall that when we created the navigation bar, it was wrapped in a `div` element with an `id` attribute:

```
<div id="navBar">
```

We can use the `id` of the element so that styles can be applied only to things within it:

```
div#navBar {
   text-align:center; margin:4px;
   font-family:Arial; font-weight:bold;
   }
```

The `div#navbar` syntax means the definition that follows will only be applied to the `div` element with the `id` navbar. We do this to center its contents (with `text-align:center`), set a margin, and define the font.

However, we can continue this syntax to define the style for links contained in the `div` element:

```
div#navBar a {
   color:#000000;
   padding: 5px 4px 5px 5px;
   border: 2px solid #808080;
   background: #cccccc;
   text-decoration: none;
   }
```

This sets the style for a link in our navbar div element. We define the color of the text (black), some padding around the text, a background color (#cccccc, a pale grey), and remove the underlining of links with text-decoration:none;. The other thing we do is set the border for each link. The border is 2 pixel wide, a solid line, and colored #808080, which is a darker grey. This is what gives each link its own little box.

The next definition, div#navBar a:hover, allows the links to behave differently when the mouse cursor hovers over them. This removes the need for any kind of onMouseOver JavaScript to produce 'roll-over' effects; the stylesheet now takes care of this.

```
div#navBar  a:hover {
   border-color: #000000;
   color: #ffffff;
   background: #336699;
   }
```

Here the definition changes the background colors, text color, and the border color. All the other settings defined by div#navbar a will be 'inherited', so there is no need to specify these settings again.

The final steps added a class attribute to the table column holding the navigation bar, and in the style.css file we set the definition for this class. We added some padding and margins to give the bar some spacing, and set the background color to a dark-blue color (#2F5376).

Changing Blocks

Our next area of customization will be blocks. We will create new blocks in a moment, but first of all we will do some quick customizations to put greater control of the display of blocks into the hands of the theme.

Time For Action—Show Right-Hand Blocks on All Pages

You will notice that the right-hand blocks are not displayed for all modules; they are displayed on the homepage, and also for some modules such as Downloads. Our next change will be to make the right-hand blocks appear on every page, for every module.

1. Open the theme.php file in your text editor.

2. Find the themefooter() function definition, and locate the following lines within that piece of code:

   ```
   if (defined('INDEX_FILE'))
   {
   ```

3. Change the first line as shown below:

   ```
   //if (defined('INDEX_FILE'))
   {
   ```

4. Save the file.

5. Now open up any module, and your right-hand blocks will be there.

What Just Happened?

The variable INDEX_FILE is set by certain modules when the 'front page' of that module is displayed. The front page is the page displayed when there is no file value in the query string of the URL. On all other pages, INDEX_FILE is not set.

The change we made in the code comments out a check for this value being set. Only if the check is true will the next section of code execute. That section of code is shown below—you will see it contains a call to blocks("right"). This is the function call for displaying the right-hand blocks.

```
if (defined('INDEX_FILE'))
{
    $tmpl_file = "themes/TheDinosaurPortal/center_right.html";
    $thefile = implode("", file($tmpl_file));
    $thefile = addslashes($thefile);
    $thefile = "\$r_file=\"".$thefile."\";";
    eval($thefile);
    print $r_file;
    blocks("right");
}
```

Since we comment out the check to see if the INDEX_FILE constant is defined, the code enclosed by the braces ({ and }) will always execute, and the blocks will always be displayed.

Time For Action—Hide Right-Hand Blocks For Certain Modules

Now we've got the right-hand blocks on every page. This can be a bit much—the presence of the right-hand blocks can make the page feel rather 'heavy'.

Next we are going to see how to turn off the right-hand blocks for certain modules. For our example, we'll turn off the blocks for the Downloads, Feedback, and Search modules.

1. Open the theme.php file in your text editor.

2. Add the highlighted lines of code to the top of the file after the color definitions:

```
$textcolor2 = "#000000";
global $packt_hideRightBlocks;
$packt_hideRightBlocks = array('Downloads'=>1,'Feedback'=>1,
                               'Search'=>1);
if(file_exists("themes/TheDinosaurPortal/tables.php")){
```

3. Find the line we commented out in the previous task in the themefooter() function definition.

4. Add the following two lines of code between the commented line and the brace:

```
// if (defined('INDEX_FILE'))
global $packt_hideRightBlocks, $module_name;
if (!$packt_hideRightBlocks[$module_name])
{
```

5. Save the theme.php file.

6. In your browser, check that the right-hand blocks are displayed on the homepage and on the Topics module page, but not on the Downloads, Search, and Feedback pages.

What Just Happened?

We created a global variable, $packt_hideRightBlocks at the top of the theme.php file. This variable is an array, and contains entries for the names of the modules that we will hide the right-hand blocks for. If we want the right-hand blocks shown for a particular module, we do not include it in the array.

We added the prefix packt_ to the variable name in order to avoid potential clashes with other global variables. The definition of the array shows we want to hide the right-hand blocks for the Downloads, Feedback, and Search modules.

Note that we had to put a global prefix before the definition of the $packt_hideRightBlocks statement to declare it as a global variable. We had to explicitly declare this variable as global because otherwise the variable will be scoped to the function that included the theme.php file, and this is the head() function in the header.php file. (This file is in the root of the PHP-Nuke installation, and is not part of a theme.) We'll talk more about this file later.

The idea now is simple—we need to get the name of the current module, and then see if there is an entry for that in our array. If there is, we won't display the right-hand blocks.

We are able to add code to the themefooter() function at just the point we were working with in the previous task. First we add the global statement, to access the $packt_hideRightBlocks and $module_name global variables from our function. The $module_name global variable is defined by the 'core' of PHP-Nuke, and contains the name of the current module.

Next we check if there is an entry in the $packt_hideRightBlocks array with the name of $module_name.

```
if (!$packt_hideRightBlocks[$module_name])
```

In fact, the code actually checks that there isn't such an entry—the ! character in front of the check means 'not'. If there is no such entry, then the code to display the right-hand blocks will be executed. Thus only a module whose name is not in the $packt_hideRightBlocks array will have right-hand blocks displayed.

- If you want to turn off this feature, and have all the right-hand blocks displayed for all modules, simply comment out the if statement line.

- If you want to use this feature to only show blocks for certain specified modules, change the check to the following:

```
if ($packt_hideRightBlocks[$module_name])
```

Now the right-hand blocks will only be shown for modules whose name is in the $packt_hideRightBlocks array.

It is also very easy to apply this method to handle the left-hand blocks. All you'd need is to set up an array called $packt_hideLeftBlocks, similar to our $packt_hideRightBlocks array, and then apply the same code to themeheader() function before the blocks("left") function call. Make sure you have some alternative form of navigation if you turn off the left-hand blocks—you could well have removed the Modules menu block!

Time For Action—Making the Block Titles Uppercase

Let's continue tweaking the block display:

1. Open the `theme.php` file in your text editor, and find the `themesidebox()` function definition.

2. Add the highlighted line immediately after the first line of the function definition:

    ```
    function themesidebox($title, $content) {
        $title = strtoupper($title);
    ```

3. Save the `theme.php` file.

4. Refresh your browser, and you will note your block titles are now in uppercase.

What Just Happened?

The `themesidebox()` function controls the display of blocks. It simply grabs the `blocks.html` template, processes it, and spits out the result, producing a block. This function is called whenever any part of the application wants a block drawn.

The block title is held in the `$title` variable, and all we did was use the PHP `strtoupper()` function to convert the current title into uppercase. After that, the block display carries on as usual.

Time For Action—Creating a New Block

Now we've got blocks all over our page—but they're not 'our' blocks. Well, not yet. Our next job is to create a new block design. Now we will really feel that we are stamping our identity on our site.

1. You will need to grab the `blockTop.gif`, `blockBottom.gif`, and `blockBackground.gif` files from the `SiteImages` folder in the code download and copy them to the `images` folder in the `TheDinosaurPortal` folder.

2. In the theme folder, you will find the `blocks.html` file. Open it in your text editor.

3. Delete the existing code, and enter this new code:

    ```html
    <table width="176px" cellspacing=0>
        <tr height="28">
            <td background="themes/TheDinosaurPortal/images/blockTop.gif">
            </td>
        </tr>
        <tr>
            <td background="themes/TheDinosaurPortal/images/blockBackground.gif">
                <div class="blockTitle">$title</div>
            </td>
        </tr>
        <tr>
            <td background="themes/TheDinosaurPortal/images/blockBackground.gif">
                <div class="blockContent">$content</div>
            </td>
        </tr>
        <tr height="28">
            <td background="themes/TheDinosaurPortal/images/blockBottom.gif">
            </td>
        </tr>
    </table>
    <br>
    ```

4. Save the `blocks.html` file, and refresh your browser. The blocks should have changed:

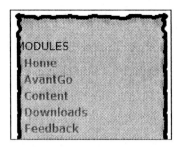

5. Now open the `style.css` file in your text editor.

6. Add the following style definitions to the end of the file:

```
div.blockContent {
  margin-left:8px; margin-right:8px;
  padding-bottom:8px; padding-top:8px;
  padding-left:0px; padding-right:0px;
}

div.blockTitle {
  background: #ffffff;
  margin-left:8px; margin-right:8px;
  color:black;
  padding-top:2px; padding-bottom:2px;
  font-size:1.2em; font-weight:bold;
  font-family:arial, verdana;
  text-align:center;
}
```

7. Save the `style.css` file, and refresh your browser. You'll see this:

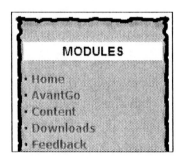

What Just Happened?

The `blocks.html` file is the template used for displaying blocks. It uses two placeholders, `$title` and `$content`, which contain the title and content of the block respectively.

Our block consists of a single HTML table, set to a width of 176 pixels:

```
<table width="176px" cellspacing=0>
```

The cellspacing is set to 0 so that all the rows are right next to each other, and no gaps appear between the rows.

The table consists of four rows, one row for the top (header) image of the block, one row for the block title, one for the block content, and one for the block footer image. Note that the image for the bottom row is the just a vertical flip of the top-row image.

The height of the top row is specified exactly as the height of its background image. This is to make sure that the entire background image is shown, since it must link up with the background image for the middle row.

```
<tr height="28">
  <td background="themes/TheDinosaurPortal/images/blockTop.gif" ></td>
</tr>
```

The next row shown displays the block title. This will be held in the $title placeholder. Note that we wrap the title in a div element with a class of blockTitle, so we can defer fine tuning of its look to the CSS file.

```
<tr>
  <td background="themes/TheDinosaurPortal/images/blockBackground.gif">
    <div class="blockTitle">$title</div>
  </td>
</tr>
```

The next row displays the block content. This will be held in the $content placeholder. Again, we wrap the content in a div to take care of the styling in the CSS file.

```
<tr>
  <td background="themes/TheDinosaurPortal/images/blockBackground.gif">
    <div class="blockContent">$content</div>
  </td>
</tr>
```

Finally, the block footer. This is constructed in the same way as the block header.

```
<tr height="28">
  <td background="themes/TheDinosaurPortal/images/blockBottom.gif"></td>
</tr>
</table>
```

The <br> at the end of the block adds a line break after the block, getting things ready for the next block to be displayed.

The styling for the block title and content is done in the style.css file. For the block content, we are only concerned with some spacing around the edges:

```
div.blockContent {
  margin-left:8x; margin-right:8px;
  padding-bottom:8px; padding-top:8px;
  padding-left:4px; padding-right:4px;
}
```

The left- and right-hand margins are set so as to ensure that the text is far enough from the edge of the image, and inside the thick black border of the block.

For the block title, we set its background color to white, and centered the text with the text-align property.

Time For Action—Making Right-Hand Blocks Different from Left-Hand Blocks

At the moment, a block is a block, wherever it is displayed. Here we'll show a simple way to choose a different template for the right-hand blocks, and so give you the opportunity to have the right-hand blocks look different from those on the left-hand side of the page.

For our example we will use the same template as the left-hand blocks, except our background images will be horizontal flips of the existing images.

1. Grab the files blockBottomRH.gif, blockTopRH.gif, and blockBackgroundRH.gif from the siteImages folder of the code download and copy them to the images folder of our theme.

2. Open the blocks.html file in your text editor, and replace the word blockBottom with blockBottomRH, replace blockTop with blockTopRH, and replace blockBackground with blockBackgroundRH.

3. Save the file as blocks_right.html in the folder of your theme.

4. Open the theme.php file in your text editor.

5. Add the highlighted lines to the top of your file:

```
define("BLOCKSIDE_LEFT", 0);
define("BLOCKSIDE_RIGHT", 1);
global $packt_blockSide;
$packt_blockSide = BLOCKSIDE_LEFT;
if(file_exists("themes/TheDinosaurPortal/tables.php")){
include("themes/TheDinosaurPortal/tables.php");
```

6. Go to the themesidebox() function definition.

7. Change the code as below:

```
function themesidebox($title, $content)
{
    $title = strtoupper($title);
    global $packt_blockSide;
    if ($packt_blockSide==BLOCKSIDE_RIGHT)
      $tmpl_file = "themes/TheDinosaurPortal/blocks_right.html";
    else
      $tmpl_file = "themes/TheDinosaurPortal/blocks.html";
```

8. In the themefooter() function, add the highlighted lines above the call to blocks("right"):

```
global $packt_blockSide;
$packt_blockSide = BLOCKSIDE_RIGHT;
blocks("right");
```

9. Save the theme.php file.

10. Refresh your browser, and compare a left-hand side block with a right-hand side block.

What Just Happened?

To make the left- and right-hand blocks different, first we had to define a new template for the right-hand block. We did this by editing the standard block template, blocks.html, and creating a new file, which we called blocks_right.html. The only difference between those two files is the different background images used; each image used for this block is simply a horizontal flip of the corresponding image for the block we created above.

With our new block template in place, we needed to create a mechanism for switching between left- and right-hand blocks. The global variable $packt_blockSide will be used to do this—a value of 0 means that left-hand block and a value of 1 means right-hand block. We defined two PHP constants, BLOCKSIDE_LEFT with the value 0 and BLOCKSIDE_RIGHT with the value 1:

```
define("BLOCKSIDE_LEFT", 0);
define("BLOCKSIDE_RIGHT", 1);
```

This was done for convenience—later in the file we will want to check the value of packt_blockSide, and rather than trying to remember if 0 means left or right, we can use the constants. Before that, we have to set the value of the $packt_blockSide variable:

```
global $packt_blockSide;
$packt_blockSide = BLOCKSIDE_LEFT;
```

Now we come to actual switching of the block templates. This goes on in the themesidebox() function:

```
if ($packt_blockSide==BLOCKSIDE_RIGHT)
   $tmpl_file = "themes/TheDinosaurPortal/blocks_right.html";
else
   $tmpl_file = "themes/TheDinosaurPortal/blocks.html";
```

If the $packt_blockSide variable is indicating a right-hand block, the right-hand block template is chosen, otherwise the standard block template is chosen. The template to be processed for the block is determined by the $tmpl_file variable, and simply switching its value like this means a different template will be used.

We're almost there—but we still haven't actually done anything to trigger the change in the $packt_blockSide variable, which will in turn lead to a different template. We'll do this in the themefooter() function. This function manages the display of the right-hand part of the page, including the right-hand blocks. On the line before the function call to display these blocks, we change the value of $packt_sideBlock:

```
global $packt_blockSide;
$packt_blockSide = BLOCKSIDE_RIGHT;
blocks("right");
```

Now the processing takes this form—the blocks() function will call the themesidebox() function to display each block. In the themesidebox() function the variable $packt_blockSide is checked, and if it has the value 1 (represented by the BLOCKSIDE_RIGHT constant) the right-hand block template is chosen, processed, and displayed.

We save the file, and we are ready to roll with our two types of blocks!

Changing Story Layout

In this section we will change the formatting of stories. First of all, we will change the format of the story summary that is displayed on the homepage. After that, we will change the format of the extended view of the story, which is viewed when clicking the Read More... link of the story summary.

Creating a Rounded Box

We're going to take a moment to cover a simple technique for producing a pretty cool effect—an HTML 'box' with rounded corners:

THIS IS WHERE THE CONTENT GOES!!!

This box can be used to house a block, but we will be using it to decorate the stories on the homepage of our site. We can even use only half of the box to easily create a rounded tab that could be used in a navigation bar!

The technique we will cover here is pretty simple; it will make use of some simple images, and some CSS properties to achieve the effect. You will find several CSS tutorials on the Web that also cover this topic, producing more robust and fancier effects.

The plan is very simple—we color in a table with a background color, and then we 'eat' chunks out of the four corners of the table, thus giving the rounded effect.

The chunks will be 'eaten' by using four tiny 'rounded' images, which we will create first. In fact, we will create only one image, and then through a combination of 'flips', proceed to produce all of the images we need.

Creating the Corner Images

The image below shows the 8x8 image we will use as our corner-removing chunk. It was originally created from cutting out the corner of a rounded box drawn in Photoshop. However, the image is small enough that you could create one like this pixel by pixel!

Since the picture we show here is in black and white, it is worth noting that the unshaded areas in the screenshot are actually the transparent areas of the image. The pixels shown in black in this picture will actually be white in the image.

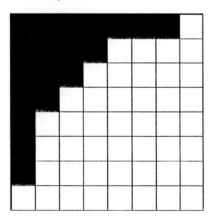

Now that we have our basic image, we ensure that the unshaded area is set to transparent, and save this file as corner-tl.gif in the images folder of our theme. You should refer to the documentation of your graphics package if you are unsure how to set part of an image as transparent.

We are now ready to generate the three other corner images:

1. Make sure that the corner-tl.gif file is open in your graphics package.
2. In your graphics package, flip the image horizontally to produce the top-right corner image. Save this image as corner-tr.gif in the images folder of the theme.
3. Now flip this image vertically to produce the bottom-right corner image. Save it as corner-br.gif in the images folder of the theme.
4. Finally, flip this image horizontally to produce the bottom-left corner image, and save it as corner-bl.gif in the images folder of the theme.

Stage one is complete; we have the four corner images.

Creating the HTML

The HTML is not complex, so we will create that next. The guts of this technique are contained in the CSS information, which we will move on to in a moment.

First of all, create a file called rounded_box.html in the theme folder, and enter the following:

```
<html>
<head>
  <link rel="stylesheet" href="style/style.css" type="text/css">
</head>
<body>
  <table class="roundedbox" cellspacing=0 cellpadding=0>
      <tr><td class="cornertl"></td><td></td><td class="cornertr"></td></tr>
      <tr><td></td><td >THIS IS WHERE THE CONTENT GOES!!!</td><td></td></tr>
      <tr><td class="cornerbl"></td><td></td><td class="cornerbr"></td></tr>
  </table>
</body>
</html>
```

The HTML is not complex as you can see. For the purposes of our example, we have added a reference to the theme stylesheet in the file with the <link> tag.

The rounded box consists of a table with three rows, with each row having three columns.

The table has a CSS class called roundedbox. We'll look at this in a moment when we tackle the CSS, but all this CSS class will do is set the background color of the table. This will fill in the entire table with a particular color. This sets us up to use our little images to eat the corner chunks out.

The first row in the table will be used for the top-left and top-right corners. The first column of this row is defined like this:

```
<td class="cornertl"></td>
```

The attribute class and the absence of anything else in the element means that all the work will be done by the CSS class cornertl, which we will see in a moment.

The third column in the first row is defined similarly:

```
<td class="cornertr"></td>
```

Another class is used here, and from its name, you can see that it will have something to do with the top-right corner. The middle column in the first column is left blank.

The second row is where the body of the box will go. The first column is left blank since that 'belongs' to the top-left and bottom-left corners. The third column is also left blank, since that belongs to the top-right and bottom-right corners. The middle column is where all the action takes place. We've just added some basic text for now.

The last row is similar to the first row, with a CSS class used in the first column and its last column:

```
<tr><td class="cornerbl"></td><td></td><td class="cornerbr"></td></tr>
```

The middle column is again left blank.

That's all there is to the block. This HTML does not look at all interesting at the moment; this shot of it in an HTML editor gives you a clearer picture of the layout of the table:

However, there is no sign of corners yet, nor any reference to any of the images we created earlier.

All will now be made clear.

Creating the CSS

The real magic of this technique happens in the CSS definitions. In the HTML we have used four classes, cornertl, cornertr, cornerbr, and cornerbl, and it is clear that in some way these are going to be used to display the images we created above. The answer is the set of CSS background properties. These allow you to control the background color of an element, set an image as the background, repeat a background image vertically or horizontally, or position the background image.

> You can read more about the background properties at http://www.w3schools.com/css/css_background.asp.

Open the style.css file in the styles folder of the theme, and add these lines to the bottom of the file:

```
td.cornertl {
    background-image: url('../images/corner-tl.gif');
    background-repeat: no-repeat;
    background-position: top left;
    width: 8px; height: 8px;
    }
```

This defines our CSS class cornertl. Let's walk through the properties that we have used.

First of all, the background image is set with the background-image property. We will use our top-left image for this background. (It is the image that has the top-left colored in, while the rest of the image is transparent.)

```
background-image: url('../images/corner-tl.gif');
```

This image should only be displayed once in this element—if this background image is shown over and over again then it will look rather strange (it will look like a collection of humps), so we use the `background-repeat` property to ensure that the image is displayed only once:

```
background-repeat: no-repeat;
```

The background-position property is used to position the image within the element, its value is obvious:

```
background-position: top left;
```

Finally, we set the width and height of the `td` element to ensure that it does not grow; this would become rather awkward for our design.

```
width: 8px; height: 8px;
```

All we have to do now is define `cornertr`, `cornerbr`, and `cornertl` similarly in the file. The definitions are very similar; we have highlighted the different lines:

```
td.cornertr {
  background-image: url('../images/corner-tr.gif');
  background-repeat: no-repeat;
  background-position: top right;
  width: 8px; height: 8px;
}

td.cornerbr{
  background-image: url('../images/corner-br.gif');
  background-repeat: no-repeat;
  background-position: bottom right;
  width: 8px; height: 8px;
}

td.cornerbl{
  background-image: url('../images/corner-bl.gif');
  background-repeat: no-repeat;
  background-position: bottom left;
  width: 8px; height: 8px;
}
```

For each class, we simply specify the corresponding corner image with the `background-image` property, and the background position with the `background-position` property. The value of the `background-position` could not be more intuitive!

The final stroke is to add the class to fill the table with a background color:

```
table.roundedbox { background: #cccccc; }
```

Now save the file and open the `rounded_box.html` file in your browser:

THIS IS WHERE THE CONTENT GOES!!!

This isn't particularly setting the world on fire, but let's apply the technique.

Time For Action—Change the Format of Stories on the Front Page

Changing the way a story is displayed on the front page of the site involves creating a new template. That's exactly what we'll do now.

1. Open the `story_home.html` file in your text editor, and delete all the text. Enter the following into the file:

```
<table class="storyBack" width="100%" cellspacing=0 cellpadding=0>
   <tr>
   <td class="cornertl"></td><td></td><td class="cornertr" width="10"></td>
   </tr>
   <tr>
   <td></td><td class="storyTitle">$title</td><td></td>
   </tr>
   <tr height=6><td colspan=3></td></tr>
   <tr>
    <td></td>
    <td>
      <table cellSpacing="0" cellPadding="4" border="0" width="100%">
        <tr>
          <td valign=top class="Normal" width="25%" bgcolor="#ff9933">
          <center><img src="$t_image" align="middle" border="1"></center></td>
          <td valign=top class="Normal" width="75%">$posted $content</td>
        </tr>
        <tr valign=top><td colspan="2" align="right"><hr>$morelink</td></tr>
      </table>
    </td>
    <td></td>
   </tr>
   <tr>
    <td class="cornerbl"></td><td></td>
    <td class="cornerbr" width="10"></td>
   </tr>
</table>
<br>
```

2. Save the file.

3. Open the `style.css` file in the `style` folder, and add the following at the end of the file:

```
table.storyBack {
   background: #ffcc33;
   }
.storyTitle {
   padding-left: 6px;   padding-right:6px;
   padding-top:6px;     padding-bottom:6px;
   background-color: #2F5376;
   color: #FFFFFF;
   font-size:14pt;      font-weight:bold;
   font-family:arial, helvetica, sans-serif;
   margin-left:8px;     margin-right:8px;
   line-height: 1.5em;
   }

.storyCat {
   color: #FFFFFF;
   font-size:14pt;
   font-weight:bold;
   font-family:arial, helvetica, sans-serif;
   }
```

4. Save the file.

5. Return to the homepage of your site. The stories will now look like this:

What Just Happened?

The story_home.html file is the template for stories displayed on the homepage. We removed all of the existing content and replaced it with our new definition. The story_home.html template is processed by the themeindex() function in theme.php, although we did not work with any of the code in this example.

The template we created is based around the HTML we put together in the previous section for the rounded box. We added two rows to that table:

```
<tr>
    <td></td><td class="storyTitle">$title</td><td></td>
</tr>
<tr height=6><td colspan=3></td></tr>
<tr>
```

The first row will display the story title through the $title placeholder, and the next row is to add a bit of space before the main part of the template. After that, we have an inner table, which is effectively placed where the THIS IS WHERE THE CONTENT GOES!!! text was in the example from the previous section.

The inner table has two columns, one for displaying the topic image and the other for showing the story text:

```
<table cellspacing="0" cellPadding="4" border="0" width="100%">
    <tr>
        <td valign=top class="Normal" width="25%" bgcolor="#ff9933">
        <center><img src="$t_image" align="middle" border="1"></center></td>
        <td valign=top class="Normal" width="75%">$posted $content</td>
    </tr>
    <tr valign=top><td colspan="2" align="right"><hr>$morelink</td></tr>
</table>
```

The $t_image placeholder is used to get the path to the topic image, and the $posted placeholder holds text about who posted the story, and when it was posted. The story text itself is contained in the $content placeholder.

The last line of the table outputs the navigation bar with the Read More... link, the number of comments, and so on. This is all contained in the $morelink placeholder.

After creating the template, we add some styles to the style.css file, storyBack, storyTitle, and storycat. The storycat style is not actually used in the template, it is already part of the $title placeholder. This style holds the definition for the category name that is displayed before the story title. The storyBack style sets the background color of the whole element. The storyTitle style is used to format the title bar, and we specify a dark blue background color (#2F5376), large white text, and plenty of space around the text with the padding settings.

Variables Available in Story Formatting

We saw a couple of the placeholders that can be used in formatting the story output. There are several others that can be used in the story_home.html template by default:

Placeholder	Description
$title	The title of the story.
$thetext	The short description of the story.
$aid	The name of the administrator who posted the story to the site.
$informant	The username of the story creator.
$datetime	The date the story was posted.
$posted	Uses $aid, $time, and $timezone to produce text of the form Posted on <time> <timezone> by <name of administrator>, and also mentions the number of times the story has been read (provided by $counter).
$content	The summary text ($thetext) of the story, prefixed by <name of the story creator> writes, and with any notes for the story attached on the end.
$t_image	The path to the topic image.
$topictext	The full title of the topic.
$counter	The number of times the story has been read.
$notes	Any notes added by the administrator when the story was posted. This is not a variable passed to the function, but can be accessed with a global statement.
$time	The time the story was posted. The variable $timezone contains the author's timezone.

Changing the Layout of the Story Extended View

To change the layout of a story's extended view, you change the story_page.html template. Our new story_page.html template is below, and it is similar to the story_home.html template. The main differences are shown highlighted:

```
<table class="storyBack" width="100%" cellspacing=0 cellpadding=0>
  <tr>
    <td class="cornertl"></td><td></td><td class="cornertr"
      width="10"></td>
  </tr>
  <tr>
    <td></td><td class="storyTitle">$title</td>
    <td></td>
  </tr>
```

```
      <tr height=6><td colspan=3></td></tr>
      <tr>
      <td></td>
      <td >
      <table class="openTable" width="100%">
        <tr><td> <span style="float:right;">
          <img src="$t_image" align="middle" border="1"
            alt="$topictext"></span>
            $content</td>
        </tr>
      </table>
      </td>
      <td></td>
      </tr>

      <tr>
        <td class="cornerbl"></td><td></td>
        <td class="cornerbr" width="10"></td>
      </tr>
    </table>
```

This time, we use `<span style="float:right;">` to have the topic image positioned on the right of the table, with the text flowing to the side of it.

The `story_page.html` template is processed by the `themearticle()` function in `theme.php`. This function has similar variables to those shown in the table for the `themeindex()` function, although in `themearticle()`, the `$thetext` variable actually contains the story introduction and the story extended text.

You will note that the same placeholder, `$content`, is used in both the `story_home.html` and `story_page.html` templates. In `story_home.html`, it holds the short description of the story, and in `story_page.html`, it holds the short description plus the extended text.

There are some lines in `themearticle()` that are worth noting, since they determine the whether the creator's name is added to the start of the story:

```
if ("$aid" == "$informant")
{
    $content = "$thetext$notes\n";
}
else
{
    if($informant != "")
    {
        $content = ".....";
    }
    else
    {
        $content = "$anonymous ";
    }
    $content .= ""._WRITES." <i>\"$thetext\"</i>$notes\n";
}
```

If the author who posted the story (`$aid`) is the same as the user who wrote the story (`$informant`), then the content of story is just the story description, story extended text, and any notes for the story. There is no mention of the story creator or who posted the story in the `$content` variable if the story creator is the same as the administrator who posted the story to the site.

If the story was written by someone other than the administrator, the content of the story becomes <username> writes, and then the story description, story extended text, and any notes for the story are enclosed in quotes and are put into italics. If the story was not submitted anonymously, a link to the Your Account details of the story creator is created for the user name. (We have replaced that part of the code with . . . . . for brevity here.)

If you want to change the way the extended text view of the story is displayed, going beyond what the template can do, these lines in themearticle() are a good place to start.

Changing the Footer

The footer is the last part of the theme. The footer template is the footer.html file, and we will create a new template for it, based on the table that we created for openTable(). Here is the new footer template:

```
</td></tr></table>
<br>
<center>
  <table class="openTable" cellspacing="0" cellpadding="0"
       width=\"50%\">
    <tr>
      <td align="center">$footer_message</td>
    </tr>
  </table>
<center>
```

The first line closes off the table that was started at the end of header.html; without it, our page would not look right. After that, we create a new table with the openTable class that we defined for the table in the openTable() function earlier. This table will be centered in the page, and have a width of 50% of the page:

There is only one placeholder in this template, $footer_message. This contains the copyright message, which must be displayed in order to comply with PHP-Nuke's license.

Our theme is complete!

Adding a Favicon

A Favicon is a small image displayed in the navigation bar of the browser, and also in the list of bookmarks:

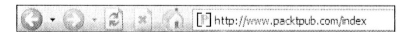

The Favicon is not something we can actually control with the theme, but it is the finishing touch for the site, and it does lead us into another interesting area of PHP-Nuke customization. Favicons behave rather strangely in Internet Explorer, and you will find that you need to add a site to your Favorites before the Favicon is displayed.

First of all, the Favicon is an image in a special format, ICO format. The file consists of a couple of copies of the same image at different sizes (16x16 and 32x32 usually). We will need to convert any standard graphical image we plan to use to this format before we continue.

You can download a free command-line tool to convert from PNG files to ICO files here:

```
http://www.winterdrache.de/freeware/png2ico/
```

There is an executable version of the application for Windows there, and instructions on how to use it. For other platforms you will have to compile the code yourself.

In the code download, there is a file called `favicon.ico` in the `SiteImages` folder that has already been converted. This should be copied to the `images` folder in the root of your PHP-Nuke installation.

All that remains now is to add a link to this file. This link is not something that is handled by the theme, since it goes between the <head> and </head> tags of the document, which are beyond the control of the theme.

What we need to do is open our text editor, and enter the following code into a blank document:

```php
<?php
echo "<link rel=\"SHORTCUT ICON\" href=\"images/favicon.ico?\">\n";
?>
```

The output of this file is the HTML required for the browser to download and display the Favicon. The location of the Favicon is indicated by the `href` attribute.

Save this file as `custom_head.php` in the folder `includes\custom_files` in the root of the PHP-Nuke installation.

Now when you refresh your browser, the Favicon will be displayed in the browser bar:

Including Custom Files

The `\includes\custom_files` folder can hold files with specific names that PHP-Nuke can process at various points. The advantage of this approach is that you can throw your code into the PHP-Nuke core 'mix' without having to hack its inner workings. This folder was new in PHP-Nuke 7.6. In earlier versions, you could use the `my_header.php` file in the `includes` folder to achieve similar results, but the `custom_files` folder in PHP-Nuke 7.6 introduced greater flexibility.

- Anything output from the `custom_head.php` file will be added between the <head> and </head> tag of the document.

- Anything output from a file called `custom_header.php` will be added to the output from the `header.php` file. This means it will be output after the </head> tag and before the theme kicks in. Similarly, anything output from the `custom_footer.php` file will be added to the output from the `footer.php` file.

- Any code in a file called `custom_mainfile.php` will be executed before any of the code in the `mainfile.php` file.

Page Output from Start to Finish

We've made many changes to customize a theme in this chapter, and now we are ready for a detailed overview of exactly how the theme controls the appearance of a page.

The theme doesn't start the page output. The page output process is started by the module that is currently in action at that point. Every part of every module that wants to display a standard page will have code like this:

```
include("header.php");
...
include("footer.php");
```

Page output actually starts in a function called header(), which is in the header.php file. The module won't call this function directly; within the header.php file is the call to the header() function, and simply including the file will get things started.

First of all, the header() function creates the META tags and TITLE tag, adds links to the required stylesheet (this is by default the style.css file in the style folder of the current theme), and opens the HTML tag.

Now the fun really starts. header() now makes the first call to one of the theme functions, themeheader() in theme.php; and the theme has come into play.

When themeheader() is executed the following happens:

- The body tag is opened.
- Any advertising banners are displayed.
- The header.html template is processed and displayed. Usually the header.html template finishes by starting a new table to hold the main page content, and starts a column in that table.
- The left-hand blocks are rendered into this column. The themesidebox() function is called to display each block.
- The left_center.html template is processed. This closes the column started earlier. For some themes, it adds a 'padding' column. Then the column that will hold the module content is started.

Now the module continues with its activities, outputting its content, probably wrapping it with the OpenTable() and CloseTable() functions found in the tables.php file. After it has finished, to close the page up the module includes the footer.php file. In footer.php is a function called footer(). Similar to header.php, the footer() function is called from within the footer.php file.

The footer() function calls the themefooter() function, and the following happens:

- The center_right.html template is processed. The main column is closed; a padding column is possibly added and a new column is started.
- The right-hand blocks are rendered. The themesidebox() function is called to display each block.
- The footer.html template is processed. It closes a column (there will be one column still left open at that point), and then renders the page footer message.

After the call to `themefooter()`, the final throes of the `footer()` function are to close the body tag and the page's HTML tag. The body tag was opened in the `themeheader()` function, but is not actually closed in the theme.

Note that the `themeindex()` and `themearticle()` functions in the theme are only involved when the News module is in action, and are not part of the general page output process.

Summary

We have transformed the look of the Dinosaur Portal in this chapter from a standard looking PHP-Nuke installation to a very distinctive looking site. To do this, we started with the 3D-Fantasy theme and gradually added our new design.

We met the main ingredients of a theme, the PHP code files `theme.php` and `tables.php`, and the HTML templates that determine how a particular part of the page will look. We saw how the templates and the PHP code interact, and how they are used to separate the design of the theme from the PHP code that drives it.

We changed the page header, adding a new banner, and then a simple navigation bar. Then we looked at using the CSS stylesheet, the `style.css` file in the `style` folder of the theme, to make formatting changes independently of both the template and the PHP files.

After that, we looked at blocks in the theme. In particular, we saw how to create a new block. We saw how to create a rounded box, and put this to use for formatting the stories on the homepage of the site.

The final activity of the chapter was to add a Favicon to the site, which is not actually part of the theme's responsibility, but it rounds off the customization nicely.

10
Programming PHP-Nuke

In this chapter we will look at programming PHP-Nuke. Specifically, this means creating new blocks and modules. Before we get stuck into that, we will have a look at what actually happens inside PHP-Nuke when a page is requested by a browser.

After that, we will create a new block, a better version of the Dinosaur of the Day block we created in Chapter 4. That, if you recall, was a static HTML block, and we had hard-coded the image of the dinosaur and its title into the block. Here we will create a block that takes the image to display and title of the dinosaur from the database. This will introduce us to data access in PHP-Nuke, a topic that you will use a lot as you begin to code more with PHP-Nuke.

After a quick look at the file and folder structure of a module, we then begin creating a new module for PHP-Nuke. This module will allow items of content to be submitted for modules that do not support user-submitted content. In this chapter, we will code functionality for users to submit encyclopedia entries for administrator approval. However, this will not involve making any modifications to the Encyclopedia module, and can be extended to cover other modules as well.

What Happens When a Page is Requested?

Let's see what happens when a visitor wants to view an article on the site, and the process that PHP-Nuke goes through to construct the page containing this information. Viewing an article means that the visitor will be navigating to a page similar to this:

```
http://localhost/nuke/modules.php?name=News&file=article&sid=1
```

The page requested by the visitor is modules.php, so let's have a look at that. Note that although there are many PHP files in the PHP-Nuke installation, there are only four files actually requested in the normal course of interaction with the site:

- index.php
- modules.php
- admin.php
- backend.php

The other files in the PHP-Nuke installation are used by these files when required.

Where Does PHP-Nuke Get Information From?

PHP-Nuke is able to collect information about what module the visitor wants to see, what operation they want to perform, and details of the user from request variables coming from these places:

- The query string in the URL: The URL of the page holds information that tells PHP-Nuke which module to select, which part of the module to use, what item of content to show, and so on. The query string information is used to select the page from the system that needs to be shown to the visitor.

- Posted variables: When a user enters information in a form, and submits this back to the server, this information will be available to PHP-Nuke. This posted information is how PHP-Nuke gets input from the user to create items of content, enter terms to search for, and so on.

- Cookie variables: There is user account information stored in a cookie (and administrator account information if the user has such an account). This is used to identify the user, so they do not have to keep logging on every time they view a page or come to the site. When the user logs out, this information is deleted from the cookie.

The information that PHP-Nuke gets from these sources has to be treated very carefully within the system. These sources are the only means through which visitors communicate with the site, and are also the channels through which hacks or attacks might be conducted on the site. The patches we applied in Chapter 2 while installing the system address precisely this issue, and they make sure that the data PHP-Nuke collects from a visitor is in exactly the right form for working with.

Requesting a Page

Once the `modules.php` page is requested, the first step followed is to include the `mainfile.php` file. This file does the following things:

- It checks and processes the request variables (namely the input to the application), to avoid possibly harmful tags, or other indicators of some form of SQL injection attack.

- It creates global variables for each request variable.

- It sets up a connection to the database.

- It gets the site configuration such as the site name, site logo, and so on, from the database.

The `mainfile.php` file also contains a number of core functions such as checking if the user is logged in or is an administrator, choosing the blocks to display, and filtering text, among others. These will be used at different points in the creation of the page.

After this file has been included, the next thing to happen in `modules.php` is that PHP-Nuke gets the requested module from the `$name` global variable, which corresponds to the `name` query string variable (as in `modules.php?name=News`), and checks if this module is active. If the module isn't active, and the visitor isn't an administrator, a 'Module Not Active' message is displayed, and the page output is done.

If the module is active, then PHP-Nuke checks if the visitor has rights to access this module. PHP-Nuke checks to see if the access is restricted to a particular user group, and if so, is the user a member of that group? PHP-Nuke also checks if the module is for subscribers only, and if so, is the user a subscriber to the site? If the visitor doesn't have the right permissions to view the module, then a 'No Access' message is displayed, and the page output is done.

If the module selected by the visitor is active, and they do have permission to view it, then PHP-Nuke can get on with passing control to that module. Control is passed to the selected module by attempting to include the `index.php` file in the folder of the selected module. However, if there is a `file` variable in the query string, then the file with that name is included instead. If these files can't be found, a 'Module Cannot Be Found' error is displayed to the visitor.

Thus if the user requests a page like `modules.php?name=News&file=article&sid=1`, the `article.php` file in the News folder will be included by PHP-Nuke. If the user requests a page like `modules.php?name=News&sid=1`, then the `index.php` file in the News folder will be included. Attempting to request a page like `modules.php?name=News&file=nosuchfile` returns a page with a 'No such page' message, since there is no file called `nosuchfile.php` in the News folder. The 'No such page' message is generated by PHP-Nuke, since it's in control of the process.

If the user has selected an active module for which they have view permission, and are requesting a page that is part of the module, then control passes to the module, and it's up to that module to do its work and create the page. We'll see how this works later in the chapter, but for now, our overview of how PHP-Nuke gets the page creation underway is complete.

Seeing how PHP-Nuke works isn't particularly exciting, what is more exciting is seeing how we can extend the power of PHP-Nuke by creating new blocks and modules. Along the way, we'll see most of the components required for 'programming' with PHP-Nuke, and you'll get a good idea of how to go about your own development projects.

Creating a Block

Our development efforts begin with creating a File block. A File block is a PHP script that is stored in the blocks folder. It must have a filename of the form `block-NAME.php`, where NAME will be used by PHP-Nuke as the title for the block. The filename should not contain any spaces.

The goal of a block is simple. It just has to create one variable, `$content`, that holds the content of the block. After that, the PHP-Nuke core will bring the theme into play to take care of displaying the block.

The block we will create is a better version of the Dinosaur of the Day static HTML block we created in Chapter 4. The block will display the name of the Dinosaur of the Day, and a thumbnail image of the lucky lizard. However, on the next day, a different dinosaur will be chosen, and the block display will be updated.

This is how the block works:

- We will create a database table to hold the date, the title of the dinosaur for that day, and a link to the thumbnail image of that dinosaur.

- We will create a text data file that will contain the name of a dinosaur and a link to its thumbnail image on each line. The data in this file will be the dinosaur pool from which the dinosaur of the day is chosen at random.

- When the block code is executed, it will look in the database table to see if there is any information for the current date. If there is, it will retrieve it and build the block output.

- If there is no information for the current date, the data from the text file will be loaded in. One of the entries in that file will be selected at random, and that data will be inserted into the database. This will become the Dinosaur of the Day. That data will then be used to create the block output.

We will use the text file to hold the 'Dinosaur of the Day' candidates rather than a database table so that we do not have to create a separate administration feature to add these details. To add more dinosaurs to the list, we simply upload a new version of the text file.

Make sure that you copy the dinosaur thumbnails from the code download into the \images\dinosaurs\tnails folder of your PHP-Nuke installation root.

Time For Action—Creating the Database Table
1. Open up phpMyAdmin in your web browser, and select the nuke database from the drop-down list in the left-hand panel.
2. Click on the SQL tab, and enter the following code into the textbox, then click Go.

```
CREATE TABLE dinop_dinoportal_dotd (
id INT( 10 ) NOT NULL AUTO_INCREMENT ,
day VARCHAR( 16 ) NOT NULL ,
title VARCHAR( 128 ) NOT NULL ,
image VARCHAR( 250 ) NOT NULL ,
PRIMARY KEY ( 'id' )
) TYPE = MYISAM ;
```

What Just Happened?
We just created our database table. There is only one table needed, with a simple design. There are four fields in the table. The id field will hold an auto-incrementing unique numerical value and the other fields will hold the current date, the title of the dinosaur, and the link to the image of the dinosaur.

Time For Action—Creating the Text File
1. Open up your text editor, and enter the following:

```
Tyrannosaurus Rex,images/dinosaurs/tnails/tyro.gif
Stegosaurus,images/dinosaurs/tnails/stego.gif
Triceratops,images/dinosaurs/tnails/triceratops.gif
```

2. Save this file as dotd_list.txt in the blocks folder.

What Just Happened?

The dotd_list.txt file will be the data source for choosing a new Dinosaur of the Day image. You will notice that we are storing the data here in the form 'name of the dinosaur', 'path to the image', so it will be easy to extract the information when we need it.

Time For Action—Creating the Block Code

1. Open up your text editor, and enter the following code into a blank file:

```php
<?php

if ( !defined('BLOCK_FILE') )
{
   Header("Location: ../index.php");
   die();
}

global $prefix, $db;

$today = date('d-m-Y');

$sql = "SELECT * from ".$prefix."_dinoportal_dotd WHERE day='$today'";

$result = $db->sql_query($sql);
$content = "";
$dino_title = "";
$image = "";

  $numrows = $db->sql_numrows($result);
  if ($numrows)
  {
     $row = $db->sql_fetchrow($result);
     $dino_title = $row['title'];
     $image = $row['image'];
  }
  else
  {
     $filename = "blocks/dotd_list.txt";
     $possibles =@ file($filename);

     if ($possibles)
     {
        $choice = rand(1, count($possibles));
        $imp = explode("," , $possibles[$choice-1]);
        $dino_title = $imp[0];
        $image = $imp[1];
        $sql = "INSERT INTO ".$prefix."_dinoportal_dotd(day,title,image)
             VALUES ('$today', '$dino_title', '$image')";
        $result = $db->sql_query($sql);
     }
     $choice = rand(1, count($possibles));

     $imp = explode("," , $possibles[$choice-1]);
     $dino_title = $imp[0];
     $image = $imp[1];
  }
  if ($dino_title)
  {
     $content = "Today's dinosaur
     is:<br><center><b>$dino_title</b><center><br>";
        $content .= "<center><img src=\"$image\"
     alt=\"$dino_title\"></center><br>";
  }
?>
```

2. Save this file as block-DinosaurOfTheDay.php in the blocks folder of your PHP-Nuke installation.

What Just Happened?

We just entered the code for the Dinosaur of the Day block, and we'll step through it now.

This first part of the code stops this file being requested directly by a visitor— the BLOCK_FILE constant is defined in mainfile.php, and without that constant being defined, the visitor would be redirected back to the homepage of the site. Block files are never requested directly by the visitor, they are included by PHP-Nuke. These first few lines of code are found in every block file:

```
if ( !defined('BLOCK_FILE') )
{
  Header("Location: ../index.php");
  die();
}
```

Now we can get started. First, we set ourselves to access some of the global variables of the application, and we will have our first look at the objects to access data from the database. The only global variables we need here are the ones for data access—$prefix, which holds the value of the database tables prefix, and $db, which is used to actually perform database operations.

```
global $prefix, $db;
```

Next, we grab today's date, formatted as digits like this 24-05-2005.

```
$today = date('d-m-Y');
```

Now we set up the SQL statement to retrieve the information corresponding to this date from the database:

```
$sql = "SELECT * from ".$prefix."_dinoportal_dotd WHERE day='$today'";
```

Now we execute the SQL statement:

```
$result = $db->sql_query($sql);
```

It is possible that there is no data corresponding to today's date, so we check the number of rows returned from this last query. If there are zero rows, there will be no information.

```
$numrows = $db->sql_numrows($result);
```

If there are some rows returned, we can start creating the block output. We use the sql_fetchrow() method to retrieve a row of data from the result of the query. This row is returned as an array, and we set some variables from the array. We'll only grab one row. If for some reason, there is more than one entry for today's date, we simply ignore the others.

```
if ($numrows)
{
  $row = $db->sql_fetchrow($result);
  $dino_title = $row['title'];
  $image = $row['image'];
}
```

Now we move on to the situation where there is no information for today's date, and we have to create it. The first thing we do is to read the contents of the dotd_list.txt file into an array—there will be one entry in the array for each line in the text file. However, we have to consider what will happen if there is some kind of problem reading the file.

```
else
{
    $filename = "blocks/dotd_list.txt";
```

Note that the path to the file for the dodt_list.txt file is \blocks\dotd_list.txt. This may seem strange, since both this file and the block file are in the same blocks folder. However, PHP will be looking for this file from the executing script, which will be one of index.php, modules.php, or admin.php, all of which are outside the blocks folder. Thus we need to add the blocks folder in the path to the dotd_list.txt file.

Now we try to grab the file itself:

```
$possibles =@ file($filename);
```

The file function opens the named file, and reads the input into an array called $possibles. The use of the @ character here will suppress any error messages—if there is a problem opening or reading the file, no untidy error messages will be displayed to the user, and execution can continue. Of course, if there is a problem reading the file then there will be a problem with $possibles. So we check this next—if there has been some problem reading the file then $possibles will be false:

```
if ($possibles)
{
```

If there is something stored in $possibles, then this check will be passed, and we can proceed to choose one element from it at random. We choose a random number, between 1 and the number of lines in the text file.

```
    $choice = rand(1, count($possibles));
```

All we have to do now is choose that element from the array (we have to subtract one from the random number because the first element of the array is 0, rather than 1), and then split up that line to get at the title and the path to the image.

```
        $imp = explode("," , $possibles[$choice-1]);
        $dino_title = $imp[0];
        $image = $imp[1];
```

We split the line using the explode() function. The explode() function converts a string to an array by splitting it at certain characters. We will split the string at the ',' character, and we get an array with two entries. The first entry is the name of the dinosaur; the second is the path of the image.

Now we have the details of our Dinosaur of the Day, we can add it to the database using an INSERT SQL statement.

```
        $sql = "INSERT INTO ".$prefix."_dinoportal_dotd(day,title,image)
               VALUES ('$today', '$dino_title', '$image')";
        $result = $db->sql_query($sql);
    }

}
```

At this point, we should have a Dinosaur of the Day, one way or another, and so we can finalize the block output. However, we check the value of the $dino_title variable just in case there has been some problem either retrieving data or creating the new Dinosaur of the Day. If there has been a problem with either of these, there will be no value for the $dino_title variable, and if so, this code will ensure that the block content will remain empty, rather than producing some useless output.

```
if ($dino_title)
{
    $content = "Today's dinosaur
is:<br><center><b>$dino_title</b><center><br>";
    $content .= "<center><img src=\"$image\"
                        alt=\"$dino_title\"></center><br>";
}
```

That's it, our block is complete! The key points of this block were the initial few lines that stopped the file from being requested directly, and this was also our first encounter with the data access code. Another thing to note from this example is the effort we made to ensure that the block output was only created if everything went smoothly. We suppressed errors when trying to read in a file, we checked that the reading of a file had actually given us some data, and then we didn't create any output if there was a problem with dino_title variable, which would be an indicator of some problem.

All this means that if there is a problem, the visitor will not be confronted with lots of error messages, which could disturb the visitor and lead to a poor impression of your site, or even break the layout of the page, or reveal some information about your code that could be used against you.

All that remains now is to set up this File block using the steps we saw in Chapter 4, and we are away!

Data Access in PHP-Nuke

In the code for creating the block we had a couple of lines with data access functions:

```
$result = $db->sql_query($sql);
$numrows = $db->sql_numrows($result);
$row = $db->sql_fetchrow($result);
```

PHP-Nuke uses a 'data abstraction layer', which means that you call functions against an object, which translates them into specific calls against the database of your choice. Generally, MySQL is the database used with PHP-Nuke, but you could choose another database server to power your site. A more pertinent advantage is that you don't need to use database-specific functions to access data in PHP-Nuke; you only need to learn about the functions of the data access object (You will still need to know some SQL to create queries that will be executed on the database).

The code for the data access object is found in the file \db\mysql.php. In fact, the db folder contains code for different types of database server, but this file is the one selected by default by PHP-Nuke for working with the MySQL database server.

The data access object is a genuine object, that is, it's an instance of a class, sql_db in this case. Classes are one of the basics of object-oriented programming, but other than this instance PHP-Nuke does not make much use of object-oriented programming. A discussion of object-oriented programming in PHP is beyond the scope of this book, and it won't particularly help here since PHP-Nuke makes so little use of it. All that we need to know is how to access the methods (functions) of the data access object.

Object-oriented programming is covered in more detail in any book on PHP programming, and you can read an article about it at http://www.devarticles.com/c/a/PHP/Object-Orien ted-Programming-in-PHP/.

The data-access object provides a number of methods that you can use to execute a query, retrieve a row of data, check the number of rows returned by the query, or get the last inserted auto-increment field. Working with the object follows a similar process to the standard way of working with data in PHP using functions like mysql_query() or mysql_fetch_field().

To access data in PHP-Nuke, you will need two global variables, $prefix and $db. The $prefix variable holds the table prefix of the database tables, and this needs to be used in your SQL queries. The $db variable is the data access object itself.

In our block example, we had these lines to create a SQL query and then execute it:

```
$sql = "SELECT * from ".$prefix."_dinoportal_dotd WHERE day='$today'";
$result = $db->sql_query($sql);
```

Note the $db->sql_query() syntax. This syntax is used in PHP to call a method on an object, in this case the sql_query() method of the $db object. The sql_query() method executes an SQL query as its name suggests. You provide a string with the query that's to be executed as a parameter.

Following the execution of a query, you can retrieve a row using the sql_fetchrow() method:

```
$row = $db->sql_fetchrow($result);
```

This method returns an array, and you can refer to the fields in the data using $row['fieldname'], as we do in the block example to get the title and image fields:

```
$dino_title = $row['title'];
$image = $row['image'];
```

If you want to insert or update data, you need to create the relevant SQL query and then use the sql_query() function to do it:

```
$sql = "INSERT INTO ".$prefix."_dinoportal_dotd(day,title,image)
        VALUES ('$today', '$dino_title', '$image')";
$result = $db->sql_query($sql);
```

This is only a small selection of the methods of the data access object. Another interesting one is the sql_nextid() method, which you can use after an INSERT statement to get the value of the last auto-increment field created. However, these are the methods that you will see the most of as you look around the code in PHP-Nuke.

Module File and Folder Structure

Before we get started creating a new module, let's have a look at the file structure of a typical module. A module is simply a collection of files (usually only PHP files) contained in a folder that goes in the modules folder in the root of the PHP-Nuke installation. The name of the folder is the name that PHP-Nuke will recognize the module by.

However, we can't just place the files into the module folder in any order. There is an organization of files, subfolder names, and filenames that modules need to follow in order to function properly with PHP-Nuke.

The image below shows the contents of the News module folder:

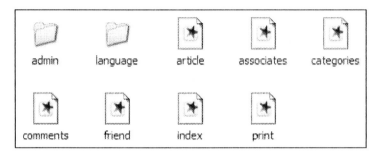

We have already seen how PHP-Nuke switches between files in the module folder based on the value of the file query string variable. If there is no value for this variable, the index.php file of the module is used. Files that sit inside the module folder are the 'front-end' files, which will be used during a standard user's visit to the module.

The code for the administration part of a module resides in the admin folder within the module folder. In earlier versions of PHP-Nuke (before 7.5), the administration code for any module would have to go into the admin folder (the one in the root of the PHP-Nuke installation), and would be mixed with the 'core' administration code. The decision to have a module's administration code contained within the module folder itself means that the module is much more self-contained, keeps people away from the core code itself, and generally makes the module easier to set up, install, and maintain. We'll see more about what is found in the admin folder when we create the administration area of our new module later in this chapter.

We saw in Chapter 4 that the Language block allows you to change PHP-Nuke's user interface language. This ability to switch languages is something that has made PHP-Nuke so popular all around the world. This multi-language support is achieved by module developers avoiding coding any 'localizable' text into the module output. Localizable text is text that needs to be translated if a different interface language is selected. Instead of coding the text, PHP constants are used, with the values of the constants defined in a **language file**. The language files are found in the language folder of the module, and there is a separate language file for each language, each with a filename of the form lang-LANGUAGE.php. All PHP-Nuke needs to do is select the correct file based on the desired language.

Creating a User Submissions Module

Writing a new module allows you to extend PHP-Nuke to get it to do exactly what you want it to do. What we will do here is to create a general-purpose module that will allow users to submit content for modules that do not support user-submitted material. We'll call it UserSubmissions. It will work in the way the Submit News module works for stories:

- The user will submit the material through a form.
- The administrator will be notified of the new submission by email.
- The administrator will be able to see a list of the submitted material in the administration area, and can edit, delete, or approve the material to go into the database.

The point of this module is that it does not touch the modules for which it allows the submission of content; everything will happen in the UserSubmissions module. In this chapter, we will only code in functionality for users to submit encyclopedia entries. It is straightforward to extend this to allow submissions for the Content module, or questions for the FAQ module.

Conceptually what the module does is to:

- Present a form to the user similar to the one the administrator would use for entering an encyclopedia entry.
- Take the user's input and store it in a 'general' way in a single database table.
- After the administrator checks the input, the data is then stored in the encyclopedia's database tables using the same kind of code that the Encyclopedia module uses.

We will see exactly what the 'general' way we store the data in is later. Basically, the module will take all the parts of the encyclopedia entry—the title, the text, the encyclopedia ID—and put them all together into one bundle, which can then be easily retrieved and broken out to form the individual pieces of data for the administrator to view, approve, or delete.

Rather than presenting the development as a series of steps for you to follow, we will break the code up into various tasks, and then examine each piece of code or activity. You can type in the code as it is presented, although it is probably easiest to grab the example code for this module from the code download, and refer to it as we go.

Module Development Steps

The steps that we will follow to create the module are these:

- Create the module folder
- Create the database tables
- Code the front end (visitor view) of the module
- Adapt the code for multi-language support
- Set up module administration
- Code the administration area

Rather unusually, we're going to start by coding the front end of the site. The reason this is unusual is that modules typically display some kind of data (that is what all the modules we have encountered in the book do), and you would first need to enter this data into the database. This data is usually entered by the administrator, through the administration interface. With some example data in place, the front end of the site will be able to display it. It will be difficult to test the front end if it is supposed to display data and there is no data to display!

This module does not require any existing data in the database to work. In fact, the data is entered by a standard visitor, and the administrator only has to look at this data, and edit or delete it. There is no facility in the administrator part of the module for the administrator to add new data into the module, which would rather defeat the point of this module! Thus we can start on the front end of the module quite happily.

Let's start off with creating the module folder.

Creating the Module Folder

Create a new folder in the modules folder called UserSubmissions. This will be our module folder. Within this folder, create two new folders called admin and language. The admin folder will contain our administration code, and the language folder will contain the user interface language files. We create another folder, inside the admin folder, also called language. This folder will hold the language files for the module's administration interface.

That's the first step out of the way, so let's move on to the database tables.

Creating the Database Tables

The module has only one database table. The table will be called <prefix>_usersubmissions. You can follow the same steps in phpMyAdmin as we did earlier for creating the block database table to create this table:

```
CREATE TABLE dinop_usersubmissions (
    id int(11) NOT NULL auto_increment,
    data text  NOT NULL,
    parent_id int(11) NOT NULL default '0',
    type varchar(36)  NOT NULL default '1',
    user_id int(11) NOT NULL default '0',
    date timestamp NOT NULL default
        CURRENT_TIMESTAMP on update CURRENT_TIMESTAMP,
    title varchar(255)  NOT NULL default '',
    user_name varchar(250)  NOT NULL default '',
    PRIMARY KEY  (id)
) COMMENT='Table for holding user submitted content' ;
```

Each row in this table will represent a single item of submitted content. The row will be identified by its id field.

With only one table, you may be wondering how this module is going to be able to hold data from different modules. The answer is that the submitted data will be bundled up into a single object, then 'serialized' and stored in the data field. When the data is needed for viewing, it will be unbundled, and 'unserialized' back into a form that can be worked with. The 'title' of the submission will be stored in the title field.

The type of module that we are storing data for will be held in the type field of the row. The details of the submitter will be stored in the user_id and user_name fields. We actually only use the user_name field in this version of the module, but we store both for future use. The date the item is submitted is held in the field called date. This field is a MySQL TIMESTAMP, and whenever a row is inserted. the current date and time will be inserted into the field automatically by the database, so we will not need to record the date and time ourselves.

The final field is parent_id. Recall how an encyclopedia entry belongs to an Encyclopedia; a content page belongs to a Content category; a FAQ question belongs to a particular category, and so on. For each of these types of content, you needed to provide a 'parent' object that the content would belong to. That is where our parent_id field comes in. The ID of the parent object will be stored in this field. For an encyclopedia entry, this will be the ID of the chosen Encyclopedia.

The Visitor Code—the index.php File

In this section, we will walk through the code for the visitor part of the module. There is only one file that we will need, index.php.

First we will consider the overall structure of the index.php file, and the parts of the code that every module should contain. Then we will look at the individual parts of code in the index.php file that perform various tasks. The tasks performed in index.php are:

- Inviting the user to submit an item (an encyclopedia entry in this case)
- Displaying the form for user input
- Preparing the user input for storage
- Storing the user input, and notifying the administrator

Overall Structure of the Module index.php File

Before our detailed exploration of the code, let's have a look at the overall structure of the index.php file. Here is a view of the code listing with the code for each function removed. There are three main parts to the code, with the parts separated by the /* ---- */ lines.

```php
<?php
if (!defined('MODULE_FILE'))
{
    die ("You can't access this file directly...");
}

define('INDEX_FILE', true);
$module_name = basename(dirname(__FILE__));
get_lang($module_name);
$pagetitle = "- $module_name";

/* ------------------------------------------------ */


function ShowTypes()
{
    ...
}

function ShowFormForInput($oid)
```

```
{
    ...
}
function AddEnyclopediaEntry($eid, $title, $text, $language)
{
    ...
}

function formatEncyclo()
{
    ...
}

function storeSubmission($type, $storageArray, $parent_id, $title_field)
{
    ....
}

function get_user_object()
{
    ....
}
/* --------------------------------------------------- */

switch($op)
{

    case "add_encycloentry":
        AddEnyclopediaEntry($usr_eid, $usr_title, $usr_text, $usr_language);
        break;
    case "add":
        SubmitContent($oid);
        break;
    default:
        ShowTypes();
        break;
}
?>
```

The first part is standard to every module in PHP-Nuke. The first couple of lines make sure that
this file can only be used through the modules.php or index.php file. This check is similar to the
one used at the start of the block code we saw earlier. With this check, no one can access the file
directly. After that, we define a constant to indicate that we are on the homepage of the module:

```
if (!defined('MODULE_FILE')) {
    die ("You can't access this file directly...");
}

define('INDEX_FILE', true);
```

The next line gets the module name. Rather than simply typing in the module name, it is taken
from the name of the folder containing the current file. The __FILE__ PHP constant contains the
full path of the current file, the dirname() function returns the name of that file's parent folder,
and the basename() function returns the filename part of this, which in this case is actually the
top-most directory.

```
$module_name = basename(dirname(__FILE__));
```

Once the module name is defined, it is passed to the get_lang() function, which includes the
language file for this module. The module name is also used to set the title of the page:

```
get_lang($module_name);
$pagetitle = "- $module_name";
```

Now we will look at the third part of the code in index.php, which contains a construct used in all PHP-Nuke modules.

At the end of the file is a switch-case construct. It checks the value of the $op variable. Depending on the value of this variable, different functions are called within the file. The $op variable holds the value of the op request variable, and determines which operation in the module is to be performed. If the value of $op is add, the SubmitContent() function is called; if the value is add_encycloentry, the AddEncyclopediaEntry() function is called. For any other value of $op (including no value) the ShowTypes() function is called:

```
switch($op)
{
    case "add_encycloentry":
        AddEncyclopediaEntry($usr_eid, $usr_title, $usr_text, $usr_elanguage);
        break;
    case "add":
        SubmitContent($oid);
        break;
    default:
        ShowTypes();
        break;
}
```

In this way PHP-Nuke is able to map visitor requests to functions in code. You will notice that some of the functions have parameters passed to them (for example, SubmitContent() has a variable called $oid passed to it). This is a convention followed by modules in PHP-Nuke wherein request variables used in a function are passed to it from the function call in the switch-case construct. If the variables aren't passed to the function, they can still be accessed as global variables from within the function, but we will follow this convention here.

> You can read more about the switch-case construct at
> http://www.php.net/manual/en/control-structures.switch.php.

By convention in PHP-Nuke, this selection process comes toward the end of the module file, since it is easy to locate. You look to the switch-case construct to see what bit of code is executed for a particular module operation.

Tracking Down the Code for a Module Operation

Check the code that was executed when a visitor clicks on a link in the Web Links module. This has a URL of the form:

```
http://localhost/nuke/modules.php?name=Web_Links&l_op=visit&lid=1
```

At the bottom of the index.php file in the Web_Links module, you will find the switch-case construct:

```
switch($l_op) {
```

Here the variable being checked is $l_op rather than $op. Looking at that switch-case construct, you find the check for visit, and can see what action is taken. In this case, it is a call to a function called visit():

```
case "visit":
    visit($lid);
    break;
```

Now you move up the file to find the `visit()` function (you can search for `function visit(` since we are looking for a function definition):

```
function visit($lid)
{
    global $prefix, $db;
    $lid = intval($lid);
    $db->sql_query("update ".$prefix."_links_links set
                    hits=hits+1 where lid='$lid'");
    update_points(14);
    $row = $db->sql_fetchrow($db->sql_query("SELECT url
            from ".$prefix."_links_links where lid='$lid'"));
    $url = stripslashes($row['url']);
    Header("Location: $url");
}
```

In this way, you are able to see the exact code that is executed when a visitor clicks on a web link. The `$lid` variable is converted to an integer, the number of clicks stored for that link in the database is increased, the user's point score is updated (with the call to `update_points(14)`), and then the URL of the web link numbered `$lid` is retrieved. Finally, the PHP `Header()` function redirects the visitor's browser to the target of the web link.

The details of the Web Links module aren't important to us now, but the point of this discussion was to illustrate how you can track down the piece of code in a module that is responsible for a particular operation. This is very useful for understanding how modules work, and especially useful if you want to tinker with the existing operation of a module.

Let's continue with our discussion of the functions in the `index.php` file of the `UserSubmissions` module.

Inviting the User to Submit an Item

The homepage of the module displays a list of the types of content that the visitor can submit. For this example, visitors can only submit a new encyclopedia entry, although the module can be extended to allow `FAQ` or `Content` submissions quite easily. When the visitor visits the homepage of the module (`modules.php?name=UserSubmissions`), PHP-Nuke will call the `ShowTypes()` function in `index.php`.

```
function ShowTypes ()
{
    global $module_name;
    include("header.php");
    title("Submit a new Item");
    OpenTable();
    $u = get_user_object();
    if (!$u)
    {
        echo "<center>You need to be a registered user to submit or
                edit new items of content<center><br><br>";
        CloseTable();
        include("footer.php");
        exit;
    }
    echo "Choose the type of content to add<br><br>";

    echo "<ul>";
    echo "<li><a href=\"modules.php?name=$module_name&amp;op=add&amp;oid=1\">
            Submit a new Encyclopedia entry</a></li>";
```

```
        echo "</ul>";
        echo "<br>";
        CloseTable();
        include("footer.php");
    }
```

The function starts with a global statement, so that our function has access to certain variables defined outside our function. Anything defined outside of a function will be defined in the global scope, hence the reason we use the global statement to get at the $module_name variable. This function will offer the visitor a choice of content types to add a new submission for; at the moment, there is only one type, an encyclopedia entry. The ShowTypes() function gets the page output underway:

```
function ShowTypes()
{
    global $module_name;
    include("header.php");
    title("Submit a new Item");
    OpenTable();
```

The title() function creates a boxed element on the page, displaying a message in a large font. We saw mention of the header.php file and the OpenTable() function in Chapter 9. The header.php file starts the page output, and renders the page header and the left-hand blocks. The call to OpenTable() defines an enclosing element for our module output.

Before we display a list of possible types of content to offer to the visitor, we need to check if the current user is actually logged in. We will not be allowing anonymous submissions, so the user must be logged in. Of course, this can be achieved by restricting the module to registered visitors only, but if this restriction isn't in place, then the code will break without first checking that the user is indeed a logged in user.

If the user is not logged in, a message will be displayed to them, and the page output will be brought to an end.

```
        $u = get_user_object();
        if (!$u)
        {
            echo "<center>You need to be a registered user to submit or
                  edit new items of content<center><br><br>";
            CloseTable();
            include("footer.php");
            exit;
        }
```

We have introduced another function here, get_user_object(). Let's talk about that now.

Getting User Information

The information about the current user is got from the get_user_object() function that is defined later in the file. The reason we have put this functionality into its own function is so that we don't have to keep typing the same code over and over again in the file to get user information. The function will return false if there is no user information (when they aren't logged in, even if they have an account), but if the visitor is logged in, it will return an array with some details.

Let's look at the function definition:

```
function get_user_object()
{
    global $user;
```

The `$user` global variable holds the user details. This variable is actually stored in a cookie in the visitor's browser, and contains information stored in a form that we have to sort out. First of all, if the `$user` variable doesn't have a value, we return `false` for the function, since there is no user information available.

```
    if (!$user) return false;
```

The next few lines of code in the function are found in many, many places throughout PHP-Nuke and its modules. When the `$user` variable is taken from the cookie variables, it is a long string, something like this:

MjpOZXNOdxN1cjo1ZD1jNjhjNmM1MGVkM2QwMmEyZmNmNTRmNjM5OTNiNjoxMDpO
aHJ1YWQ6MDowOjA6MDpUaGVEaW5vc2F1c1BvcnRhbDozMg

This long string has to be processed and then converted to an array. However, this process is not done only once, for the benefit of the rest of the application. Anytime you want to work with user information you will need to follow this process, which is why we are putting it into its own function. Our function takes care of these details, and we only have to deal with the results.

First, we check if the `$user` variable is not an array. If it isn't, we make it into one. The string is actually encoded, so it needs to be decoded first. Note that we do not actually change the `$user` variable itself, we make a copy `$user2`, and work on that.

```
    if(!is_array($user))
    {
        $user2 = addslashes($user);
        $user2 = base64_decode($user2);
```

After this decoding, the string will be something like this, and is getting easier to work with:

2:testuser:5d9c68c6c50ed3d02a2fcf54f63993b6:10:thread:0:0:
0:0:TheDinosaurPortal:32

The final step in our function is to split the string at each : character to produce an array.

```
        $user2 = explode(":", $user2);
    }
```

Now we have an array, which we will return from the function:

```
    return $user2;
}
```

The reason we don't change the `$user` variable itself into an array is because there are some parts of PHP-Nuke that do the above decoding and splitting process themselves, without checking if `$user` is already an array. If the variable is already an array, then that process will fail, and the values returned will be unexpected.

The advantage of using our `get_user_object()` function is that we don't have to worry about any of the details of cleaning and preparing the user information, we just call the function to check if the information is available, and if it is, it will be ready for us as an array.

Returning to our showTypes() function, we call the get_user_object() function, and then check the value returned:

```
if (!$u)
{
...
```

You should always check that the user information is there before attempting to use it. Once we have the user information as an array, we can get such things as the name of the user, and their user ID. The user ID is the first element of the array, and the user name is the second element.

The remainder of the code in the showTypes() function displays a list of the types of content that users can submit, with links to begin the process. Note how the link is built using the $module_name variable rather than typing in the name of the module itself. We are only using one type of content in this chapter, an encyclopedia entry:

```
echo "Choose the type of content to add<br><br>";
echo "<ul>";
echo "<li><a href=\"modules.php?name=$module_name&amp;op=add&amp;oid=1\">
        Submit a new Encyclopedia entry</a></li>";
echo "</ul>";
echo "<br>";
```

And finally, the function closes page output, first with the call to closeTable() and then by including the footer.php file, which takes care of the right-hand blocks and the page footer, in the same way as discussed in Chapter 9.

Preparing the ShowTypes() Function for Languages

Before we move on to the other functions, we prepare our showTypes() function to make use of language constants. You will notice that we used four pieces of text in the showTypes() function. We will move these out of the function and into the language file as language constants. We create a file called lang-english.php in the languages subfolder of the UserSubmissions folder and add these lines:

```
<?php

define("_SUBMITNEWITEM", "Submit a new Item");
define("_CHOOSETYPE", "Choose the type of content to add");
define("_SUBMITNEWENCYCLOENTRY", "Submit a new Encyclopedia entry");
define("_YOUNEEDTOBEAUSER", "You need to be a registered user to submit or
edit new items of content");
?>
```

This is the English language file, and contains the text that we used in the showTypes() function. We have given the constants names that are very similar to the text that they hold. The final step is to modify the showTypes() function to use these constants. The lines with the new constants are shown highlighted:

```
function ShowTypes()
{
    global $module_name;
    include("header.php");
    title(_SUBMITNEWITEM);
    OpenTable();
    $u = get_user_object();
    if (!$u)
    {
        echo "<center>"._YOUNEEDTOBEAUSER."<center><br><br>";
```

```
                CloseTable();
                include("footer.php");
                exit;
        }
        echo _CHOOSETYPE."<br><br>";

        echo "<ul>";
        echo "<li><a href=\"modules.php?name=$module_name&amp;op=add&amp;oid=1\">"
                ._SUBMITNEWENCYCLOENTRY."</a></li>";
        echo "</ul>";
        echo "<br>";
        CloseTable();
        include("footer.php");
    }
```

For the remainder of the code, we will use the language constants from the start, and show the constants afterwards. If you wish, you can begin the process of translating the text into other languages!

This is the result of our module so far. A table that displays the list of content types the user can enter:

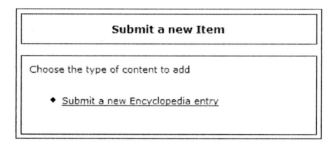

There is only one link for the user to click. This will take them to a page of the form:

```
modules.php?name=UserSubmissions&op=add&oid=1
```

The value of oid will be used to determine what form they are shown, as we shall now see.

Displaying the Form for User Input

The next function is called ShowFormForInput(). This function shows the form for the user to enter their content, and is executed when the op request variable has the value add. The function checks the value of the $oid variable to see what type of content they want to enter. Before we check the value of $oid, we explicitly convert it to an integer with the intval() function.

We have only one option for the value of $oid:

```
function ShowFormForInput($oid)
{
    global $pagetitle, $module_name;
    $oid = intval($oid);
    if ($oid==1)
    {
        $pagetitle = "- $module_name : "._ADDENYCLOENTRY;
        include("header.php");
        title (_ADDENYCLOENTRY);
        OpenTable();

        formatEncyclo();

        CloseTable();
```

```
            include("footer.php");
    }
    else
            header("Redirect: modules.php?name=$module_name");

}
```

Anything other than the value 1 for $oid will have the user redirected to the module homepage. PHP's header() function is used to perform the redirection.

The ShowFormForInput() function doesn't display the form itself, it calls the formatEncyclo() function. This function actually displays a form for the user to enter their new entry.

Here we are following a coding convention whereby a function called from the switch-case construct at the end of the file has the first letter of its name capitalized. A function that is called from within one of these functions will have the first letter of its name in lower case, such as formatEncyclo(). This simple convention makes it easy to distinguish between functions that correspond to user operations of the module (ShowFormForInput()), and the functions that support them (formatEncyclo()).

The ShowFormForInput() function uses a new language constant, _ADDENYCLOENTRY:

```
define("_ADDENYCLOENTRY", "Add a New Encyclopedia Entry");
```

The form for entering the encyclopedia entry itself is identical to the form used by the administrator to submit an encyclopedia entry. The first part of the function creates a form with a textbox for the title of the encyclopedia entry, and a text area for the text of the entry. Note the name of the title textbox is usr_title, and the name of the entry text area is usr_text.

```
function formatEncyclo()
{
    global $db, $prefix;
    global $module_name;
    echo "  <form action=\"modules.php?name=$module_name\" method=\"post\">\n
        <p><b>Title:</b><br>\n
        <input name=\"usr_title\" size=\"50\" type=\"text\" value=\"\">\n<br>
        <br>
        <b>Term Text:</b><br>
        If you want multiple pages you can write <b>&lt;!--pagebreak--&gt;
        </b> where you want to cut.<br>
        <textarea name=\"usr_text\" cols=\"60\" rows=\"20\"></textarea><br>
        <br>
        <b>Encyclopedia:</b><br>
        <select name=\"usr_eid\">\n";
```

After the form, we need to display a list of the active encyclopedias to the user so that they can select one to put their entry in. The SQL statement to get the list of encyclopedias is easy to obtain from looking at the code in the Encyclopedia module:

```
$sql = "SELECT eid, title FROM " . $prefix . "_encyclopedia
        WHERE active='1'";
```

Now we have the SQL statement, we can execute the query against the database, retrieve the rows, and build a drop-down SELECT element.

We loop through all of the returned rows, getting the title of the encyclopedia and its ID, and create the options for the drop-down list. Note that we use the stripslashes() function to strip away slashes from the title, since the code in the encyclopedia administration for adding an encyclopedia uses addslashes() on the title before storing it in the database.

> It is always wise to apply addslashes() to any text being stored in the database to avoid problems with quotes in the text.

```
$result = $db->sql_query($sql);
while ($row = $db->sql_fetchrow($result))
{
    $eid = intval($row['eid']);
    $title = stripslashes($row['title']);
    echo "<option value=\"$eid\">$title</option>\n";
}
```

We finish the SELECT HTML element:

```
echo "</select>\n<br><br>";
```

The next element of the form is a hidden field with the name op. This holds the value add_encycloentry. When the user submits the form, this value of op will be used to determine the next action.

```
echo " <input name=\"op\" value=\"add_encycloentry\" type=\"hidden\">";
```

Finally, we add a submit button to the form, and close up the form:

```
        <input value=\"Submit Item\" type=\"submit\"></p>
        </form>";
}
```

After the user clicks the button to submit their item, the page is posted back to the server. The $op variable in that page will have the value add_encycloentry, thus the AddEncyclopediaEntry() function is called from the switch-case construct at the end of the file.

Preparing to Add the Encyclopedia Entry

There are three parameters passed to the AddEncyclopediaEntry() function. These parameters are the selected encyclopedia ID, the title of the new entry, and the text of the new entry. Here is the function:

```
function AddEnyclopediaEntry($eid, $title, $text)
{
    global $module_name;
    $eid = intval($eid);

    if ($title=="" || $text=="" || $eid<1)
    {
        $pagetitle = "- $module_name : "._ADDENYCLOENTRY;
        include("header.php");
        title (_ADDENYCLOENTRY);
        OpenTable();
        echo "You need to supply a title, some text, and select an
            EncyclopediaEncyclopedia!<br><br>";
        echo "[ <a href=\"javascript:history.go(-1)\">Go Back</a> ]<br><br>";

        CloseTable();
        include("footer.php");
        exit;
    }

    $storageArray = array('title'=>$title,
                          'text'=>$text);
```

```
    storeSubmission("encyclo", $storageArray, $eid, $title);
    $pagetitle = "- $module_name : "._THANKYOUSUBMISSION;
    include("header.php");
    title (_THANKYOUSUBMISSION);
    OpenTable();
    echo "<center>"._THANKSTEXT."<br><br>";
    echo "[ <a href=\"modules.php?name=$module_name\">"._ADDMOREITEMS."
        </a> ]</center><br><br>";

    CloseTable();
    include("footer.php");
}
```

First we convert the $eid value, the encyclopedia ID, to an integer. It is supposed to be an integer, so we make sure it is with the intval() function.

```
function AddEnyclopediaEntry($eid, $title, $text)
{
    $eid = intval($eid);

    if ($title=="" || $text=="" || $eid<1)
    {
```

If the visitor hasn't submitted a title or some text for the entry, or an encyclopedia ID, we won't accept their submission. We display a message to them that they have missed filling in some details, and allow them to go back to the form and enter the information.

```
        $pagetitle = "- $module_name : "._ADDENYCLOENTRY;
        include("header.php");
        title (_ADDENYCLOENTRY);
        OpenTable();
```

Now comes our message, and the link to go back a page. Note that the link isn't a URL, but a JavaScript call to step back one page in the browser history, which is the same as the user clicking the Back button in their browser.

```
        echo "You need to supply a title, some text, and select an
            Encyclopedia!<br><br>";
        echo "[ <a href=\"javascript:history.go(-1)\">Go Back</a> ]<br><br>";
```

Now we finish the page output, and end PHP-Nuke:

```
        CloseTable();
        include("footer.php");
        exit;
    }
```

So we must have a title for the entry, some text, and an encyclopedia ID. All that remains now is to prepare all of this for storage. We create an array with the title and text, and then we call the storeSubmission() function to take care of the storage:

```
    $storageArray = array('title'=>$title,
                          'text'=>$text);
    storeSubmission("encyclo", $storageArray, $eid, $title);
```

We pass four parameters to the storeSubmission() function. The first parameter is a string indicating the type of content we want to store. The second parameter is an array containing the data that we want to store (the title, text, and language of the entry). The third parameter is the parent ID of the content.

The fourth parameter is the title of the entry. We pass this again so that it can be stored separately from the other data, because that data will be stored in a very general way. By passing the title separately, the title can be easily retrieved to identify the item in a list for the administrator. We'll see that later.

The final part of the function displays a message to the visitor, thanking them for their submission.

```
$pagetitle = "- $module_name : "._THANKYOUSUBMISSION;
include("header.php");
title (_THANKYOUSUBMISSION);
OpenTable();
echo "<center>"._THANKSTEXT."<br><br>";
echo "[ <a href=\"modules.php?name=$module_name\">"._ADDMOREITEMS.
     "</a> ]</center><br><br>";

CloseTable();
include("footer.php");
```

And here is the list of the new language constants used in this function. These need to be added to the lang-english.php file in the languages folder.

```
define("_THANKYOUSUBMISSION", "Thank you for your submission.");
define("_THANKSTEXT","We will check your submission in the next few hours,
if it is interesting, and accurate we will publish it soon.");
define("_ADDMOREITEMS", "Add More Items");
```

Storing the Submission

The final function, storeSubmission() is the real guts of this module. It is intended to take data for different types of content, and store it in one form. The storeSubmission() function does not need to know how the data is structured, where it came from, or how to display it. All this function needs to do is store it.

The function requires quite a few global variables. It needs the database access variables, $prefix and $db, and it needs the module name, $module_name. After it has finished storing the data, the function will send a notification email to the administrator, telling them that an item has been submitted, and providing them with a link to view the submission. To do this, we need the $admin_file global variable, which holds the name of the administration file, since the link to view the submission will point to an administration page.

We also need the $nukeurl, $sitename, and $adminmail variables. These variables hold the values of some of the site's configuration settings (the site URL, the site name, and the email address of the administrator). For each site configuration setting, a global variable is created in mainfile.php file. This snippet of code from mainfile.php shows the definition of the first few site configuration variables:

```
$result = $db->sql_query("SELECT * FROM ".$prefix."_config");
$row = $db->sql_fetchrow($result);
$sitename = $row['sitename'];
$nukeurl = $row['nukeurl'];
$site_logo = $row['site_logo'];
$slogan = $row['slogan'];
$startdate = $row['startdate'];
$adminmail = stripslashes($row['adminmail']);
```

You can see that all the columns are retrieved from the `<prefix>_config` table, which holds the site configuration settings. All the site configuration settings are stored in this one table, with each column corresponding to a setting. In `mainfile.php`, there are a number of lines that go through this and define a variable for each setting. If you want to access one of the site configuration settings in your code, look to this part of the `mainfile.php` file to find the name of the corresponding variable.

Returning to our `storeSubmission()` function, it begins in the usual way with `global` statements to make sure we can access all the variables we need:

```
function storeSubmission($type, $storageArray, $parent_id, $title_field)
{
    global $prefix, $db, $module_name, $admin_file;
    global $nukeurl, $sitename, $adminmail;
```

Recall that only registered users can submit items. We make one last check to make sure that the visitor is indeed a registered user of the site, and is logged in. If they're not, they're redirected to the module homepage.

```
$u = get_user_object();
if (!$u)
{
    Header("Location: modules.php?name=$module_name");
}
```

If our user is logged in, we can get their ID and username from the result of the `get_user_object()` function:

```
$user_id = $u[0];
$user_name = $u[1];
```

Now comes the bit where we take the submitted data and transform it so that it is ready for storage. Remember we created an array from the submitted data in the `AddEnyclopediaEntry()` function. Arrays are not particularly easy to store in a MySQL database, so we use the PHP `serialize()` function to convert the array into a single string. The `serialize()` function takes an object and returns a simple string representation of it. There is an `unserialize()` function, that takes that string representation and recreates the object. The idea should be becoming clear now— we serialize the array and store a string representation of it, and when the administrator needs to view the data to approve the submission, the string will be unserialized so that the data can be easily extracted.

```
$storage = serialize($storageArray);
```

We use the `addslashes()` function to prepare the text variables for storing in the database. The `addslashes()` function escapes ' and " characters in a string by adding a \ character in front of them. Without escaping them, the database will reject any values containing ' or ". We don't escape the `$type` variable, since we created that ourselves, and we are certain it has no ' or " characters.

```
$storage = addslashes($storage);
$title_field = addslashes($title_field);
```

Now we are ready to create the SQL statement to insert the details of the submitted item into our `<prefix>_usersubmissions` table:

```
$sql = "INSERT INTO ".$prefix."_usersubmissions(
    type, parent_id, data, user_id, user_name, title)
        VALUES ('$type', '$parent_id', '$storage', '$user_id',
                '$user_name', '$title_field')";
```

Now we execute the query:

```
$db->sql_query($sql);
```

Our work is almost done. The final step is to create the email that is to be sent to the administrator. Creating the text is easy; the important step is to create the URL for the administrator to view the submission. The URL will be of the form: `<admin_page>?op=UserSubEdit&sid=xxxx`, where xxxx is the ID of the row we just inserted. To get that ID, we use the `$sql_nextid()` function of the database access object. This function returns the last created auto-increment field on the database connection, which should be the value of the ID column in our table. This is precisely the value we need to make the URL.

```
$lid = $db->sql_nextid();
```

Now we create the body of the email to send, set a FROM address, the TO address, which is the administrator's email address, the `$adminmail` variable, and the SUBJECT of the email.

```
$mailBody = "A new piece of user-submitted content has been added to the
            site.<br><br>";

$mailBody .= "Visit this link to check it out.<br><br>";

$mailBody .= "<a
href=\"$nukeurl/".$admin_file.".php?op=UserSubEdit&sid=$lid>Here</a>";

$from = "$sitename <$adminmail>";
$to = $adminmail;

$subject = "A new piece of content has been submitted";
```

Now we use PHP's `mail()` function to send the mail, and our function is done.

```
mail($to, $subject, $mailBody, "From: $from\nX-Mailer: PHP/" .
        phpversion());
}
```

If you do not have access to a mail server on your testing machine, then comment out the last line with the `mail()` function.

That brings us to the end of the visitor part of the module. The module is ready for testing, although after making your submissions there isn't much else that happens, since only the administrator sees the submissions. That is our next task.

The User Submission Administration Area

Before we get onto writing the administration code, we will set up our module to feature in the Modules Administration menu. After that, we will see how PHP-Nuke selects the correct bit of code for performing the desired administrative operation; it is not as straightforward as the way that the module is selected for the visitor end of the site.

After that, it will be time to complete the administration code for the UserSubmissions module.

Creating the Modules Administration Menu Entry

To create the Modules Administration menu, PHP-Nuke looks for a file with a name of links.php in the admin folder of each module folder that the current administrator user has access to. (Recall that an administrator may have super user power or may have access restricted to certain modules.) If such a file is found, then a menu entry can be added to the Modules Administration menu.

The links.php file provides the following information to PHP-Nuke:

- A link to the main page for administering that function
- A title for its Modules Administration menu entry
- An image for its icon in the Modules Administration menu

Here is the links.php file that we will use for our UserSubmissions module. Any links.php file in an admin folder should resemble this:

```php
<?php
if (!defined('ADMIN_FILE'))
{
  die ("Access Denied");
}

global $admin_file;
adminmenu($admin_file.".php?op=UserSubs",
          "".USERSUBMISSIONS."",
          "usersubs.gif");
?>
```

The first line checks what page is attempting to make use of this file; if the page is not an administration page, execution is stopped, and the message Access Denied is displayed. (The ADMIN_FILE constant is only defined in the file admin.php.)

The adminmenu() function takes the three parameters that we listed earlier, and creates the menu entry. The first parameter is the link to the main page of the module's administration area. The second parameter is the title of the entry in the menu, _USERSUBMISSIONS. Again PHP-Nuke uses language constants.

> Note that we have to define this _USERSUBMISSIONS constant used in a language file in the core \admin\language folder, *not* the \admin\language folder in the module itself. If the constant is defined only in the module's language file, the text _USERSUBMISSIONS will be displayed in the Modules Administration menu rather than the value of the constant.

The final parameter is the image for the menu entry, usersubs.gif, and it is the name of an image file found in the \images\admin folder. (The usersubs.gif image can be found in the code download for this chapter.) Although the module code is self-contained, the image file of the menu entry needs to be located in the \images\admin folder.

After working its way through all the modules that the current user has access to, and executing each links.php file, PHP-Nuke is able to produce the Modules Administration menu.

To add our language constant, we will add it at the end of the \admin\languages\
lang-english.php file:

```
define("_WEBLINKS","Web Links");
define("_IMAGESWFURL","Image or Flash file URL");
define("_USERSUBMISSIONS", "User Submissions");

?>
```

After adding the highlighted line to that file, save the file.

Selecting the Correct Administration Area

PHP-Nuke uses the value of the op request variable to determine what part of the administration
area to present to the user. This variable can be in the URL of the page, as seen here in the URL
for the Downloads administration area:

```
http://localhost/nuke/admin.php?op=downloads
```

Alternatively, the op variable can be a hidden field in a form when the administrator is entering
some information. When the page is submitted, the value of the op field will 'override' any value
of the op query string variable, and will be used to determine the action.

Once PHP-Nuke has the value of the op variable, it begins a lengthy process to see which part of
the system will 'claim' it.

First of all, PHP-Nuke 'tries' all PHP files with a name like case.something.php in the case folder
of the admin folder in the root of the installation. The case.messages.php file looks like this:

```
switch($op)
{
    case "messages":
    case "addmsg":
    case "editmsg":
    case "deletemsg":
    case "savemsg":
    include("admin/modules/messages.php");
    break;
}
```

The switch-case mechanism is used to match the value of $op against one of the strings. The
strings here are a list of all of the 'operations' the messages administration area uses. Any URL of
the form admin.php?op=messages, admin.php?op=addmsg, admin.php?op=editmsg,
admin.php?op=deletemsg, or admin.php?op=savemsg will be matched here.

If a match is found, the file \admin\modules\messages.php is included, and execution passes to
there. That is the file that will do the work for the messages administration area.

PHP-Nuke loads in all the files in the \admin\case folder and checks to see if there is match of the
value of $op. If there is, code for that part of the administration area will be executed. If there is no
match found in any of the files in \admin\case, then PHP-Nuke moves on to the module folders
as it did with the Module Administration menu above. It looks through all the module folders that
the user has access to, and checks for the file \admin\case.php.

Here is the case.php file for the User Submissions module. All the case.php files are similar to this:

```php
<?php

if (!defined('ADMIN_FILE'))
{
    die ("Access Denied");
}
$module_name = "UserSubmissions";
include_once("modules/$module_name/admin/language/lang-".
                currentlang.".php");

switch($op)
{
    case "UserSubDelete":
    case "UserSubEdit":
    case "UserSubs":
    case "UserEncycloAccept":
    case "UserSubAccept":
    include ("modules/$module_name/admin/index.php");
    break;

}

?>
```

If there is a match here, then the index.php file in the admin folder of that module is included, and code execution continues there. In this way, all the administration functionality of the module can be kept inside the module folder itself. Note that this setup means that there is only one file for the module's administration code, the index.php file in the admin folder. Unlike with the front end of a module where PHP-Nuke selects a different file based on the value of the file query string variable, PHP-Nuke will not choose a different file in the admin folder, unless you add code for that yourself.

PHP-Nuke will look through all the module folders to try to match the value of the op query string variable. If there is no match after all this, a blank page is displayed, and that's the end of that.

We are now ready to code the administration area of the module. If you check out the Modules Administration area in the administration area, you will see the icon for our module. However, clicking on it does not produce anything since there is no code there yet!

Creating the Administration Code

The administration code is contained in a single file, index.php, in the admin folder of the module.

Let's begin with an overview of the structure of the code; again it is broken up into parts by /* -- -- */ comment lines:

```php
<?php
if (!defined('ADMIN_FILE'))
{
    die ("Access Denied");
}

$module_name = "UserSubmissions";
$aid = substr($aid, 0,25);
$query = $db->sql_query("SELECT title, admins FROM ".$prefix."_modules WHERE
title='$module_name'");

$row = $db->sql_fetchrow($query);
```

```
$admins = $row['admins'];

$auth_user = 0;

$query2 = $db->sql_query("SELECT name, radminsuper FROM ".$prefix."_authors
WHERE aid='$aid'");

$row2 = $db->sql_fetchrow($query2);
$name = $row2['namer'];
$radminsuper = $row2['radminsuper'];

if ($row2)
{
  if (stristr(",".$admins.",",",".$name.",") )
     $auth_user = 1;
}
if ($radminsuper == 1 || $auth_user == 1)
{
/* ---------------------------------- */
function UserSubs()
{

}
function UserSubDelete($sid)
{

}
function UserSubEdit($sid)
{

}
function editEncycloEntry($sid, $row)
{

}
function removeFromPending($sid)
{

}
function UserEncycloAccept ( $sid, $title, $text, $eid, $user_name, $user_id)
{

}
/* ---------------------------------- */

switch($op)
{
    case "UserSubEdit":
    UserSubEdit($sid);
    break;
    case "UserSubDelete":
    UserSubDelete($sid);
    break;
    case "UserEncycloAccept":
    UserSubAccept($sid, $usr_title, $usr_text, $usr_eid,
                  $user_name, $user_id );
    break;
    case "UserSubs":
    UserSubs();
    break;
}
}
else
{
  include("header.php");
  GraphicAdmin();
  OpenTable();
  echo "<center><b>"._ERROR."</b><br><br>You do not have administration
```

```
            permission for module \"$module_name\"</center>";
    CloseTable();
    include("footer.php");
}
?>
```

The first part is standard to all modules. The first line checks if the ADMIN_FILE constant has been declared. This constant is only defined in the admin.php file, and this check makes sure the file isn't being requested directly or from a non-administration part of the system. If the check fails, the Access Denied message is displayed.

The next line sets the $module_name variable. We can't use the basename(dirname(__FILE__)) setup here that we used in the front end of the module, since that will return admin, rather the name of the module folder. If you really don't want to type in the name of your module, you can use the following instead:

```
$module_name = basename(dirname(dirname(__FILE__)));
```

but it is quicker to type in the module name here!

The rest of the lines in this top chunk of code check to see if you have permission to administer this module. Each module has a row in the <prefix>_modules table in the PHP-Nuke database. This row contains information about the module, including a list of the administrators who are permitted to access this module. This list is stored in the admins field of the row. We grab that from the database:

```
$query = $db->sql_query("SELECT title, admins FROM ".$prefix."_modules WHERE
title='$module_name'");

$row = $db->sql_fetchrow($query);

$admins = $row['admins'];
```

Now we grab the 'credentials' of the current administrator from the database. Administrator details are stored in the <prefix>_authors table, and the author is identified by their aid. We get the name of the administrator, and find out if they are a super user.

```
$query2 = $db->sql_query("SELECT name, radminsuper FROM ".$prefix."_authors
WHERE aid='$aid'");

$row2 = $db->sql_fetchrow($query2);
$name = $row2['name'];
$radminsuper = $row2['radminsuper'];
```

If the current administrator is a super user, $radminsuper will have the value 1.

Now all we have to do is check if the administrator's name is in the list of module administrators. This list, held in the $admins variable, consists of the names of the administrators for this module, separated by commas, including a comma at the end of the list. To check if our administrator's name is in that list, we add a comma to the start and end of the name, and use the stristr() function to find an occurrence of that string inside the $admins variable. We add a comma to the start of the $admins variable so that every name in the list is surrounded by commas, and this way there can be a match for the exact name use the stristr() function. If there is a match, $auth_user is set to 1.

```
if ($row2)
{
  if (stristr(",".$admins, ",".$name.",") )
      $auth_user = 1;
}
```

The only way this administrator can access the administration area is if they have super user powers or if $auth_user is 1, which implies that they have administrative rights for this module:

```
if ($radminsuper == 1 || $auth_user == 1)
{
```

The second chunk of code in the file is only executed if the administrator passes this test. This is where all the action happens and we will talk about that in a moment.

The bottom chunk of code after the switch-case construct in the file handles the situation where the user does not have the required administrator permissions to access the file. It simply displays the administration area with a message that they have no access to this module's administration. This gives us a good opportunity to see how the administration page is created:

```
include("header.php");
GraphicAdmin();
OpenTable();
echo "<center><b>"._ERROR."</b><br><br>You do not have administration
        permission for module \"$module_name\"</center>";
CloseTable();
include("footer.php");
```

The first line starts the page output in the same way as the front end of the module, by including the header.php file. Next comes the call to GraphicAdmin(). This displays the administration menus. Whenever you create an administration page, you will need to call this function to display these menus.

After that, page output continues as usual with OpenTable(), the error message, CloseTable() and then including footer.php to wrap things up.

Now that we've seen the overall shape of the code in the file, let's begin to dig into the individual functions in the file.

Displaying the List of Submitted Items

The main part of the administration area will display a list of all the submitted items. The type of content, the title, the user who submitted it, and some buttons to view or delete the item will be displayed. This is similar to the administration functionality we have seen throughout PHP-Nuke.

The main operation is the UserSubs() function, and is the default function called when the page is viewed:

```
function UserSubs()
{
    global $db, $prefix;
    global $admin_file;

    include("header.php");

    GraphicAdmin();

    $contenttypes = array('encyclo'=>"Encyclopedia");
    title(_USERSUBADMIN);

    OpenTable();

    echo "<center>";
```

```
$sql = "select id, title, type, user_id, user_name,  UNIX_TIMESTAMP(date)
        AS theDate from ".$prefix."_usersubmissions order by date desc";
$result = $db->sql_query($sql);
echo "<table border=1>";
echo "<tr><td>ID</td><td>Submission Type</td>
<td>Title</td><td>User</td><td>Date</td>
<td colspan=3>Functions</td></tr>";
while($row = $db->sql_fetchrow($result))
{
    $type = $row['type'];
    $id = $row['id'];
    $title = $row['title'];
    echo "<tr><td>$id</td>";
    echo "<td align=\"center\">".$contenttypes[$type]."</td>";
    echo "<td>$title</td>";
    echo "<td>".$row[user_name]."</td>";
    echo "<td>".date("l dS of F Y h:i:s A", $row['theDate'])."</td>";
    echo "<td><a
            href=\"".$admin_file.".php?op=UserSubApprove&sid=$id\">
            <img  src=\"images/unban.gif\" alt=\"Approve\"
            title=\"Approve\" border=0></a></td>";
    echo "<td><a href=\"".$admin_file.".php?op=UserSubEdit&sid=$id\">
            <img src=\"images/edit.gif\" alt=\"Edit\" title=\"Edit\"
            border=\"0\"></a></td>";
    echo "<td><a
            href=\"".$admin_file.".php?op=UserSubDelete&sid=$id\">
            <img src=\"images/delete.gif\" alt=\"Delete\"
            title=\"Delete\"></a></td>";
    echo "</tr>";
}
echo "</table>";
echo "</center>";
CloseTable();
include("footer.php");
}
```

The function begins with the usual global declarations, $db and $prefix for data access, and $admin_file for the name of the admin file. Next, it starts the page output, and displays the administration menus with a call to GraphicAdmin().

An array called contenttypes is created:

```
$contenttypes = array('encyclo'=>"Encyclopedia");
```

This array will hold the module names that correspond to values in the type field of the stored, submitted data.

Now we retrieve the current list of submitted items:

```
$sql = "select id, title, type, user_id, user_name, UNIX_TIMESTAMP(date) AS
theDate FROM ".$prefix."_usersubmissions ORDER BY date ASC";
$result = $db->sql_query($sql);
```

Note the UNIX_TIMESTAMP() function. This is a MySQL function, and it returns the TIMESTAMP field, date, as a UNIX timestamp. This is a number counting the number of seconds between the Unix Epoch (January 1 1970 00:00:00 GMT) and the time specified. Retrieving the date in this form means we do not have to do any further formatting with the date to work with it. The 'AS theDate' part creates an alias for this field, so that we can subsequently refer to it as theDate. Note that we order the submissions by the date on which they were submitted.

Now we create a table to display the list of submitted items:

```
echo "<table border=1>";
    echo "<tr><td>ID</td><td>Submission Type</td>
    <td>Title</td><td>User</td><td>Date</td>
    <td colspan=2>Functions</td></tr>";
```

We loop through all the retrieved rows and retrieve the type of content, the ID, and the title:

```
while($row = $db->sql_fetchrow($result))
{
    $type = $row['type'];
    $id = $row['id'];
    $title = $row['title'];
```

We begin the display of a single row in the table. The first column displays the ID of the submitted item, the second column the type of content it is, the third column shows the title, the fourth column the name of the user who submitted it, and the fifth column the date:

```
echo "<tr><td>$id</td>";
echo "<td align=\"center\">".$contenttypes[$type]."</td>";
echo "<td>$title</td>";
echo "<td>".$row[user_name]."</td>";
echo "<td>".date("l dS of F Y h:i:s A", $row['theDate'])."</td>";
```

The final two columns in the table show the icons for editing (and approving) the item, and deleting the item:

```
echo "<td><a href=\"".$admin_file.".php?op=UserSubEdit&sid=$id\">
        <img src=\"images/edit.gif\" alt=\"Edit\" title=\"Edit\"
        border=\"0\"></a></td>";
echo "<td><a href=\"".$admin_file.".php?op=UserSubDelete&sid=$id\">
        <img src=\"images/delete.gif\" alt=\"Delete\" title=\"Delete\"
        border="0"></a></td>";
echo "</tr>";
}
```

The icon for editing is edit.gif and the icon for deleting is delete.gif. Both these files are found in the images folder of PHP-Nuke and are the same as those used throughout the administration area. The alt attribute is used as substitute text in case there is some problem displaying the image file. We have added the title attribute to give a visual cue about the function of the icon (the text that appears as you hover the cursor over it).

Each of these images is enclosed by a link to the relevant function in our administration area. The ID of the submitted item is held by the $id variable, and will be passed to the pages through the sid query string entry. Note that we use the $admin_file variable in the links rather than typing in admin.php. This ensures that our module supports the renaming of the administration file.

The rest of the function finishes off the page output:

```
echo "</table>";
    echo "</center>";
    CloseTable();
    include("footer.php");
}
```

Now when you visit the administration area of the UserSubmissions module, you will see the list of your submitted items.

ID	Submission Type	Title	User	Date	Functions
1	Encyclopedia	Tyrannosaurus Rex	testuser	Thursday 10th of November 2005 10:02:40 PM	

User Submission Administration

Let's set about coding the first administrative function, to allow the administrator to view and approve the submitted item.

Editing and Approving the Submitted Item

The UserSubEdit() function allows the administrator to view, edit, and approve or reject the submitted item.

```
function UserSubEdit($sid)
{
    global $admin_file, $db, $prefix;

    $sid = intval($sid);

    $sql = "select * from ".$prefix."_usersubmissions where id=$sid";
    $result = $db->sql_query($sql);
    $row = $db->sql_fetchrow($result);
    if (!$row)
      Header("Location: ".$admin_file.".php?op=UserSubs");

    $arry = unserialize($row['data']);
    $row['data'] = $arry;
    $type = $row['type'];
    switch($type)
    {
        case "encyclo":
            $ok = editEncycloEntry($sid, $row);
            break;
        default:
          Header("Location: ".$admin_file.".php?op=UserSubs");
    }
}
```

This function requires the global $admin_file, $db, and $prefix variables, and begins by converting the $sid variable to an integer. The next thing done is to retrieve the submission from the UserSubmissions table:

```
$sql = "select * from ".$prefix."_usersubmissions where id=$sid";
$result = $db->sql_query($sql);
$row = $db->sql_fetchrow($result);
```

If there is no row of data returned, we redirect to the main User Submission Administration page:

```
if (!$row)
  Header("Location: ".$admin_file.".php?op=UserSubs");
```

If the check is passed, it means that we must have some data, so we unserialize the contents of the data column; remember this column contains a serialized array that we created in the storeSubmission() method of the visitor area.

```
$arry = unserialize($row['data']);
```

We store the array back in the $row variable, so that all our data is back together again.

```
$row['data'] = $arry;
```

Now we need to process the data based on the type of content, stored in the $type field of $row.

```
$type = $row['type'];
switch($type)
{
```

For a case of type encyclo, we call the editEncycloEntry() function to display the data to administrator. If the there is any other value for type, we will redirect to the main User Submission Administration page:

```
    case "encyclo":
        $ok = editEncycloEntry($sid, $row);
        break;
    default:
        Header("Location: ".$admin_file.".php?op=UserSubs");
}
```

This UserSubEdit() function is similar to the ShowFormForInput() function of the module front end, in that it will select a different type of form to show to the administrator based on the type of content being looked at.

Displaying the Submitted Item

The editEncycloEntry() function displays the submitted item to the administrator. It contains code similar to the formatEncyclo() function of the front end that displayed the form to the visitor, the difference being that the visitor saw an empty form, but the administrator will be seeing a form populated with the submitted item data.

```
function editEncycloEntry($sid, $row)
{
    global $db, $prefix, $admin_file;

    $usr_eid = $row['parent_id'];

    $eid = intval($eid);
    $data = $row['data'];
    $usr_text = $data['text'];
    $usr_title = $data['title'];

    include("header.php");
    GraphicAdmin();

    OpenTable();

    echo "  <form action=\"".$admin_file.".php?op=UserSubs\"method=\"post\">\n
            <p><b>Title:</b><br>\n
            <input name=\"usr_title\" size=\"50\" type=\"text\"
            value=\"$usr_title\">\n<br>
            <br>
            <b>Term Text:</b><br>
            If you want multiple pages you can write <b>&lt;!--pagebreak--
```

```
                  &gt;</b> where you want to cut.<br>
                   <textarea name=\"usr_text\" cols=\"60\"
                  rows=\"20\">$usr_text</textarea><br>
                   <br>
                   <b>Encyclopedia:</b><br>
                   <select name=\"usr_eid\">";

              $sql = "SELECT eid, title FROM " . $prefix . "_encyclopedia WHERE
                    active='1'";

        $result = $db->sql_query($sql);
        while ($row2 = $db->sql_fetchrow($result))
        {
            $eid = intval($row2['eid']);
            $title = stripslashes($row2['title']);
            echo "<option value=\"$eid\" ";

            if ($eid == $usr_eid)
              echo "selected";

            echo ">$title</option>\n";
        }
        echo "</select>\n<br><br>";
        echo "<br><br>";

        echo "<input name=\"user_name\" value=\"".$row['user_name']."\"
              type=\"hidden\">\n";
        echo "<input name=\"user_id\" value=\"".$row['user_id']."\"
              type=\"hidden\">\n";
        echo "<input name=\"sid\" value=\"$sid\" type=\"hidden\">\n";
        echo " <input name=\"op\" value=\"UserEncycloAccept\" type=\"hidden\">";
        echo "<input value=\"Accept\" type=\"submit\">";
        echo "<a
              href=\"".$admin_file.".php?op=UserSubDelete&sid=$sid\">Delete</a>";

    echo "<a href=\"".$admin_file.".php?op=UserSubs\">Ignore</a>";
    echo "</form>";
    CloseTable();
    include("footer.php");
    }
```

The code begins by picking out and cleaning data from the $row variable:

```
          $usr_eid = $row['parent_id'];

          $eid = intval($eid);
          $data = $row['data'];
          $usr_text = $data['text'];
          $usr_title = $data['title'];
```

After beginning the page output, we create the form for the administrator. This code is almost identical to the code in formatEncyclo(); the difference this time is that we actually fill in the fields in the form (shown highlighted):

```
echo "  <form action=\"".$admin_file.".php?op=UserSubs\" method=\"post\">\n
           <p><b>Title:</b><br>\n
           <input name=\"usr_title\" size=\"50\" type=\"text\"
           value=\"$usr_title\">\n<br>
           <br>
           <b>Term Text:</b><br>
           If you want multiple pages you can write <b>&lt;!--pagebreak--
           &gt;</b> where you
           want to cut.<br>
           <textarea name=\"usr_text\" cols=\"60\"
           rows=\"20\">$usr_text</textarea><br>
```

```
                    <br>
                    <b>Encyclopedia:</b><br>
                    <select name=\"usr_eid\">";
```

The next thing is to create the drop-down list of Encyclopedias. Again, this is similar to the code in formatEncyclo(), except this time we have to select the Encyclopedia chosen by the submitter (these lines are highlighted):

```
            $sql = "SELECT eid, title FROM " . $prefix . "_encyclopedia WHERE
                    active='1'";

    $result = $db->sql_query($sql);
    while ($row2 = $db->sql_fetchrow($result))
    {
        $eid = intval($row2['eid']);
        $title = stripslashes($row2['title']);
        echo "<option value=\"$eid\" ";

        if ($eid == $usr_eid)
          echo "selected";

        echo ">$title</option>\n";
    }
    echo "</select>\n<br><br>";
```

We add some hidden fields that contain the details of the user who submitted the item, the ID of the item itself, and a value for op to determine the next action when the page is submitted:

```
        echo "<input name=\"user_name\" value=\"".$row['user_name']."\"
                type=\"hidden\">\n";
        echo "<input name=\"user_id\" value=\"".$row['user_id']."\"
                type=\"hidden\">\n";
        echo "<input name=\"sid\" value=\"$sid\" type=\"hidden\">\n";
        echo " <input name=\"op\" value=\"UserEncycloAccept\" type=\"hidden\">";
```

Finally, we add a submit button, and some links for the administrator to delete the item outright, or just ignore the item and return to the main User Submission Administration page:

```
        echo "<input value=\"Accept\" type=\"submit\">";
        echo "<a href=\"".
                $admin_file.".php?op=UserSubDelete&sid=$sid\">Delete</a>";

        echo "<a href=\"".$admin_file.".php?op=UserSubs\">Ignore</a>";
        echo "</form>";
```

With this form, the administrator is able to view the submission, and make some modifications if they choose. If they are happy with the submission, they can click the Accept button and the data will be added to the encyclopedia database. When they click the Accept button and the page is submitted, the value of op will be UserEncycloAccept, and the process of inserting the submitted item into the encyclopedia begins.

Accepting the Submitted Item

And at last we come to inserting the data into the encyclopedia.

```
    function UserEncycloAccept( $sid, $title, $text, $eid, $user_name, $user_id)
    {
        global $db, $prefix, $admin_file;

        $sid = intval($sid);
        $eid = intval($eid);
```

```
    if ($sid<1 || $eid<1)
      Header("Location: ".$admin_file.".php?op=UserSubs");

    $text .= "<br><b>Submitted by: ".$user_name."<b><br>";

    $text = stripslashes(FixQuotes($text));
    $title = stripslashes(FixQuotes($title));

    $db->sql_query("insert into ".$prefix."_encyclopedia_text values(NULL,
                    '$eid', '$title', '$text', '0')");

    removeFromPending($sid);

    Header("Location: ".$admin_file.".php?op=UserSubs");
}
```

We begin by preparing, and checking the ID of the submitted item, and the Encyclopedia it is supposed to be going into. If we have no value for either of these, we redirect the administrator to the main administration page.

Before we insert the data, we add a note to the end of the entry text indicating who added the entry:

```
$text .= "<br><b>Submitted by: ".$row['user_name']."<b><br>";
```

We have to prepare the text and title before storing it in the same way that the Encyclopedia module does. You can see what needs to be done in the encyclopedia_save() function in the index.php file of the encyclopedia administration code. We do it here too:

```
$text = stripslashes(FixQuotes($text));
$title = stripslashes(FixQuotes($title));
```

We insert the data into the encyclopedia table.

```
$db->sql_query("INSERT INTO ".$prefix."_encyclopedia_text
                VALUES(NULL, '$eid', '$title', '$text', '0')");
```

Now we remove the submitted item from the list with a call to removeFromPending(), and redirect the administrator to the main User Submission Administration page since we are done.

```
removeFromPending($sid);
Header("Location: ".$admin_file.".php?op=UserSubs");

}
```

Removing a Submitted Item

The removeFromPending() function is where the deleting action happens. We create a SQL statement to delete the entry from the UserSubmissions table, and then execute that query:

```
function removeFromPending($sid)
{
    global $db, $prefix;
    $sql = "DELETE FROM ".$prefix."_usersubmissions WHERE id=$sid";
    $db->sql_query($sql);
}
```

This deleting functionality is kept separate from the function called by the administrator to delete an item because more than one operation will want to delete the item from the list.

Deleting a Submitted Item

The UserSubDelete() function is how the administrator deletes a submitted item. This function doesn't do too much; it calls the removeFromPending() function that actually removes an item from the database. After the entry has been deleted, the administrator is redirected to the User Submission Administration main page:

```
function UserSubDelete($sid)
{
    $sid = intval($sid);
    if ($sid<1) return;
    removeFromPending($sid);
    Header("Location: ".$admin_file.".php?op=UserSubs");
}
```

And that completes the code for this module.

Extending the Module

To extend this module for other types of content from different modules (including your own), you will need to make changes to both the front end of the module and the administration end.

Extending at the Front End

At the front end, you will need:

- A form for the visitor to enter their submission—you will need to add a new check against the value of $oid in the ShowFormForInput() function in the front end index.php file, and then create a new function like formatEncyclo() for displaying the form.

- A function for serializing the submitted data—like the AddEncyclopediaEntry() function. This will require you add a new entry to the switch-case construct at the end of the index.php file.

Extending at the Administration End

At the administration end, you will need to:

- Create a new entry in the contenttypes array in the UserSubs() function.

- Add a new entry in the $type switch-case construct in the UserSubEdit() function, and a new function for displaying the submitted item similar to editEncycloEntry(). In that function, you will need to state a new value for the op hidden field, and make sure you add this value both to the switch-case construct near the end of the index.php file, and also in the case.php file, or else that action will never get recognized by PHP-Nuke.

- Finally, you will need a new function to insert the submission into the relevant database.

Summary

In this chapter, we have seen a lot of code. We began with a look at how PHP-Nuke handles requests for a page.

After that, we created a new block, a better version of the Dinosaur of the Day block we created in Chapter 4. We created a block that displayed an image and the title of a dinosaur from the database, adding that information to the database if there was none there. This introduced us to data access in PHP-Nuke, a topic which we used throughout the chapter after that.

After a quick look at module file and folder structure, we began creating a new module for PHP-Nuke, a UserSubmissions module. The steps that we followed to create the module were:

- Creating the module folder structure
- Creating the database table
- Coding the front end (visitor view) of the module
- Adapting the code for multi-language support
- Coding the module administration area, and adding the module to the Modules Administration menu

A
Installing XAMPP

In this appendix we will walk through downloading, installing, and setting up the XAMPP package. XAMPP is a free package that has a collection of free applications assembled to provide you with an easy-to-setup web server (Apache), database server (MySQL), and server-side scripting language (PHP). XAMPP lets you experiment with these technologies and develop your own web applications.

Setting up an AMP (Apache, MySQL, PHP) environment has typically required configuring the different applications to work on their own, and then to work with each other. With XAMPP this interplay has already been set up for you, and the system comes ready configured and ready to go. In addition to being easy to get started, XAMPP includes a number of useful extensions, code libraries, and other applications, all already configured so you don't need to spend a long time trying to get them working together.

> Note that we are installing XAMPP here as a 'development' or 'testing' environment only. We will only be using XAMPP for testing and exploring the technologies, and not as a 'production' environment for serving our website to the outside world. Setting up a production web server and a database server, and securing and optimizing them is a topic beyond the scope of this text.

There is a version of the XAMPP package available for Windows, Linux, Mac OS X, and the Solaris operating system. XAMPP is free to download, and the package contains the following:

- The AMP environment of Apache, MySQL, PHP.
- PHP 4 and PHP 5, and many extensions.
- phpMyAdmin, the leading web-based interface to MySQL.
- The PEAR library. PEAR (PHP Extension and Application Repository) is a framework for reusable PHP components, and is a favorite among professional PHP developers. You can find out more about PEAR at pear.php.net.
- eAccelerator, a PHP caching utility to speed up the serving of your pages.
- FileZilla, an FTP server.
- An implementation of OpenSSL for running your site under HTTPS.

The advantage of the XAMPP package is that everything you need is collected together for you, tested, and ready to go. The downside is that you will have a very large file to download. On the brighter side, you only have to download one file rather than downloading lots of files, and then trying to get them working.

The home of the XAMPP package is the site www.apachefriends.org/en/. The installation walkthrough in this chapter may not solve all your problems, and only covers Windows. If you find yourself in need of further help, check out the XAMPP documentation page at:

    http://www.apachefriends.org/en/faq-xampp.html

Details of the XAMPP package itself can be found at:

    http://www.apachefriends.org/en/xampp.html

On that page, you will find a link to the XAMPP version of your particular operating system. We will be choosing XAMPP for Windows. Clicking the XAMPP for Windows link on this page brings you to:

    http://www.apachefriends.org/en/xampp-windows.html

You will find that there are several options for downloading XAMPP. First, you can choose from one of three types of package:

- XAMPP
- XAMPP add-ons
- XAMPP Lite

Each of these packages is available in different download formats, a Windows installer file, a ZIP file, or a self-extracting 7-ZIP archive:

XAMPP for Windows 1.4.16, October 05th 2005		
Version	Size	Content
XAMPP Windows 1.4.16		Apache HTTPD 2.0.54, MySQL 4.1.14, PHP 5.0.5 + 4.4.0 + PEAR + Switch, MiniPerl 5.8.7, mod_ssl 2.0.54, Openssl 0.9.8, PHPMyAdmin 2.6.4 pl1, XAMPP Control Panel 2.1, eAccelerator 0.9.4, Webalizer 2.01-10, Mercury Mail Transport System für Win32 und NetWare Systems v4.01a, FileZilla FTP Server 0.9.10a, SQLite 2.8.15, ADODB 4.65, Zend Optimizer 2.5.10a, XAMPP Security. For Windows 98, 2000, XP. See also README
Installer [MD5]	25 MB	Installer
ZIP [MD5]	68 MB	ZIP archive
EXE (7-zip) [MD5]	22 MB	Selfextracting 7-ZIP archive
Upgrade Package 1.4.16		With MySQL 4.1.14, PHP 5.0.5 + PEAR, PHPMyAdmin 2.6.4 pl1, FileZilla FTP Server 0.9.10a for the XAMPP **version 1.4.15**. See also CHANGES
Installer [MD5]	16 MB	Installer
ZIP [MD5]	50 MB	ZIP archive
EXE (7-zip) [MD5]	16 MB	Selfextracting 7-ZIP archive

We will be choosing the Installer version of the full XAMPP package. This is some 25MB to download. You can choose the Upgrade Package if you already have an earlier version of XAMPP installed on your system.

The XAMPP add-ons package consists of more open-source technologies, such as Python, Perl, Tomcat, and Cocoon. We will not need them in this book. The XAMPP Lite package is half the size of the full XAMPP package, but it does contain everything that you will need to run the code in this book. However, the Lite package does not come as a Windows installer.

Clicking the Installer link takes you to a page where you select the 'nearest' Sourceforge mirror site from which to download the file. You can download the file from any of the sites listed, so you might want to pick the one nearest to you. The downloaded file will have a filename of the form:

    xampp-win32-1.4.16-installer.exe.

The 1.4.16 part is the current XAMPP version.

We will install the XAMP package into a folder called c:\apachefriends\. You can either create this folder before you begin, or from within the installation process.

We begin by double-clicking on the file, and we will be presented with a dropdown to choose the language of our installation. Select English and click OK to move on to the welcome page, which displays a simple message, and you can click Next to move to the start of the process.

You will be presented with a dialog asking you to choose the location for XAMPP to install its files into. XAMPP will create a folder called xampp in the Destination Folder specified, and add its files in there. Clicking the Browse button allows you to create the apachefriends folder if you have not already done so, and then the folder can be selected:

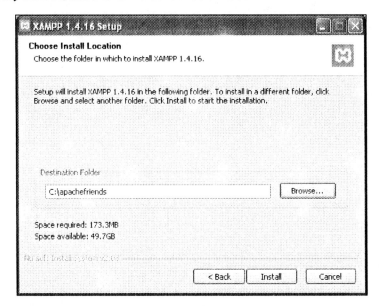

Click Install to continue and the installation begins. The files are extracted and copied to the specified folder. A command-line window will open at one point, right before the end; do not be disturbed by that! After the command-line window closes, the installation is complete, and you are presented with the end screen. Click Finish to complete the installation.

After clicking Finish, you will be asked if you wish to install the XAMPP servers as Windows services. This will save you the trouble of having to start them manually every time you boot up.

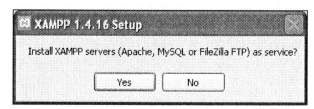

Click Yes to begin installing these servers as Windows Services.

If you are running the IIS server or Skype VOIP application, then exit them before attempting to install Apache as a Windows Service. Otherwise, the Apache service will fail to install as a Windows Service, with XAMPP reporting a problem with port 443 (for Skype) or port 80 (for IIS).

You will first be asked if you wish to install Apache as a Windows service. Again, click Yes. Then you will be asked if you wish to install MySQL as a Windows Service. Again, click Yes. The next choice is if you want to install Filezilla FTP as a Windows Service. We don't have need of an FTP server in this book, so you can click No.

After this, you are presented with a congratulatory message, and an option to view the Control Panel:

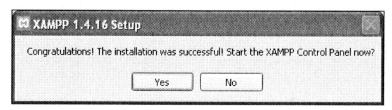

The XAMPP Control Panel is used to control and monitor the status of the services that XAMPP has installed. When the Control Panel is running, you will see an icon like:

in your System Tray, and you can double-click it to get the XAMPP Control Panel back on your screen. If you have closed the Control Panel, you can open it again from Start | Programs | apachefriends | xampp | CONTROL XAMPP SERVER PANEL. Alternatively, you can control and monitor these services in the usual way from the Windows Control Panel, (Start | Settings | Control Panel), by using the Services area found in Administrative Tools.

With our servers installed as services, we are ready to go. Open up your browser, and enter http://localhost/ into the navigation bar. You should see the following splash screen, inviting you to select a language. We will select English:

Now you will be taken to your XAMPP homepage. In future you will directly be taken to this page when you enter `http://localhost/` into your browser, bypassing the language splash screen.

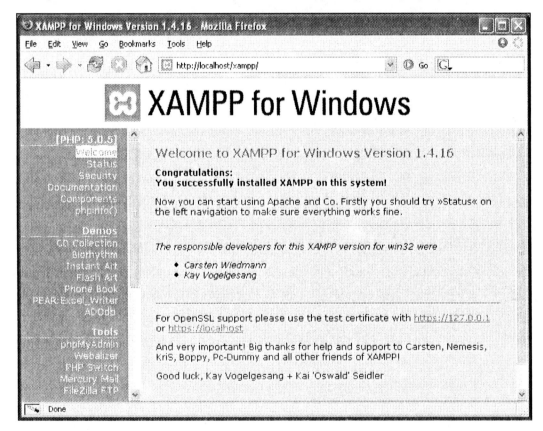

You will find a range of options in the left-hand panel for you to test out what comes with XAMPP. Of particular interest is **phpMyAdmin**, which we will be making use of in many parts of the book, and which is likely to become a very important tool as you work more with PHP and MySQL. You can click the link in the left-hand panel, or enter its URL (`http://localhost/phpMyAdmin/`) directly into the browser to get started with it.

There is one step left. By default, XAMPP is configured to run PHP 5. We will need to set XAMPP to run PHP 4. PHP-Nuke is written in PHP 4, so it is sensible to be running this while using PHP-Nuke. Although there is great compatibility for PHP 4 applications running under PHP 5, there is no particular reason to run PHP 5 for PHP-Nuke, so we will make the switch.

There is a file called php-switch.bat in the apachefriends\xampp\ folder that allows you to make the switch between PHP 5 and PHP 4 (and back again). However, before you can use it you need to stop the Apache Service.

Open up the XAMPP Control Panel, and click the Stop button next to the Apache service. You should see a message reporting the service has been stopped:

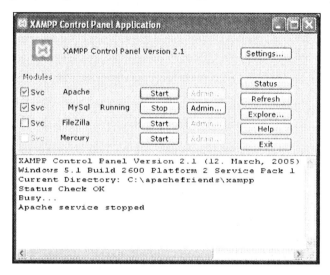

Now double-click the file php-switch.bat in the apachefriends\xampp folder, and a command-line window will open, and you will be prompted to choose the version of PHP.

Simply press *4* followed by *Enter*, and XAMPP will switch over to PHP 4 for you. Once it has completed, you will see a message containing this report:

```
OKAY ... PHP SWITCHING WAS SUCCESSFUL
```

Press any key to close the window. You will now have to restart Apache from the Control Panel by clicking the Start button, and then you can return to your browser and visit your XAMPP home page. Once you are finished with the Control Panel, click Exit to shut it down.

You can use php-switch.bat to switch back to PHP 5 again if you want to continue working with PHP 5, but remember to stop the Apache service before using it.

Before we finish off, it's worth noting two important folders in your XAMPP installation.

- htdocs: This folder is your 'document root'. A file placed in this folder will be made available by the web server. We will be copying our installation of PHP-Nuke into this folder to get it working properly.

- apache: This folder contains a file called `apache_installservice.bat`. If Apache failed to install as a service during the installation process, then you can run this file to try again. Also in the apache folder is a folder called `bin`. This contains most of the binary files of the XAMPP installation, and also a number of configuration files. In particular, it contains the PHP configuration file, `php.ini`. There are two `php.ini` files in the standard installation of XAMPP, but if you need to make changes to 'the PHP configuration file', you should make changes to the `php.ini` file in the `apache\bin\` folder or you may find your changes do not have any effect.

Your XAMPP installation is now set up and working, and you are ready to begin installing PHP-Nuke!

Index

X

XAMPP package
about, 289
apache folder, 294
configuration, 293
contents, 289
control panel, 292
download options, 290

htdocs folder, 294
installation, 291
Installer version, 290
php-switch.bat file, 294

Y

Your Account module, 29, 83

Thank you for buying Building Websites with PHP-Nuke

Packt Open Source Project Royalties

When we sell a book written on an Open Source project, we pay a royalty directly to that project. Therefore by purchasing *Building Websites with PHP-Nuke* Packt will have given some of the money received to the PHP-Nuke project.

In the long term, we see ourselves and you—customers and readers of our books—as part of the Open Source ecosystem, providing sustainable revenue for the projects we publish on. Our aim at Packt is to establish publishing royalties as an essential part of the service and support a business model that sustains Open Source.

If you're working with an Open Source project that you would like us to publish on, and subsequently pay royalties to, please get in touch with us.

Writing for Packt

We welcome all inquiries from people who are interested in authoring. Book proposals should be sent to authors@packtpub.com. If your book idea is still at an early stage and you would like to discuss it first before writing a formal book proposal, contact us: one of our commissioning editors will get in touch with you.

We're not just looking for published authors; if you have strong technical skills but no writing experience, our experienced editors can help you develop a writing career, or simply get some additional reward for your expertise.

About Packt Publishing

Packt, pronounced 'packed,' published its first book "*Mastering phpMyAdmin for Effective MySQL Management*" in April 2004 and subsequently continued to specialize in publishing highly focused books on specific technologies and solutions.

Our books and publications share the experiences of your fellow IT professionals in adapting and customizing today's systems, applications, and frameworks. Our solution-based books give you the knowledge and power to customize the software and technologies you're using to get the job done. Packt books are more specific and less general than the IT books you have seen in the past. Our unique business model allows us to bring you more focused information, giving you more of what you need to know, and less of what you don't.

Packt is a modern, yet unique publishing company, which focuses on producing quality, cutting-edge books for communities of developers, administrators, and newbies alike. For more information, please visit our website: www.PacktPub.com.

Printed in the United States
46563LVS00003BA/46